Music and Worship
in the Church

Music and Worship in the Church

Revised and Enlarged Edition

Austin C. Lovelace
William C. Rice

ABINGDON

NASHVILLE

MUSIC AND WORSHIP IN THE CHURCH
Revised and Enlarged Edition

Library of Congress Cataloging in Publication Data
Lovelace, Austin Cole.
    Music and worship in the church.
    Bibliography: p.
    Includes index.
    1. Church music—Protestant churches. I. Rice,
William Carroll, joint author. II. Title.
ML3100.L7   1976   783'.026   76-13524

ISBN 0-687-27358-7

MANUFACTURED BY THE PARTHENON PRESS AT
NASHVILLE, TENNESSEE, UNITED STATES OF AMERICA

Preface

MOST BOOKS ON CHURCH MUSIC ARE WRITTEN FOR THE SPECIALISTS—THE organist, the choir director, and occasionally the minister. While this book is also addressed first of all to these "specialists," the greater audience it seeks is every person in the church.

When music is stripped of all its technical language (and hocus-pocus with which some pseudo musicians would surround it), it reveals itself to be a part of life—as natural a form of expression as speech. It can be an aid to worship in the form of organ music, anthems, and responses and can become a means of worship in the singing of hymns and doxologies and in congregational chants and responses.

Any music in the church must therefore be judged in its relationship to worship, and for its highest potential must depend in the final analysis on the attitude of each person who shares in any way in the praise of God. The minister, first and foremost, must stand on firm ground and give support to the technical guidance of the "experts"—the director, the organist, the soloists and choirs—in co-operation with the music committee. To each of these this book would speak.

A secondary, but perhaps more important, concern of this book is the dedicated, volunteer lay leaders of the church and church school who seek guidance in the specialized and often unfamiliar field of church music. An attempt has been made to provide a manual for them which suggests philosophical guidance and practical help in improving the quality and use of music in every area of the church's life.

The congregation itself is encouraged to consider its attitude toward and role in church music. As long ago as 1887 Waldo S. Pratt warned:

It is not always remembered that since congregational singing is essentially expressive, it can flourish only where there is a congregational spirituality that craves expression. . . . Congregational singing will not flourish without

5

encouragement from the pastor and the church musicians, and without effort from the individual members of the congregation itself. It will not run itself, nor advance without guidance, nor attain its full stature until every regular worshiper feels a personal responsibility about it.[1]

Our suggestion to the minister and musicians, then, is that they share the book with all. There is at least one chapter which can speak to the needs of everyone in the church, from the music specialist to the man in the pew. Church music will not improve of itself, nor make forward strides without guidance, nor attain its full stature and potential until every person in the church assumes a personal responsibility for singing a new song unto the Lord. Toward the achievement of this goal this book is dedicated.

Austin C. Lovelace
William C. Rice

Postscript—1976

The two hundredth anniversary of the United States offers a unique opportunity for looking back and ahead. Church music has moved a long way since the first hymnal was printed in 1640 and since William Billings introduced the fuguing tune into worship (through the back door by way of the singing school).

When this book was first written, there was not much of worth being written in the area of hymnody, but in the last fifteen years excellent new writers have appeared, and the number of new hymnals is phenomenal world wide. There is a renewed interest in worship, with movements both traditional and innovative. Publishers continue to publish huge amounts of new music despite rising costs. Workshops for church musicians are frequent and widely attended.

It is an exciting time in which to work, but the need for examination of goals and ideals is perhaps more necessary than ever. There is always the danger that in the frantic pace of today we may not be sure of

[1] *The Church Music Problem* (New York: The Century Company), pp. 22-23.

where we are going, but we are getting there fast. This two hundredth anniversary is a good time to stop and examine basic attitudes.

This revision adds two chapters which attempt to face some of our problems and to offer a philosophy and some practical advice to help chart a course for the days ahead. We are confident that the future of church music can be faced with optimism, and it is our hope that this book may have some small part in helping to guide that course.

Contents

I

Worship and Music

WORSHIP AND MUSIC WERE BLENDED IN MAGNIFICENCE AT THE DEDICATION of Solomon's temple:

All the Levitical singers, Asaph, Heman, and Jeduthun, their sons and kinsmen, arrayed in fine linen, with cymbals, harps, and lyres, stood east of the altar with a hundred and twenty priests who were trumpeters; and it was the duty of the trumpeters and singers to make themselves heard in unison in praise and thanksgiving to the Lord, and when the song was raised, with trumpets and cymbals and other musical instruments, in praise to the Lord,

"For he is good,
for his steadfast love endures forever,"

the house, the house of the Lord, was filled with a cloud, so that the priests could not stand to minister because of the cloud; for the glory of the Lord filled the house of God. (II Chr. 5:12-14.)

Singers, instrumentalists, choir directors, ministers, and people all shared in the worship of God. Even the music committee—if we think of the Levitical group as directing the program—had its part to play in making music in praise to God. Here was music with a purpose, succeeding in bringing to all the sense of the presence of God, "For the glory of the Lord filled the house of God."

Louis F. Benson suggested that the organic relation between music and religion is revealed in even a superficial study of comparative hymnology.

It shows us that relation as already a condition and not a theory in early religions. It reveals the actual employ of hymns in ritual and life from a time earlier than all written records. It shows especially a relatively high develop-

11

ment of worship-music and poetry in one of those national religions, the Hebrew, and how in the divine providence that Jewish Psalmody became the inheritance of the Christian Church, passing into it directly and unquestioned.[1]

Further illustrations of this fundamental relation which immediately come to mind are the use by Christ and his disciples of a hymn at the institution of the Lord's Supper (connecting church song with the most characteristic feature of Christian worship, Holy Communion); the early Christians in the catacombs "singing hymns to Christ as God"; the singing missionaries sent from Rome to all corners of Europe to found choir schools and to evangelize the heathen with song, word, and deed; the powerful use of music in the Reformation, about which Luther said, "Next to theology, I give the first and highest honor to music"; and the place of music in the Wesleyan revival in England. Every high moment of spiritual awakening in the history of the Church has been accompanied by a revival of song, for singing is as close to worship as breathing is to life itself.

Church music today does not seem to obtain the same results, however. Music and worship are often dull, lifeless, perfunctory, and void of meaning. Many musicians and ministers are dissatisfied with things as they are but appear uncertain as to what direction reform should take.

Today many denominations are re-examining their historical foundations, with special study of the meaning of worship and the value of certain worship patterns. Seminaries are critically rethinking the theological foundations of faith and practice and world bodies are attempting to formulate a statement concerning the true nature of the Church. H. Richard Niebuhr in the foreword to *The Purpose of the Church and Its Ministry* stated:

The general reason for the inquiry is . . . the conviction that "the unexamined life is not worth living"—a principle that has been given a special form in the Christian demand for daily and lifelong repentance. Institutions and communities no less than individuals are subject to this requirement. . . . We tend to repeat customary actions unaware that when we do today what

[1] *The Hymnody of the Christian Church* (Richmond, Va.: John Knox Press, 1956), p. 27.

12

we did yesterday we actually do something different since in the interval both we and our environment have changed; unaware also that we now do without conscious definition of purpose and method what was done yesterday with specific ends in view and by relatively precise means.[2]

When one turns to the contemporary scene of church music there are to be found many signs of activity. Like a spring garden there is growth in profusion, but a serious question can be raised as to whether there may not be more weeds than flowers. In the words of Albert Schweitzer, "The fertilizing rain brought up a crop of toad-stools." [3] Organs in great numbers are being purchased, ranging from a few behemoths larger than necessary to deformed and maimed stepchildren —the electronic spinets. Salesmen attempt to make every church group feel that it is not in accord with the latest worship trends if it does not have some kind of organ, disregarding the fact that the product which they sell may have a tone which is unearthly and less than heavenly. Many music committees purchase an organ without ever considering the quality of sound, which after all should be a chief consideration in purchasing a musical instrument.

In some churches the multiple choir program has mushroomed to incredible proportions; in many cases it is the central focus around which the rest of the life of the church revolves. While we have yet to see a "perambulator choir" wheeled into the sanctuary to sing an anthem, we, along with many ministers and musicians, are disturbed by the low standards of music and performance in many such programs and by the tendency to exploit individuals in presenting spectacular productions in the sanctuary in place of worship. Some choirs, bedecked in sensationally colored robes, stoles, choir achievement stripes, et cetera, bid fair to outdo not only Solomon and the lilies but Joseph in his multicolored coat as well.

Literally thousands of anthems are published each year, most completely devoid of inspiration or value. Added to these are the output of the jukebox and jazz hucksters in the "sacred" field, along with the musically and theologically bankrupt "gospel hymn" collections which stream from the presses and are plugged on radio and television in a com-

[2] (New York: Harper & Brothers, 1956), p. viii.
[3] *The Quest of the Historical Jesus* (London: A. and C. Black, Ltd., 1954), p. 96.

13

mercial exploitation of religious emotions. Most of the music written to-day is produced for the moment and for the pleasure of men; it is a reflection of ourselves and not of God. It is small wonder that few great composers are interested in writing music for the church.

New congregational hymnals have appeared with increasing regularity and excellence during the last few decades; yet congregational singing in most churches is at a low ebb despite the new hymnals, the increase in choir membership, and the hiring of professional and full-time leadership. Few congregations can be found which sing with the fervor which has marked great periods of spiritual rebirth and vitality. Many congregations are treading the wine press of a dozen or so "old favorites" from which no further sustenance can be extracted.

The overwhelming majority of books published recently dealing with church music fall in the "how to" category, with full details on how to keep a program moving without friction; but almost never is the question raised as to whether or not the program is valid and worthwhile. Is church music guilty of activity without real purpose?

The current picture is one of emotion, commotion, and promotion. Hymns and anthems are chosen to please the congregation or to secure a specific emotional response. Many of the texts (particularly of the jukebox variety) take a firm stand in favor of God, mother, the Bible, and heaven but have little more to offer as spiritual food. In certain churches the music program is one of pointless commotion, with no relationship between choirs, hymn singing, music in the church school, or the services of worship. In others the program is a masterful job of organization and promotion with the choir program like an incredible invention of Rube Goldberg, with all the wheels turning smoothly but producing nothing. And in some the organ pipes gather dust and cobwebs, replaced by plucking and strumming, amplified to decibels that shatter the ear and blow the mind.

The Church does not fulfill its role if it is merely an effective organization with a busy program; it must also be a living organism. In the final analysis the Church is concerned with worship in the sense of the total response of each individual to the call of God. It is concerned with the whole man and every area of life. In Christ men see the perfect example of doing the will of God; in him they see the perfect love of God (with totality of heart, soul, and mind) and self-sacrificing love

14

for men—worship which begins with consummate at-oneness with God and issues in unselfish service to all mankind. Worship as seen in this vast concept, is central to the life of the Church and is the goal of all endeavor.

It is not within the scope of this book nor the capacity of the writers to present a comprehensive theological statement of the meaning of worship, for this has been done more ably and fully by many authors, some of whom are listed in the bibliography. Rather it will be our purpose here to suggest certain characteristics of music which relate it and make it a means of and aid to worship, and to list certain abuses and wrong attitudes toward worship which hinder music from fulfilling its vital and living relation to worship.

There are four main characteristics of music which give it an organic relation to worship. The first similiarity between the two lies in the element of mystery which surrounds both. Beauty cannot be easily explained and defined. Why is Brahms' "German Requiem" a moving and beautiful work? Explaining chords, rhythms, or form does not really answer the question. Precisely what makes the four opening notes of Beethoven's "Fifth Symphony" so gripping and compelling? There is really no answer. Why does a particular chord in one composition add mystery and excitement while in another it is tame and even tasteless? No one can really say.

When we turn to the area of religion we find mystery. Albert W. Palmer reminds us that

Christianity grew up amid the so-called mystery religions of the Graeco-Roman world. It has also its great mystery, which was symbolized in this sacrament [of communion], the mystery of God above and beyond the evil and suffering of the present age and revealed to men in the beautiful human life and sacrificial death of Jesus Christ.[4]

The mind of man cannot comprehend the wonders of God; it can only see the occasional flashes of light which shine through the glory holes of life. In the awesome areas of life's mystery music helps man to express the inexpressible.

Second, music and worship are both inextricably intertwined with the

----

[4] *The Art of Conducting Public Worship* (New York: The Macmillan Company, 1939), pp. 137-38.

emotions; both are capable of expression that is personal and universal. The urge and desire to worship a Being beyond the confines of the known and finite is common to all men, and the use of some form of communication (speech, music, literature, drama, sculpture, painting) is also common to all men.

Music is a language in its own right, and, as an art, a means of communication. Using pitches, rhythms, harmonies, timbres, and form it is as capable today of running the gamut of emotions from exaltation through gaiety, joy, excitement, solemnity, and fear to extreme dejection and sorrow as it was in the days of the biblical singers—Miriam, David, and Zechariah. The instruments of today are only refinements of the flutes, stringed instruments, trumpets, and drums with which the children of Israel praised God, and the God we worship is the same yesterday, today, and always. Thomas Hornblower Gill suggests that even our urge to song is one with all people:

> Their joy unto their Lord we bring,
> Their song to us descendeth;
> The Spirit who in them did sing
> To us His music lendeth:
> His song in them, in us, is one;
> We raise it high, we send it on—
> The song that never endeth.

From time to time the Church has been fearful of the emotional power of music and has attempted to curb its ecstatic moments. Yet the emotions are a powerful force for good and cannot be divorced from the total man. The Reverend Howard A. Johnson, Canon Theologian of the Cathedral Church of St. John the Divine, New York, states his views strongly:

Here I feel impelled to enter the lists as a champion of ecstasy. The Christian Religion, after all, gives us grounds for excitement. The Preface to the Prayer Book states that it is the Church's aim to do that which most tends to "the exciting of piety." In the furtherance of this aim music has been and can be the Church's great ally. While music most certainly engages the mind, it can do more than that: it can set the foot to tapping, the body to tingling. More important still, it can penetrate to the subconscious depths of the soul. Many Americans are afraid of enthusiasm and exaltation, either because they have seen the shallow emotionalism induced by fanatic preaching and cheap

16

music in certain revivalistic sects, or else because they have not been able to shake off a dubious puritanical heritage which regarded the organ as the devil's bagpipe and beatified "Thrift, Industry, and Sobriety" as the chief purpose and point of Christianity. Most of us, in fact, still recoil at the extravagance of pouring out an alabaster cruse of oil exceeding precious. To what purpose is this waste? Some music, yes; but keep it simple, and it hadn't better be very rhythmic or rich or exciting. We confound matters further still by driving a quite unreal cleavage between "sacred" and "secular" music. That there are different *genres* of music, that this is a useful, though rough, working distinction, I would not deny; but I do object when people tell me that the difference lies in the fact that secular music is *sensuous*, and therefore suspect, whereas sacred music is not. Nonsense! All music is sensuous. That is, it addresses itself primarily to the senses. And why are we afraid of the senses? For a reason that does us no credit. Unconsciously, we are Gnostics, Manichees, oriental dualists, splitting man into two parts, assigning him a pure and religious part, the spirit or soul, and an inferior and somehow impure part, the body with its senses. But this is heresy. It is to forget that the good God created the whole man, body as well as soul, and that he addresses himself to the whole man in the hope of winning the whole man, body and soul. . . .

It should be evident from what I have said that I who like *pianissimo* am also an advocate of the loud, the joyous, the ecstatic. In other words, gooseflesh is nowhere more properly at home than in church.[5]

Although there is an affinity between music and worship in terms of emotional potentialities, a major difficulty arises at this point: no two persons will see the same meaning in a painting, nor will two persons react identically to the impact of a drama. While music has often been called the universal language, it would be impossible to get any group of persons to agree on a simple specific meaning of any one composition. However, tests by psychologists indicate that the general mood of music (triumphant, playful, sad, pensive) is commonly experienced and agreed upon by a group of listeners. No one in his rightful mind would mistake a Sousa march for a prayer hymn. Yet our critical faculties are often dulled through association and tradition to accept without question hymn tunes and anthem settings as appropriate when the music

[5] *The American Guild of Organists Quarterly,* "Something About Church Music," January (1959), p. 8. Used by permission.

belies the mood and thought of the text. Only that music which is an honest and inspired expression of the feelings and thought of the composer and can become an accepted honest expression of the congregation in worship is worthy of acceptance.

The third point of contact between worship and music lies in their creativity. Worship is a creative encounter of man with God, a living and vital relationship which depends upon the active and unceasing quest of man in response to the call of God. One cannot say, "I have worshiped today so have no further need of worship." Each moment of worship is a new, fresh, creative, and spiritual quest.

Music is closely related at this point of creativity, for the source of all great church music is the elusive moment of inspiration which is a glimpse of God revealed to the composer. Through the use of symbols (notes, key signatures, bar lines, et cetera) the composer is able to put on paper a guide to an approximation of the correct interpretation of his work, but so long as the notes are but specks on a sheet of paper music does not come to life. The actual production of sounds which the composer has indicated depends upon the imagination and re-creative powers of the conductor and performers as well as the sympathetic listening and imagination of the hearers as they follow the musical ideas and attempt to understand the composer's intentions and feelings.

It is at the point of re-creation that music is vastly different from the plastic arts. Once a painting or piece of sculpture is complete there is nothing further to be done by the creator. It will remain the same in its physical form; the only differences possible are in the change of the viewer's attitude and perception. But sing a note and let the tone die. Where is it then? It cannot be seen, it cannot be touched, it cannot even be heard anymore. If we are to experience it again the note must be re-created, and yet in its re-creation it will not be exactly the same. It may be louder, less vital, slightly different in pitch and vocal color, and our reaction to the note will be different since we are now able to compare it with the memory of the previous sound.

Music, like worship, can be and must be created over and over—there is no end and no perfect completeness. A total comprehension of God is impossible; a perfect performance is an elusive impossibility. Yet man is called by the voice of God and an inner compulsion to attempt the impossible. One only need think of Toscanini and his constant and ceaseless study of the Beethoven symphonies—never happy with any performance, always seeking a more perfect recreation of the magnificent creations of the great master. In worshiping God, does man ever perfectly worship and adore? Does he ever reach the point of doing the perfect will of God? No, but each worship encounter and each creative moment is a new and fresh approach—one more step in the spiritual quest for perfection of which Charles Wesley sang:

> Finish then Thy new creation;
> Pure and spotless let us be;
> Let us see Thy great salvation
> Perfectly restored in Thee:
> Changed from glory into glory,
> Till in heaven we take our place,
> Till we cast our crowns before Thee,
> Lost in wonder, love, and praise.

Finally, music has an affinity to language, for both are forms of communication evolving from the impulse to give voice to the feelings and to express thoughts. Plainsong and the chant are merely heightened speech, making use of the rising and falling inflections of the words themselves to provide the melodic line. The use of high and low pitches heightens the emotional impact of words, and the timbre or quality of the voice in speech—which changes with varying emotions—is merely sustained or dramatized in song. Excitement in speech finds its counterpart in quicker tempos in music.

However, there is a vital difference between speech and music which Archibald T. Davison points up in *Church Music: Illusion and Reality*.[6] The appeals of speech and music are in opposite directions. While both are dependent upon the doorway of the senses, music tends to appeal more quickly and strongly to the emotions while speech is designed to appeal more immediately to the intellect. In speech the mind is primarily aroused by the meaning of the words; then the imagination works upon the idea and an emotional response may result. In music the body becomes aware of some organization of sound such as a flowing melody or a martial rhythm. The emotions are immediately stirred and the imagination begins to relate the sounds to some mental picture.

---

[6] Cambridge, Mass.: Harvard University Press, 1952.

←──────────── Speech

EMOTIONS   IMAGINATION   INTELLECT

Music ──────────────→

The intellect is rarely used by most listeners; modern man is so bombarded with recorded and broadcast sound that he turns his mind off and becomes a nonlistener in self-defense. Yet he can never gain a full appreciation of music until he learns to listen for melodic, rhythmic, and harmonic patterns and to comprehend musical forms.

Thus both music and speech are capable of following the same channel, although in different directions, and music and poetry joined in perfect union and urging the mind and heart in one direction can be a vital and moving aid to worship. Handel's famous "Hallelujah Chorus" from the *Messiah* is a perfect matching of words and music in an oratorio, and Ralph Vaughan Williams' magnificent tune, "Sine Nomine," is a perfect match for the words, "For all the saints." In sharp contrast is the music set to the words of the song, "Standing on the promises." From the title one would be led to think of strength, faith, foundation, but when the tune is played there is nothing strong, secure, or foundational about the music. The tune seems to say "jumping" or "dancing" on the promises. A far better choice is the hymn, "How firm a foundation," with the tune, "Foundation," based on only five notes of the scale.

While music and poetry are closely related, music will have an optimum impact only when it parallels the poetry and forms a perfect union with it. A little critical listening to and evaluation of anthems and hymn tunes in current use would reveal many mismatches of words and music, and even the church would have to agree that in many cases there is just cause for divorce. Further discussion of the relation of words and music must be deferred to the chapter on the choir's music.

It will perhaps be fruitful at this point to examine some of the present attitudes toward worship and the use of music in worship which have been stumbling blocks in many churches. One attitude is that of music as a servant or "handmaiden of religion." In a very real sense this is correct, for a hymn tune is excellent only as it is subservient to the words, undergirds the thought and captures the dominant mood. Likewise a prelude which prepares the minds of the listeners for the service which follows "serves" its purpose. Yet music has been forced by many to do things unrelated to true serving. When a song leader suggests that a few hymns be sung till everyone arrives, when hymn stanzas are omitted without care or thought, thereby spoiling the sense (and even forcing the congregation to sing fragments of sentences), when the organist is expected to "noodle a bit" to cover an awkward movement in the service or to drown out the confusion of the late-comers, or when hymns are interspersed with fun songs willy-nilly in fellowship singing; then music is being forced to serve, not as a handmaiden, but as a prostitute.

Other misuses of music are the result of sincere but often misguided attempts to plan "worship experiences." The danger here is that the service will be planned only to secure some psychological response, which carried to the extreme can become psychological manipulation, a man-made trap to secure a particular reaction which is not necessarily a response to God's call.

Another misleading phrase, "enriching worship," has come to the fore with the stirrings for a more liturgical pattern of worship. Enrichment unfortunately may take no more substantial form than adding a little musical fertilizer (in the form of numerous, lengthy, and often irrelevant choir responses), fancy lighting effects, including a neon cross, chime notes striking the hour, and a misnomer called "The Sacrament of Silence" during which the organist is expected to play "Sweet hour of prayer" with *vox humana* and full tremolo. Such additions to a service of worship are about as effective in revitalizing true worship as feeding sugared water to a dying man in need of a blood transfusion.

There is a fallacy in the attitude that worship takes place in the chancel area with the people sitting in the church as spectators. In sports the American people are fast becoming spectators instead of participants, and this attitude has invaded the church. An usher illustrated this all too clearly when he said, "This is the forty yard line, folks; you can get a good view of the show from here." Unfortunately, the congregation is often called an audience—present to hear the choir sing the anthems and hymns and to hear the oratory of the preacher. The newspaper account which spoke of the finest prayer ever offered to a Boston audience may be amusing, but it is also a sad commentary on the state of worship.

21

A more wholesome attitude toward worship can be developed through thinking of worship as a verb instead of as a noun. Worship is active, not passive. It is an act which every person must make in response to the searching lovingkindness of God, for God has acted first, seeking us in many ways to reconcile us to himself long before we were ready to seek him. In creation, in giving us life, in history, in prophecy, in the still small voice, in the "love which over and around us lies," in the lives of saints of all generations, in the scriptures, in the "fellowship of kindred minds," in the life and call of Christ—everywhere and anywhere we turn, God has already acted calling us to commune with him and to answer him.

> I sought the Lord and afterward I knew
> He moved my soul to seek Him, seeking me.[7]

As a result of God's acts, we are called to action individually and corporately. When Moses stood before the burning bush he was commanded to take off his shoes because he stood on holy ground. His first act was inspired by the presence of the living God, but next Moses was expected to put on his shoes and to lead the children of Israel out of the land of Egypt. Merely to be awestruck in the presence of God is imperfect and inadequate worship. With awe, praise, adoration, and thanksgiving must go confession of sin, listening to God's Word, and finally consecration and dedication of self to the tasks to which we are called.

God acts first, but man also acts in worship, and his actions take personal and corporate forms. In a service of worship a hymn may be an act of giving thanks, of confessing, of praying for guidance, or of consecrating oneself to the will of God. While a hymn is corporately sung, each individual must make a personal appropriation unto himself if it is to have its fullest meaning and value. Although the great congregation includes the apostles, the saints, and the martyrs of all generations, and even the choirs of heaven, the uniqueness of every person in the sight of God must not be forgotten. Each person must make his own offering of praise and prayer to God and must face the judgment and will of God just as surely as did Cain and Abel when they brought their

---

[7] Anonymous.

gifts to the altar. Isaac Watts put it thus, "Let every creature rise, and bring peculiar honors to our King." Each individual has a unique and personal act which he alone must make before God and the household of God, and there is no person so insignificant that he cannot make some real contribution to the worship life of the church.

> What shall I render to the Lord
>   for all his bounty to me?
> I will lift up the cup of salvation
>   and call on the name of the Lord,
> I will pay my vows to the Lord
>   in the presence of all his people.
>   (Ps. 116:12-14)

In the service of worship we hear God speaking to us in many ways—through the scripture, the sermon, hymns, and prayers and in return we respond with our prayers, hymns, and offering (of self as well as money). This conversation between God and man has been beautifully stated by Charles Wesley:

> Talk with us, Lord, Thyself reveal,
> While here o'er earth we rove;
> Speak to our hearts, and let us feel
> The kindling of Thy love.
>
> .   .   .   .
>
> Here then, my God, vouchsafe to stay,
> And bid my heart rejoice;
> My bounding heart shall own Thy sway,
> And echo to Thy voice.

Worship, however, is more than action and interaction between God and man; it must be worthy action. Worth-ship, the original meaning of the word, suggests that our worship be worthy of the God whom we praise.

> Worthy art thou, our Lord and God,
> to receive glory and honor and power,
> for thou didst create all things,
> and by thy will they existed and were created.
>   (Rev. 4:11)

23

Our gifts to the God who created us, sent his Son to us, and guides us by his Holy Spirit should be worthy of acceptance. If this be true, our gifts should represent some cost to us. A shallow hymn, a sloppily sung anthem, are hardly fit gifts to bring as an offering to God, for they cost us little or nothing. If more work is required to sing a better hymn or to prepare a finer anthem, should we do less than our best to bring "a living sacrifice, holy and acceptable unto God, which is your spiritual worship"?

Worship must also be creative action. Unless our minds and hearts are seeking signs of God—his presence, his goodness, his loving care—we will be unable to respond. We will have eyes and see not, and ears and hear not. In the words of Elizabeth Barrett Browning in "Aurora Leigh":

> Earth's crammed with heaven,
> And every common bush afire with God;
> And only he who sees takes off his shoes—
> The rest sit round it and pluck blackberries.

Awareness of the burning bush was crucial to the encounter of Moses with God, and the fate of the people of Israel depended on his perception. But surely, we would say, a burning bush would be easy to see— no one could miss that. Yet week after week the congregation is in the presence of God, repeating holy words, handling holy things, till constant thoughtless repetition has dulled the mind into a rote performance of high and holy exercise. Only as each person attempts to make all things new as he approaches the throne of grace can worship take place. The most familiar hymn should be approached with a fresh and creative frame of mind, and the unfamiliar hymn should be welcomed with an open and receptive mind, for

> Sometimes a light surprises
> The Christian while he sings.[8]

God seeks to reach us through many avenues, and the person who listens, seeks, and is sensitive to creative moments truly worships. New insights and perceptions await the searching, open mind, but the person who slams the hymnal shut on Sunday morning when a new hymn is

---

[8] William Cowper.

24

announced is preventing a creative moment and in effect is slamming shut the door to communion with God.

While worship involves worthy and creative action, it must also be based on firm foundations of belief. What a man believes affects how he acts, for "whatsoever a man thinketh in his heart, so is he." In the preface to *Hymns and the Faith*, based on the study of forty-nine most commonly sung hymns, Erik Routley says:

It will be found that the papers that follow form a conspectus of Christian belief which . . . covers the whole of the credal country. Without straining the texts by an inch it has been possible to say something about all the cardinal doctrines of the Church. That is to say, our normal canon of popular hymns does really provide all the cardinal doctrines of Christendom.[9]

If this is true, the hymnal offers excellent opportunities to learn the faith and to guide worship; at the same time the responsibility for choosing the best possible expression of truth becomes obvious.

Some of Routley's illustrations may serve to highlight his opening statement:

Creation—"O worship the King, all-glorious above"
Providence—"Through all the changing scenes of life"
Gratitude—"Now thank we all our God"
Time and Eternity—"O God, our help in ages past"
Mystery—"God moves in a mysterious way"
History—"Praise, my soul, the King of Heaven"
Sanctification—"Love divine, all loves excelling"

In sharp contrast to the solid foundations exemplified in these hymns is the flimsy basis of the popular song, "I Believe," used by a choir director first as an anthem and then as a hymn. The "punch-line" of this pseudoreligious item is, "Every time I hear a new-born baby cry, then I know why I believe." Such sentimental twaddle is often foisted on congregations by well-meaning but misguided leaders who confuse an emotional tug at the heart strings with true worship.

While there is danger in choosing material which is not based on strong foundations of doctrine, there is also the danger of dishonest worship. In answer to the question, "Are ye able?" youth glibly

---

[9] (Greenwich, Conn.: The Seabury Press, 1956), p. x.

25

answer, "Lord, we are able," without very much thought as to whether or not they are really willing to go to the death for their beliefs. Unthinking singing is a form of dishonesty, for the singer mouths thoughts which are not his and have no grip on his mind or heart. Something is wrong when the congregation sings, "O Jesus, I have promised to serve Thee to the end," and then fails to give to a fund for carrying the message of Christ to the ends of the earth. Likewise there are some hymns which are either vague in thought (such as "Hark, hark, my soul!") or sub-Christian in their content (such as the last stanza of "My faith looks up to Thee," which presents an unchristian view of death). Each individual must constantly be on guard lest his worship become a matter of outward form, without personal integrity or honesty.

In the minutes of the first Methodist Conference held on Friday, June 29, 1744, at the Foundry in London, John Wesley was asked:

Q. How shall we guard against formality in public worship; particularly in singing?
A. 1. By preaching frequently on that head. 2. By taking care to speak only what we feel. 3. By choosing such hymns as are proper for the congregation; generally hymns of prayer or praise, rather than descriptive of particular states. 4. By not singing too much at once; seldom more than five or six verses. 5. By suiting the tune to the nature of the hymn. 6. By often stopping short and asking the people, "Now! do you know what you said last? Did you speak no more than you felt? Did you sing it as unto the Lord; with the spirit and with the understanding also?"

His suggestions are startling, but are worthy of consideration if extreme measures are needed to arouse a congregation out of formal and meaningless worship.

Lest worship be thought of as entirely a personal matter, the corporate nature of worship needs to be stressed. We are indeed all brothers in Christ, and the Church is a community of the faithful. The sense of fellowship and brotherhood which comes from worship together is a most important factor, and this sense of community is aided by singing hymns and by sharing wholeheartedly in all of the congregational responses. In The Art of Conducting Public Worship Albert W. Palmer quoted Raymond Calkins:

26

There is all the more reason for embracing this opportunity (for active participation in the liturgy) at the hour of common worship because of the difficulty which many people recognize of speaking about the reality of religion in private. A feeling of reserve, due in part to reverence, but also in part to false timidity or downright lack of personal conviction, keeps them from uttering in personal ways during six days of the week the faith that is, or should be, in them. All the more reason, therefore, for uttering in corporate fashion, on the first day, their common faith at the hour of common prayer and worship.[10]

To which the author added, "As the Psalmist puts it: 'Let the redeemed of the Lord say so'!" The psalmist also added other imperatives:

> Let the peoples praise thee, O God;
> let all the peoples praise thee! (67:5)

Paul exhorted:

Let the peace of Christ rule in your hearts, to which indeed you were called in one body. And be thankful. Let the word of Christ dwell in you richly, as you teach and admonish one another in all wisdom, and as you sing psalms and hymns and spiritual songs with thankfulness in your hearts to God. (Col. 3:15-16)

Corporate worship is involved in common thought, common devotion and worship, and common appreciations.

Worship which is honest, worthy, creative, and based on faith will result not only in action and interaction, but also reaction. It is stirring to talk with God, but it is equally important that we hear his commands and obey. Our response to worship may be highly individualistic or corporate. It may be the response of a Schweitzer to the needs of a continent, or of a community to the need for clearing slums, but true worship always results in changed lives. Our prayer is:

> Lord, speak to me, that I may speak
> In living echoes of Thy tone.[11]

If we leave a service with only such thoughts as "Wasn't the music

[10] *Concerning Public Worship*, p. 11.
[11] Frances R. Havergal.

lovely; what a wonderful sermon!" and our lives are no different in the days that follow, then worship has not occurred. When Moses came down from the top of the mountain after talking with God we are told that "the face of Moses shone." When Isaac Watts stood amazed before the love of God as he surveyed the wondrous cross, his action was complete surrender:

Were the whole realm of nature mine,
That were a present far too small;
Love so amazing, so divine,
Demands my soul, my life, my all.

Here is worship in the sense of complete response to the love of God.

This brief review of attitudes toward worship and the abuses and misuses of music inevitably leads to the conclusion that there is a desperate need, not for more attention to program, but for a searching re-evaluation of the use of music on the part of every person who in any way is a part of the music and worship leadership of the church.

The primary problem which faces the contemporary minister or church musician is the reuniting of music and worship in their historical role on sound theological foundations. Any music program which is evolved must stand on solid ground and should be able to give satisfactory answer to these questions:

1. Does the music speak the feelings and thoughts of the true worshiper? Is it related to life itself?

2. Does the music express universal truths as well as individual emotions? Does the music help each individual to grow in Christian stature?

3. Does the music speak of eternal mysteries? Does the greatness of the music suggest the greater majesty of God?

4. Is the music creative in design and performance? Does it help make the time of worship one of new insights, new visions, and new approaches to God?

5. Have the composer and performers assumed moral responsibility for creative integrity and excellence of craftsmanship in presenting the Word of God?

There is a serious need in the contemporary scene to broaden the base of the music program in terms of a concept of worship which goes beyond the eleven o'clock "worship service" on Sunday morning. Worship which is concerned with the whole of life also includes Christian education, stewardship, and evangelism, and there is no organic distinction between them. Yet in many churches there is one type of music and hymnal for the eleven o'clock worship service, an entirely different kind of hymnal and song for the "Sunday school," and often a third for evangelistic meetings. The value of a music program is further weakened and made ineffectual if the director limits his time and energy only to the choirs and the Sunday morning music, and if he fails to treat the children's and youth choirs as more than either a musical or an educational project. Music can be an evangelizing agent in drawing persons to the Church and to its message; it can be a means of "teaching one another" and of helping persons to grow spiritually; and as a method of stewardship of time and talent the choir program is an effective means of serving God and man. Yet in each area (evangelism, education, and stewardship) the ultimate concern is worship in its fullest sense.

The purpose of this book, then, is not to restore a particular pattern of worship or to explain a program of music and worship, but to lead the minister, musician, and layman into a deeper appreciation and understanding of their respective roles in initiating and fostering a valid relation of music to worship and of working effectively in a program worthy of this bond.

II

The Minister

SINCE WORSHIP IS CENTRAL TO THE LIFE OF THE CHURCH, AND THE GOAL
of church music is to aid worship and to serve as a means of worship,
leadership should come first of all from the spiritual head of the
congregation—the minister. One of his chief concerns is the planning,
correlation, and co-ordination of the entire worship life of the church.
There is no area which does not demand his guiding hand as pastor of
the flock. It is not enough that he alone understand the role of music,
for he bears the responsibility for guiding the total music program toward
the goal of true worship through every area of the church's life by
interpreting to the various leaders (worship committee, director,
organist, pianists, church-school leaders) their responsibility for their
segments of the total work. If the minister is effective and successful in
his leadership the church-school teacher will understand why it is
important to choose hymns carefully for each age group; the choir
director will see that his job is of much greater scope than teaching
anthems to a choir; the pianists and organist will see that their manner
of hymn playing and their choice of music may further or hinder
worship; the music committee will see its job as more important than
merely organizing and supporting musical activity; and the congregation
will assume its role of active participation in a total program of music
which reaches every person and leads to a deeper sense of worship.

Unfortunately, a minister may be so impressed with the complexities
of his job that he cannot "bother with music problems." As Samuel
A. Devan painted the picture:

He is expected to combine the financial acumen of John D. Rockefeller,
the spiritual fervor of St. Bernard of Clairvaux, the scholarship of Spengler,
the organizing ability of a German bureaucrat, the aggressiveness of Napoleon,
the smoothness of a politician, the tenderness of a parent, the magnetism of

30

Lloyd George, the manners of Chesterfield, with the literary force of St. Paul, and the evangelistic impetus of John Wesley. It is hardly to be wondered at if occasionally some individual falls a little short of expectations in some one of these particulars.[1]

As a preacher, theologian, diplomat, pastor, administrator, financier, counselor, and psychiatrist he has little time left for involvement in the music program. Therefore the minister often prefers to stay clear of any entanglement with music, particularly so if it is the war department.

He cannot and must not take a hands-off attitude, however, for the relation of music to worship is so vital and the amount of time spent musically in a service of worship is so extensive (up to fifty per cent) that the effective minister is compelled to develop some basic philosophy of music and worship, administer policies, select and guide personnel, and promote the cause of church music in the entire life of the church. As minister and spiritual leader he is responsible for making the music of the church spiritually enriching and edifying. If he finds the music of the congregation, the choirs or the church school failing to feed the sheep he must take action as shepherd of the flock. Therefore he must know what is good spiritual musical food and see that it is fed in the worship and educational life of the church.

He must prepare himself to assume his role of leadership in the music area, remembering that leadership does not imply carrying the whole load or doing the job alone. The wise minister will work through the music committee to secure competent musical leadership to direct the music program in the congregation, choirs, and church school. He can exert true leadership and guide the thinking of the music committee by recommending books, by discussing the philosophy of music and worship with them, by encouraging and supporting musical leaders, by delegating authority, by utilizing the available and potential talent in the church, and by helping each person see his responsibility to use good music effectively in every area of the church's life.

In most churches the leadership must be secured from the membership of the church—a housewife who has had some musical training in college, a young piano or organ student with leadership potential, or a

[1] *Ascent to Zion* (New York: The Macmillan Company, 1942), p. 215. Used by permission of Mrs. Winifrede Devan.

local music teacher, possibly in the public schools or a nearby college. Sometimes a church will be unable to pay anything, and sometimes only a token salary, but every church that can possibly do so should be encouraged by the minister to secure a full-time director of music whose training has been specifically in the ministry of music. The person who assumes the job should have his responsibilities clearly defined in collaboration with the music committee and the minister and definite lines of communication and command outlined.

While the minister will confer with the music committee in outlining the general phases of the music program, he must work even more closely with the director and the organist. It is to this relationship that we turn first. The necessity for working co-operatively has already been suggested, but few ministers share sufficiently with their musicians in planning. J. H. Jowett discussed this problem in his book, *The Preacher: His Life and Work:*

Enlist his spirit in your own exalted purpose. Make him realize, by the fellowship of your own deepest desires, that he is a fellow-labourer in the salvation of men to the glory of God. Let the music be redeemed from being a human entertainment, and let it become a divine revelation. Let it never be an end in itself but a means of grace, something to be forgotten in the dawning of something grander. Let it never be regarded as an exhibition of human cleverness but rather as a transmitter of spiritual blessings: never as a terminus, but always as a thoroughfare. And therefore take counsel with your organist. Tell him what you want to do next Sunday. Do not be shy about leading him into the deeper things. Do not keep him in the outer courts: take him into the secret place.[2]

Sharing of purpose and material is crucial whether the church be large or small, or whether the musician be full-time paid or part-time volunteer, and should begin with the minister planning the program and sermon topics as far in advance as possible. More and more ministers are making it a practice to outline their preaching themes a year in advance—sometimes following the liturgical year. The advantage of this to the musician becomes evident when it is realized that selecting music on approval for study, choosing appropriate anthems, ordering enough copies for the choir, and rehearsing the anthem for four to six weeks

[2] Used by permission of Harper & Brothers.

can add up to months. Learning the theme of the service or the sermon topic on Wednesday is of little help to a choir director on Thursday night, for only a top professional choir could manage to learn an anthem in one rehearsal and even then its presentation would lack the polish and depth of insight which comes only from living with an anthem over a period of time. If the sermon subject and hymns are not chosen until Saturday night, the minister cannot expect the anthem to be appropriate (except by lucky chance), and he cannot expect the choir to give leadership on the hymns since they will not have been rehearsed. *The Choir Loft and the Pulpit*, jointly written by Clarence and Helen A. Dickinson and Paul Wolfe, consists of a series of orders of worship used at the Brick Presbyterian Church in New York for an entire year with all material jointly chosen in a planning session. It includes organ music, anthems, hymns, prayers, scripture readings, responses, and sermon topics and themes with texts. This type of careful planning avoids such ludicrous situations as the use of "Ho! everyone that thirsteth" before a temperance sermon; more important it brings to the service of worship a unity of purpose and thought which is conducive to true worship.

An indication of the joint responsibility for the service is expressed in an article by Howard A. Johnson:

From the point of view of theology, of poetry, and of music, the music presented in a parish ought to be something of which the pastor and the organist have a concordant opinion. If the congregation doesn't like it, it ought to be something that both priest and organist can together defend. The integrity of both persons is at stake. The organist must not be asked to play music which musically is indefensible. The priest must not be expected to defend any compositions which, however brilliant they may be as music, are theologically objectionable, liturgically inappropriate, or devotionally disturbing.[3]

The director and organist who are deemed worthy to be co-partners in the planning and carrying out of worship, should be named in the bulletin of the church. They should also be included in any staff or group meeting which plans or discusses the work and life of the church. Regardless of whether the musician is full or part time, as a co-worker

[3] "Something About Church Music," p. 4.

33

in serving the church he deserves the friendship, confidence, and moral support of the minister. If his judgment cannot be trusted the wrong person has been chosen.

A competent leader should receive an adequate salary, for a servant is worthy of his hire. There should be no dictation to him in the music field provided there has been agreement on the general policies of the church. Most conflicts arise out of lack of mutual respect and co-operation and the failure to come to an understanding of purpose and plan before the director is hired. Particularly annoying to a director is a minister who casually invites people to join the choir without knowing whether or not they can sing. Names of prospects should be turned over to the director, for it is his responsibility to handle the musical matters of the church. A pastor may suggest a title of an anthem or of an organ piece, but the final decision must rest in the hands of the musician. In short, Christian ethics should apply to the minister and musician relationship.

Battles and hard feelings can be avoided if the advice of *The Choir Loft and the Pulpit* is heeded:

If the pastor and the musician are to play their much needed parts in the life of the church, there must be the closest kind of collaboration and mutual confidence between them. The whole tone of the service will depend upon their teamwork. The first thing for each of them to understand is that each of them is human. . . . Musicians are not more temperamental than ministers, and neither of them has any monopoly on concert psychology. . . . To this initial understanding of our common humanity might be added a few fairly well tested rules of procedure. The first is that the minister is the commanding officer in the church. He is given that position not only by church law but by common sense. . . . A second general principle to be observed is division of responsibilities. Certain parts in the service will come under the direction of each. . . . A third principle to be observed is what might be called staff work. Church services are much like armies, and failures and defeats can be traced to inadequate staff preparation. . . . From all that has been said it should be clear that the minister of the pulpit and the minister of the choir loft are fellow laborers. There are not two services; there is one. The service is not to the glory of either of them or to the glory of the choir; it is to the glory of God. If that vision is caught, if there is some willingness to accept and understand the human limitations of each, two men can work together with much confidence and happiness. Best of all, through their combined gifts, the Church which they serve will come to feel the greatness of worship. The congregation will see the Lord high and lifted up, His glory filling the temple.[4]

There is also a relation to the choir to be considered. On Sunday mornings at the conclusion of the service the pastor is usually found greeting people at the door, while the choir quietly retires to the robing room and out the rear exit. If the sermon was helpful the pastor hears about it; if the music was helpful usually no word reaches the choir. Expression of appreciation should be given by the minister to them, but this word should take place, not in the order of worship, but in other places and in other ways. A visit to the choir rehearsal occasionally to thank the choir for their contribution, to share future plans and hopes, and to remind the singers that they are co-ministers in worship will do much to increase the effectiveness of the choir's work. It is also well for the minister occasionally to attend rehearsal if only to sit in the men's section and to sing with the choir under the leadership of the director.

Perhaps most important of all is the relationship of the minister to future leadership. He should take an interest in all of the choirs of the church, offering encouragement to individuals with musical potential. He should seek out from the director the names of young persons with talent who should be trained to serve the church, and then encourage the officers of the church to assist financially in their training if necessary. Some churches which cannot afford professional leadership can pay for piano or organ lessons for young people who in turn will be able to take over the music work of the church and to serve more skillfully. By all means the minister should see that the church organ is made available to qualified students for practice under competent supervision. One church arranged private lessons for a talented girl who soon became the chief organist, and group lessons for three other girls who became substitute organists for many of the weekday services. The minister can also help the musical program by securing books and materials and by encouraging the music leaders to improve themselves and their leadership. He can keep abreast of new developments in church music by

[4] Clarence and Helen A. Dickinson and Paul Wolfe (New York: The H. W. Gray Company, 1943), pp. 26 ff. Used by permission.

attending church-music conferences and workshops and by bringing his organist, director, and other music leaders. It is his duty to know what his denomination is doing in the field of church music. If it is developing a program he should support it; if it is not, he should insist that it do so.

As the importance of music to worship is recognized, more and more seminaries are offering courses in the philosophy and practice of church music, but unfortunately many such courses are still elective, and hundreds and even thousands of ministers arrive in the local church with inadequate personal training to guide the music committee with competence. Yet there is no need for despair, for many excellent books are available to the seeking pastor to clarify his own thinking before he attempts to lead the music committee. Several of the best are listed in the bibliography.

The ability to judge what music is proper for worship and what is not can be developed without a complete musical education. Joseph W. Clokey in chapter five of *In Every Corner Sing* suggests a series of questions which will help even a comparatively untrained person to be discriminating in choosing appropriate music. By guiding the volunteer and untrained music leaders the minister can lift the level of music and worship in any church.

The minister who is concerned about the faith and beliefs of the church members will stay alert to the theology which is sung in the church school and in the youth groups, as well as in the services of worship, for it should not be contrary to the doctrines of the church but should be doctrinally sound and spiritually edifying. A little investigation will reveal many instances where the church-school songs are working at cross purposes to and undercutting the theology which the minister preaches. Changing such a situation is clearly the job of the minister.

It is particularly important that the question of "association" be faced and understood, for it presents one of the knottiest problems in church music. Every person has a tendency to avoid the untried and unknown and to cling to that which is familiar. When a person says, "I know what I like," he is really saying, "I like what I know." Calm, detached judgment of an "old favorite" is most difficult, for it is possible for an individual to relate an extremely poor piece of doggerel with

36

a pleasant and even meaningful experience. When he makes the mistake of insisting that the song should have the same value to everyone else, he overlooks the fact that the value of association is purely personal and the song is not necessarily endowed with eternal value thereby. Particularly in the church school, teachers and song leaders are inclined to cling to the songs of their childhood without recognizing that many are weak, and some even insidious in their theology. Because a person may have a fondness for a ditty called "Give, said the little stream," which he sang as a child, he has no right to foist it on the children of today if on close study it is obviously insipid and has little value.

It is also the minister's duty to guide in the ordering of worship services and every movement of the liturgy. In fact, it is his responsibility to supervise all of the factors, both physical and personal, that may affect a service. In carrying out the order, all signals involving the director, organist, choir, and ushers should be carefully cleared to avoid such distractions as the minister's rising to speak before the organist has finished the prelude, his announcing a change of hymns on the spur of the moment, or the ushers' coming forward before the offertory is completed. Particularly annoying is the statement following the prelude, "We will now begin our worship by. . . ." In a carefully planned and executed service there is usually no excuse for announcing hymn numbers or signalling the congregation to stand at certain points if proper announcements appear in the bulletin. Ordinarily the choir's standing and sitting are sufficient cues to the congregation. If a statement is made concerning a hymn it should be for the sole purpose of arousing the congregation to better singing by calling attention to something of particular interest or value concerning its historical, biographical, literary, or theological background. It is not necessary to say, "We will now stand and sing to the glory of God number . . . ," or to read all of the first stanza after announcing the hymn number.

Following the suggestion of John Wesley, quoted earlier, the minister might from time to time preach sermons on the subject of worship— the congregation's duties, the place of music, the reasons for using a particular order of worship. Few congregations know what worship really is, why certain acts take place, and even fewer understand the place of music in worship. The minister should not hesitate to experiment with the order and items in an order of worship, but a balance of liturgical materials of the past as well as the present should be maintained.

David H. Hislop in *Our Heritage of Public Worship* suggested:

Worship must have proportion of spiritual content. By this I mean we must relate authority and freedom in public worship. . . . There is a relation between the authority of God that imposes restraint and the freedom of the Divine Spirit that calls for spontaneity, between the authority of the classic tradition in which man has worshiped and the freedom of the immediate mood which envelops the worship. To balance rightly restraint and spontaneity, authority and freedom, is to give proportion to a service, and that too is an element in the beauty of worship.[5]

Every minister should be able to sing, or at least should make an attempt to sing the hymns. Unfortunately there are some who brag that they are monotones. A true monotone is an extreme rarity, and such a boast is a camouflage and subterfuge to avoid facing up to a musical responsibility. Any minister will find study with a competent voice teacher helpful, since correct singing carries over into effective speech, which is one of his main assets in the pulpit. Every prospective theological student should be encouraged to join church choirs and choral groups, taking advantage of every opportunity to learn good vocal methods and fine choral literature.

The congregation will be encouraged to share wholeheartedly in hymn singing if the minister himself sings the hymns with vigor. If he sits poring over his sermon notes during the hymn or spends the time gazing over the congregation he indicates by his action that hymn singing is not important. But if a service is broadcast or a public address system is used, the minister who sings, no matter how well, should stay a good distance from the microphone in order to avoid a solo performance.

The effective minister is a constant student of the hymnal. Knowing the hymnal involves not only a study of the historical background of hymns, their authors and composers, but also a careful study of the individual texts and tunes. Every hymnal contains certain indispensable aids to this study. The table of contents is an outline of the beliefs of the church; the topical index is an extension of the basic outline, broken

[5] London: T. & T. Clark, 1935, pp. 305-6.

38

down into many smaller sub-headings so that hymns on almost any subject or topic can be found. Some books also include a scriptural index, listing scriptural references to be found in the various hymns. In searching for the most appropriate hymn it is wise to have available hymnals of many denominations since hymn editors of another book may list additional supplementary suggestions on a given subject. The indexes of authors and composers are useful to the student who wishes to study the historical development of hymns.

The minister is directly responsible for congregational participation in the service, for the choice of hymns rests primarily in his hands. However, this concern should be shared with the organist and director, for the minister often may choose a hymn text without knowing whether or not the tune is singable, whereas the musician, if left to his own devices, may judge a hymn on the value of the tune without too much reference to the text. There is also the factor of appropriateness of hymns to the various liturgical seasons, to the needs of the specific service, and the relation to other parts of the service. If minister and musician will spend time together in choosing hymns, each will receive benefit from the counsel of the other. Carefully maintained records of hymns sung and frequency of use will help guide in choosing hymns wisely.

Often a fine text which is wedded to a poor tune can be salvaged for congregational use by substituting an alternative tune using the same meter; therefore the metrical index is invaluable to the minister and the church musician for making the best possible choice. If an alternative tune is chosen, these rules should be followed: (1) Let the congregation know what is done and why (either by announcement or by printed notice in the bulletin). (2) Ask the organist and choir to rehearse the new tune and warn the choir to sing the melody only. (3) Choose a tune which is very familiar to the congregation. It is quite difficult to sing the words on one page while trying to watch a tune elsewhere in the book. (4) Choose a tune which has the same meter and the same accents. A meter may be either trochaic ($/\cup/\cup$) or iambic ($\cup/\cup/$), in which case the accentuation is reversed. (5) Choose a tune which has the same mood as the text. For instance, "O God, our help in ages past" can be sung metrically to the tune usually associated with "Amazing grace! how sweet the sound," but the tune has none of the stateliness of

Watts's fine text and does not belong with it. (6) Always counsel with the director or organist to ensure the best choice possible.

Familiarity with the hymnal can only come from individual study of every single hymn in the book. This investigation should be carried on in conjunction with the hymnal handbook so that the fullest meaning and beauty of each hymn can be found. It is particularly important that each text be read as a poem—a difficult procedure where the text is interlaced between the two staffs of music, but most rewarding as a spiritual exercise. The studious minister will set aside some definite time for this research, and when his own church hymnal is completed will turn to hymnals from other denominations to discover that no one book has a monopoly on all of the best devotional material available.

The alert minister can indicate the importance he attaches to hymns by using them in ways other than singing. A sermon may grow out of the thought pattern of a hymn (e.g., "Thou art the Way" or "Come, Holy Ghost, our hearts inspire") or a series of sermons built around a group of hymns which develop a theological subject. Hymns may be used as spoken or sung calls to worship, prayer responses, scripture responses, responsive readings, or litanies. Many may be read as prayers, by the minister alone or with the congregation. Hymns may be listed by number in the bulletin for use as meditation before the start of the service. Hymns may be interspersed with slides of famous paintings for a special service of worship, and of course a group of hymns can be used to develop a theme in a hymn festival. Hymns read or sung at funerals may be particularly helpful if chosen to give faith and hope. The opportunities are unlimited for using hymns in a creative and imaginative way, and this subject will be discussed further in the section dealing with the congregational choir practice.

One of the pitfalls every minister should avoid is a closed mind toward church music. He may be tempted to feel that because he had a course or two in church music at seminary he has learned all there is to know in the field. Or he may feel that because he knows a hundred hymns or so that there is nothing more to learn about hymns. Or most dangerous of all, he may try to force a certain type of music program on a new congregation because it worked very well in another church where he was pastor, failing to realize that no two congregations are alike in size, constituency, temperament, or culture. One congregation may need a long period of education in church music before it can comprehend and accept the best music. Another may already be receptive to a program far beyond the sights of the minister himself, and he will have to grow up musically to the level of the new congregation. The wise minister will keep abreast by reading and study; he will also keep his hand on the musical pulse of the people.

No minister has the right to hide behind the excuse, "I can't carry a tune in a bucket" or "I don't know anything about music," for his role as minister carries with it the responsibility to know something about church music. By study of the books listed in the bibliography he can fill in gaps of knowledge; by private voice study he can improve his musical ability; and by securing and supporting the finest leadership possible he can develop a true ministry of music. The minister, then, is probably the most important person to church music, for its level cannot rise higher than his estimation of its importance in the life of the church.

III

The Music Committee

A COMMITTEE HAS BEEN CALLED, AMONG OTHER THINGS, A GROUP WHICH keeps minutes and wastes hours; yet the work of every church is organized and directed by committees, occasionally with conspicuous success. Not only does a committee draw people into closer living contact with the work of the church, but it relieves a minister of needless pressures in a taxing schedule. In many churches it is through the music committee that the minister works to develop and guide the music program, but there is often less than unanimity of thought as to who should serve on the committee and what the scope of its responsibilities and duties should be.

There are instances where the choir director is chairman of the music committee, thus making him his own boss! One famous Presbyterian minister informed the chairman that his job was to leave the director of music alone and see that everyone did likewise. On the other extreme there are committees that run matters with an iron hand—choosing the anthems, naming soloists for each Sunday, and dictating all policies. Others run bazaars, present operettas, and hold rummage sales to raise money for their own program, operating independently of the church budget. Some are afflicted by "chairmanitis" with the members serving only as a rubber stamp the few times they meet. When a group of church musicians recently was asked who hired them, some said the music committee, some the pastor, and some the governing board.

The first step toward a sane approach to the music committee is to recognize that it is not an independent group in the church, for the music committee must work in close co-operation with the worship committee and the education committee. It must first of all have some clear understanding of the place and role of music in worship before it can move intelligently forward in securing leadership and outlining an effective program. It must also plan a continuing educational program in music for the entire church, including the church school, so the worship and church-school programs do not work at cross purposes musically as so often happens when the children are taught one type of hymn—or song —in church school while another is used for worship services. Evans E. Crawford, instructor in practical theology at Howard University, said in a lecture at the St. Louis Area Pastors' School in July, 1959, "We'll hold a revival and save seven souls, but neglect our church school and lose a whole generation." The church-school program should provide opportunities in preparation for worship, and the hymns taught should be of the highest caliber, taken chiefly from the church hymnal. A study of this problem should be undertaken jointly with the education committee so each group benefits from the viewpoint and experience of the other.

In piloting the music program of the entire church, the committee is concerned with equipment (organ and pianos), hymnals for every group, and music leadership (pianists, music leaders). It should guide the choice and use of music for every age group—children, youth, and adults—including fun and fellowship singing. In all areas of the church's life the committee should work for unity of purpose and values.

The membership of the music committee should include persons with musical judgment who can guide the program intelligently and musically. At the same time it should also include those who are not musicians but who may be able to assist in other ways. Perhaps every music committee should have at least one person who has complained loudest—he may get a new understanding of church music and may even be converted! Members should be:

1. Sympathetic to the cause of good church music
2. Promoters and salesmen of the program
3. Sources of advice and counsel to the music leadership
4. Sensitive to the reactions of the congregation and able to interpret and bridge differences
5. Constructive critics of the program.

The committee should represent the mind of the entire church, with members from the governing board, the finance committee, the choral groups (probably the choir presidents), key musicians who can help recruit singers, the chairman of the choir mothers' guild, the education

43

committee, and the congregation at large. Membership should be on some system of rotation so a chairman does not serve for a lifetime and so new blood is constantly brought into the committee.

The pastor, organist, and director should be ex officio members, and there should be a representative from the education committee because of the liaison necessary between the two groups. Likewise, a member of the music committee and the director of music should also attend the education meetings. In at least one denomination the director is an ex-officio member of the education committee.

The primary job of the committee is to secure competent leadership in music and then to support the program which is jointly established. The actual hiring is usually done by the governing board, but upon recommendation of the music committee in consultation with the pastor. Every church that can do so should hire a well-trained, full-time director of music, for such a person will be able to develop a program which is truly a ministry to the congregation. There are many schools which offer training in church music, and each year more and more trained leaders are available.

The committee must decide whether it is desirable to secure two persons—an organist and a director—or one person to handle both jobs. This decision should be based on the availability of a highly trained and competent musician (many persons who try to play and direct are incompetent to do so), the scope of the choir program (one person can spread his energies and interest too thin if there are many choirs), and the physical arrangement of the choir loft and organ console (it may be physically impossible for the organist to see and direct the choir.) If there are two persons, the chief authority for leadership must be clearly defined to avoid friction. In most churches the director would be the head, but care should be taken to secure a director who is musically competent. Few things are as conducive to war in the choir loft as the situation where the organist—receiving the smaller salary—is a superior musician to the director but must take direction from a musical inferior. Other needful personnel might include clerical help, either volunteer or part-time paid, and assistants to the organist for certain services or to the director to help with youth choirs. An important part-time position could well be that of a supervisor of church-school music, who may also work with the children's choirs.

As a prelude to securing leadership, the committee, with the minister, should study the church—its membership, size of age groups, location in the community, musical facilities and potentialities to determine how many choirs are actually possible, how many prospects can be found for these choirs, how often the choirs are needed to lead in worship services, when rehearsals can best be scheduled, what the needs of the church school for hymn playing and musical leadership are, what opportunities present themselves for recreational use of music, and what outside musical events may be expected (choir festivals, civic oratorio groups, conference music events).

The following questions should be raised and answered:

1. What is the musical atmosphere of the church? What is its history in terms of attitude and growth? Is it conservative, progressive, or static? The success or failure of previous choirs should be thoroughly investigated and the present interest evaluated. While difficult to measure, the level of musical understanding and appreciation of the congregation will affect the development of a choir. It will also determine the point at which the musical education of the congregation must start.

2. How large an adult choir can and should be maintained? Perhaps seating facilities limit the number unnecessarily, in which case consideration should be given to making some structural changes. It should be obvious that a church of one hundred fifty members cannot maintain a choir equal in size to that of a church with five hundred members. Under certain circumstances, especially when leadership and material are not available, the church with a very small membership should not try to organize a choir of any kind, but should expend its energies in developing the music of the congregation. Size and quality bear little relation to each other in matters pertaining to church music, however. Some churches with few members have effective programs far superior to those maintained by many large congregations. A choir of six or eight dedicated singers possessing average ability and having good leadership can be a strong force in a church of fifty members.

3. How many choirs are needed? Again, mere numbers are unimportant. There must be a *need* for every choir and an opportunity for it to sing with reasonable frequency. If a church has two or more worship services each Sunday, the maintenance of several choirs can perhaps be easily justified. It is unfortunate that some ministers and musicians are

more concerned about the number of choirs maintained than about the opportunities provided for the growth of individual members, or for the contribution made to the life of the church.

4. What funds are available? Provision should be made for the cost of equipment, including a basic library, and for excellent leadership. There are some persons who feel that a church should never pay any musicians—director, organist, or singers. A good case can be made for not paying singers, but any church is wise to spend its money for the best possible leadership available. Good musical leadership can minister to the spiritual needs of the church, but poor leadership will doom a program to failure; better to abandon any efforts for starting a choir plan than to settle for less than the best that can possibly be obtained. A study made in 1952-53 showed that the amount of money being spent at that time on the music program was disgracefully small.[1] A random selection of 3,000 churches received questionnaires, and 1,279 replied in time to be considered. Of the 808 with fewer than 500 members, 124 had spent nothing on the music program the previous year, 19 had spent up to ten dollars, and a total of 531 had spent less than five hundred dollars. In churches of less than 250 members, the situation was much worse. Even in the larger churches the amounts spent were discouragingly small. Before any attempt is made to set up a music program, the congregation should realize the financial obligation it must assume if the program is to succeed. Musical instruments must be purchased and maintained, hymnals and anthems bought, teaching materials provided, books purchased for the library, choir robes secured and kept clean and in good repair—all these expenses, and many others, are involved in a good music program.

After due consideration has been given to the equipment needs and problems peculiar to the church, the duties of the leadership should be spelled out clearly so there will be no question as to the responsibilities of the organist and/or director. With the pastor there should be determined what staff duties and conferences are expected, how many church services are to be held each week, and what special functions such as family or fellowship dinners will call for the guidance of the musicians. Policies concerning music for funerals, weddings, vacation church

[1] William C. Rice, *A Century of Methodist Music: 1850-1950* (Iowa City: State University of Iowa).

46

schools, youth activities, camping programs, and other areas of the church life should be carefully considered. Organist fees for weddings should be set, as well as a definite policy concerning the type of music to be used at weddings.[2]

The music committee should determine a policy concerning the recruitment of choir personnel for all age groups. Particularly in the case of younger choirs they should provide assistance in arousing interest among the church-school departments and classes and various youth groups to promote the choir program. They can also form telephone committees to present the choir to parents of young children. At the adult choir level the committee should limit itself to locating prospective singers and suggesting these names to the director for action. In no instance should they invite a singer to join the choir without the approval of the director.

The committee may assist with the procuring of leadership for the choir mothers' guild. By helping with robing, transportation, telephoning, social events, and such things, the guild can take a heavy load off the shoulders of the director and at the same time increase parents' interest through participation. Assistant pianists and song leaders as well as part-time clerical help to take care of filing and repairing music, mimeographing letters, and similar work can also give valuable help to the director.

One of the most important jobs of the music committee is the establishment of a definite policy concerning the use of the church organ. First of all, the organ should be protected from indiscriminate use by outsiders. In instances where part of the organist's salary comes from wedding fees, the committee should make it a rule that only the church organist or someone approved by him is to play for weddings. In all events a fee for the organist should be collected by the church and then turned over to him. At the same time, the committee should never allow the organist to assume sole possession of the organ, jealously guarding the console key against any outside use. The organ belongs to the church, not the organist, and it should be used by students under supervision. In fact, the organist should be encouraged to give organ lessons to young people with musical talent, and the organ should be made available for

[2] See "Music Committee" in the bibliography.

47

practice as far as it is feasible, because the church is often the only possible place for organ practice. A pipe organ actually needs to be used extensively since the electrical contacts tend to corrode and the leather valves to harden and crack unless the organ is used regularly. The electric company on request will place a check meter to determine how much current is used if the finance committee is concerned about the expense and insists on some charge for practice time. The cost will prove to be negligible, particularly in view of the responsibility of the church for providing future leadership.

The committee would also be wise to provide an adequate budget for the proper upkeep and maintenance of the organ. In many cases it should plan for enlarging and improving the instrument where it is small or totally inadequate. Occasionally the committee may be called on to supervise the purchase of an instrument; needless to say, they should consult the organist and director concerning space requirements, placement, size of instrument, specification, and builder before making any decision. There is much debate about the relative merit of electronic instruments and pipe organs, and too often purchases are made on the basis of price alone. We do not presume to be final authorities in the matter, but wish to submit a few items in consideration of this problem.

1. Whatever organ is used as the basic church instrument should give a quality sound, consisting of the four basic classes of tone—diapason, flutes, reeds, and strings. The tone should have a good ensemble sound.

2. The pipe organ is specifically planned, built, and installed to fit the needs of a particular church. The same should be true of any electronic instrument.

3. A good piano built by a reputable firm will serve as an effective church instrument when lack of space and/or money prevents the purchase of a pipe organ. The tone—which is affected by the size and length of strings, characteristics of the sounding board, and the action—should be even throughout the entire compass and should have a full, singing quality. A good studio upright is superior to a tiny grand; to get the maximum benefit of the longer strings and sounding board, a grand piano should be at least six feet in length.

4. Spinet pianos and spinet electronic instruments are unsatisfactory church instruments. The tonal and mechanical limitations of each are

such that no accompanist can do an adequate job with them. A reputable dealer will not attempt to sell a spinet organ for church use.

5. Most electronic instruments do not provide the accompanist with the tonal strength and variety needed for good hymn playing or for anthem and solo accompaniment. A small two-manual-unit pipe organ with carefully chosen and voiced stops can compete favorably in price and versatility with most electronics and will provide better support and tonal variety. Any committee considering the purchase of an organ would be wise to investigate thoroughly the possibility of a small pipe organ by consulting various builders and studying various specifications such as those found in *The Diapason* and *The American Organist*.

6. Unfortunately, a pianist is able to "play" an electronic instrument with little or no specific training, to the great detriment of the instrument and the church. Certain electronic instruments are sold on the basis of this seeming advantage, which quickly becomes a disadvantage as the pianist transfers her technique to a keyboard instrument that is very little related to the piano. On the other hand, a pipe organ is much more difficult to play, even poorly, without some organ instruction.

The effectiveness of any electronic instrument will depend to a great extent upon the number, quality, and placement of speakers and upon the type of tone generator used. The speakers should have a frequency ranging from 16 vibrations per second or lower to 20,000 vibrations per second or above, and sufficient volume potential to fill the required space easily and without distortion. Electronically produced and/or amplified tone loses a great deal of its quality if the producing and/or amplifying units are forced to operate at maximum output. Since sanctuaries differ so greatly in their response to sound, considerable experimentation should be done before the speakers are permanently placed, and even then the way left open for further adjustments.

If the accompanying instrument is inadequate, the situation can be improved by the use of string, brass, or woodwind instruments. There is solid historical precedent for such use; the Old Testament refers on many occasions to the cymbal, harp, lyre, psaltery, and horn. At various times the Christian church has used "modern" instruments. We are well into another era that, while not yet comparable to the period of the Gabrielis, is bringing instrumental music into general acceptance in many Protestant denominations. Numerous large churches now de-

49

pend upon different combinations of instruments for accompaniments and for solo or ensemble presentations. Because of its wide range of tonal coloring, the organ will blend well with most instruments. Orchestral instruments can improve the music of almost any church, large or small, and make a valuable contribution to worship, provided they are chosen and used with discretion and good taste.

The committee should also make a point of providing good instruments for the church school. Where do church pianos come from? Most have been discarded by good church families who suddenly tired of looking at those worn out instruments that served only to take up room and accumulate dust and rats' nests in the family living room. All gift pianos, like horses, should be looked "in the mouth." Maintenance on many is expensive, on some, impossible. Since children are in their formative years—musically as well as otherwise—only fine pianos in good tune should be used in the church school. It is impossible to worship, much less teach, with the "donated" instrument found in most churches.

As indicated previously, the budget items for the music program should be handled by the music committee, the requests being established in co-operation with the director and forwarded first to the finance committee and then to the governing board for approval. But the spadework must be done by the music committee, which determines the needs of the program and requests the necessary funds.

The committee should arrange a few social times for the choirs each year as a way of expressing appreciation for their work and service. This recognition may take the form of a party, picnic, dinner, or an all church-choir family event. Any of these require careful planning, and the music committee should assume full charge of all details.

Primarily the music committee is an advisory group, working with the minister and director of music. It should choose fine leadership and then support the program that is projected. It should not try to advise where it is incompetent; the committee's main function is to promote, not to judge. By helping the director in the recruitment of new singers, handling business matters, and educating the congregation it guides the music program of the church. Therefore its concern stretches beyond hiring a director, beyond the adult choir, beyond the morning worship service, to the effective use of music in the total life of the church.

50

IV

The Director

THE CHOIR DIRECTOR IS THE PERSON USUALLY CONSIDERED TO BE DIRECTLY responsible for the music of the church. While his authority does not supersede that of the minister, he does have the opportunity to develop a program that will extend throughout the entire church and reach all of its people, whether young or old. How much he can accomplish will depend upon his training and ability, the amount of time he can give to the church, his personal interest in and dedication to the Kingdom, and the environment in which he must work. There is a common tendency to differentiate between the part-time director whose work in the church is primarily avocational and the full-time musician; further distinctions are often made between the well-trained musician and the amateur with very little training. We feel, however, that differences which exist are principally of degree and not of kind. Because of the unusual demands of his position, the choir director who serves any church effectively must be more than an ordinary person. His qualifications cover a wide range of abilities and interests; at certain places they duplicate those of the pastoral minister with whom he must work so closely. Waldo Selden Pratt, in *Musical Ministries in the Church*, said, "The musical leader is an assistant pastor." [1]

He has an unusual opportunity to lead the congregation in worship; he can go beyond the organist and, under certain circumstances, even the minister, because of the singular characteristics of his medium of communication—choral music. The director must not forget that the congregation needs and expects his unique kind of leadership. Since the choir is his principal medium of expression, he must help his singers to be a dedicated, priestly group whose greatest concern is worship. In

[1] Reprinted by the permission of the publisher, G. Schirmer, New York.

51

conduct, attitude, standards, and musicianship, the choir will never rise above their director. He must be more than an accomplished conductor; he must be an inspiring leader.

The qualifications of the effective director include characteristics that might at first glance seem to be unrelated to the management of a successful church music program. For example, his personal life may appear to have no bearing upon the conduct and performance of his choirs. However, we feel a church musician must be completely dedicated to his work, whether it be on a full- or part-time basis. It follows, then that he must be a sincere Christian. Unless his whole life is a demonstration of applied Christianity, he is cheating his church, his singers, and himself. There is a very practical reason beyond the moral implications for the director's having a strong Christian personality—his musicians will be more attentive, responsive, and responsible because they respect him as a person. Problems of discipline, attendance, diligence, and reliability will be solved with relative ease by the director who has the respect of the people with whom he works.

The mental, emotional, and physical demands made upon the choir director are far beyond what one might assume. Since physical health depends heavily upon mental health, it is reasonable to expect that he be a strong yet gentle person. Gentleness does not imply weakness; on the contrary a Christian life is built on firm foundations. It does not mean opinionated or stubborn or imply the possession of a closed mind. The truly strong person is sure of himself without being cocksure; he is firm but not unyielding when good judgment tells him to yield; he has his own opinions, but his mind is always open to the opinions of others; he is confident of his knowledge but is ever searching for more light and truth. Confidence in himself and in others brings with it security, emotional maturity, and a reasonably calm, even temperament. He cannot carry his feelings on his sleeve nor bring his personal problems to the rehearsal room and the sanctuary, for the church is not well served by the overly sensitive person who "gets his feelings hurt." It is important that he be able to evaluate others on the basis of their true worth rather than upon his emotional reaction to them. His qualities of stability and maturity will create similar responses in those with whom he works.

A calm, even temperament does not, however, call for the cultivation of a cowlike placidity; there must be spark and sparkle. Few things can be more depressing or enervating than working under someone who is dull and stolid. A choir cannot help reflecting the personality of the director, and unless he is vibrant with energy, radiating a feeling of expectancy, the singing of his group is likely to be lifeless and ineffective.

It is important that the director be poised. It has been said that poise is a state of mind, and certainly it does reflect one's thoughts, emotions, confidence, and belief in others. There is a great difference between genuine poise and the kind that is a front to cover feelings of insecurity and uncertainty. Artificiality and insincerity cannot be hidden for long; the intimate atmosphere of a choir rehearsal will inevitably uncover the true personality of the director.

An important ingredient in the development of poise is a sense of humor. The ability to laugh at himself or at circumstances can carry the director over many a rough spot. Again, one must separate the genuine from the artificial. The real humorist is kind, considerate, and gentle in his dealings with others. Sarcasm, jibes, and "practical" jokes at the expense of others are devices that the effective director never uses.

The poised person is well on his way toward being physically attractive. Physical beauty is perhaps the least important element in determining the attractiveness of a man or woman. Cleanliness of body and spirit; a vibrant face, especially the eyes; a radiant, straightforward approach to everyone; a cheerful kind of self-confidence that stems from an over-all belief in the greatness of God and the goodness of man—these are the important characteristics of beauty.

Vivacity, stability, and poise contribute to the development of a socially mature person who mixes well with all kinds of people. While he welcomes opportunities for solitude and introspection, his tendency is toward gregariousness. The flexible director who understands and loves people is able to adjust to most situations that confront him because his concern is not primarily with himself but with others. He is not an extrovert in the accepted meaning of the word; neither is he an introvert. He is a well-balanced person, able to hold his own with farmers, doctors, housewives, and young people, as well as with musicians.

The director's position demands that he be co-operative, for many kinds of people and many facets of church and community life are affected by his work. He cannot expect everything to move toward him on a one-way street. He will need to reserve time and energy for activities and events that bear no obvious relation to his program. Aside from the practical aspect of close co-operation with the whole church and community, there will be personal and spiritual benefits to all concerned. Lives are enriched by contact with other lives. Because musicians tend to live inside themselves too much, they have great need for these outside contacts.

Too much emphasis cannot be placed upon the value of a reputation for dependability under all circumstances. The director expects his singers to be dependable; he cannot expect more of them than he himself demonstrates. A relationship between pastor and musician, and among all the people concerned with the church, that is built upon complete trust provides a strong and satisfying experience.

It is important that he have some training in matters pertaining to church administration, church history, theology, worship, and Christian education so that he will be comfortable in his association with the pastor and more effective in his relation to all areas of the church's life. He may be given positions of official leadership not directly related to music, but that will ultimately tie his program more effectively into the life of the church. He must be conversant with policies, methods, procedures, and trends in Christian education in order to assist in the promotion of an effective plan for the use of music in Christian education. Workshops and conferences sponsored by various agencies of the church can give much help in these areas, since the present emphasis in such schools is upon the development of a music program for the whole church. In other words, the church musician is no longer an isolated individual; he is very much in the center of the church life.

Thus far the discussion has been limited to characteristics other than musical. It is the sincere opinion of some leaders in church music that training and skill in music provide the starting point for the successful church musician, and may be considered more important than aspects of the director's personality. On the other hand, increasingly large numbers of leaders in this vital area of Christian life feel quite strongly that the characteristics discussed in the first part of this chapter should be considered on a par with and complementary to the musical characteristics. We are inclined to the latter view.

The director is, to a degree, performer, teacher, conductor, composer, arranger, voice coach, and musicologist, and therefore must develop himself beyond the attainment of great technical proficiency.

It is surely better to seek musical leaders who are broadly intelligent about their art than those who are merely clever in doing things with their fingers or their vocal cords. Church music needs competent knowledge far more than flashy brilliance of execution or even what is called a pronounced musical "temperament." [2]

Certain facets of the director's musical qualifications can be classified as innate ability. While he need not be a genius, he must have talents well above the level of average musicians. Such items as pitch discrimination, the ability to hear various colors (timbre), an excellent sense of rhythm, and an over-all sensitivity to the beautiful in music must be present in a marked degree. Hard work and constant study will increase the value and use of those abilities, but there is little to be done if they are lacking or exist at a low level.

The director who has the necessary innate abilities must constantly strive to develop them and add to his knowledge, especially in areas of vocal techniques. His medium of communication is the human voice; therefore he should be able to work intelligently with singers of all ages and stages of development. He need not be a soloist, but he should be able to demonstrate the basic principles of correct singing. He must be a good diagnostician, with an understanding of the cause of poor intonation, poor tone quality, poor diction, and other vocal problems. His knowledge of the limitations as well as the possibilities inherent in each voice will affect the progress made by his choirs. Since he will probably work with children as well as adults, it is exceedingly important that he understand the varying characteristics of the child, the adolescent, and the mature voice. His understanding should enable him to make singing a joyful experience, which in turn will permit him to strive for increasingly high levels of achievement. In order to reach these levels he must understand and apply certain important principles of good choral singing:

1. *The production of appropriate sounds* is necessary for the best development of the meaning intended to be conveyed by a particular

[2] Pratt, *Music Ministries*, p. 138.

combination of words. It follows, then, that considerable attention must be given to the kinds of sounds being produced. Beautiful tone quality is the basis of all good singing, but some music demands sounds that do not depend upon pure beauty for their effectiveness. Bach, in his "Passion According to Saint Matthew," expects the choir to portray at one time a sorrowing people and at another a raving mob; certainly the sounds will be different. A delightful, gay little carol about the Baby Jesus should have color quite unlike that of the meditative chorale "O sacred Head, now wounded."

2. *Tone colors* are obtained by balancing and blending the diverse sounds produced by individual members of the choir. It is at this point that many directors fail. Untrained and trained singers alike are often unable to fit their voices into the tonal structure without proper— frequently courageous—guidance. Heavy voices, light voices, weak voices, and wavering voices must all be brought into proper perspective.

3. *Good intonation* is not something that happens of its own accord. The singers as well as the director must be willing to put forth the mental and physical effort needed to produce accurate singing. A good tape recorder will work near miracles in solving intonation problems, as well as problems of balance, blend, diction, attack, and the like. Proper posture, correct support, careful listening, and careful thinking will usually eliminate off-pitch singing if the minds of the singers are kept alert. Continued poor intonation may be due to certain physical causes, such as poor ventilation, bad acoustics, or the mental, physical, or emotional condition of the singers. The director must determine the cause of poor intonation and see that it is eliminated even if it means raising or lowering the pitch of the anthem.

4. *Good diction* has many excellent by-products. With careful attention to the words, the director can lead his choir to absorb and recreate the meaning of the music more effectively. Attack and release benefit from crisp consonants and pure vowels, as do balance, blend, and intonation. Aside from the need for the congregation to understand the words, careful diction is important because of its effect upon the whole singing process.

5. *Knowledge of theory and musicology* will increase the effectiveness of any singer and add to his enjoyment of music. While few directors find it advisable to give their choirs formal lessons in these areas, the efficient

director who carefully plans every rehearsal will teach his singers a great deal of theory and general musicianship without their being conscious of his teaching. Brief comments and explanations can be given as needs arise, but long dissertations on keys, modes, or music history will serve no useful purpose and may antagonize the choir. Most singers want to learn and will be very receptive to information that is not forced upon them.

Too often the director does not understand or consider the problems of the accompanist. In order to work more comfortably with his accompanist, he should have considerable knowledge of the keyboard; he need not, however, be a performing artist. Certainly he must be familiar with the opportunities and limitations faced by the accompanist so that he will not expect the impossible. He is responsible for eliminating material that is not playable and for obtaining the proper balance between accompaniment and choir. It should not be necessary to emphasize that his attitude toward, and consideration for, his co-worker will have a marked effect upon the final musical presentation. Unfortunately, many directors make problems for themselves by their treatment of accompanists.

Strangely enough, one of the most important areas of the director's training and experience is often neglected—that of conducting. He must be a good conductor. To some minds graceful hands and beautiful posture are an indication of good conducting. Others look for tousled hair, wildly gesticulating arms and body, and streams of perspiration. None of these obvious elements provides a dependable basis for evaluation. The conductor's one task is to communicate with his singers in such a way that they will produce the sounds which are called for by a particular piece of music at a particular time and in a particular place. What he does in public will generally reflect what has been done in rehearsal. The more effectively the choir has been trained, the less actual conducting is called for in performance.

The size and shape of the choir area sometimes add to the director's problems. Finding a place for him to stand while he is conducting is no easy task in many churches. Sometimes it is physically impossible for him to conduct adequately without being in the center of activity. In certain churches he is able to stand at one side of the chancel and, with or without mirrors, do an effective job. In others a screen may be constructed to hide him from the congregation. Unfortunately, the screen may be more obnoxious than his gesticulations. Whatever the physical situation, the director should remember that he is not the center of attention. Neither his gestures, his robe, nor his posture should be such that the congregation is conscious of him as an individual.

Conducting is more individualized than any other phase of public performance except acting. One director will obtain the same effect with a raised eyebrow that another works obviously—and perhaps in vain—to produce. It is almost impossible to establish rules for the conductor beyond the movements followed in beating the basic time patterns. However, a few items should be kept in mind by the director who wishes to make a real contribution to worship.

1. Gestures should be minimal. The very least activity that will produce the desired results is the best activity.

2. Theatrical effects must be avoided at all costs. The church choir director who stands in full view of the congregation has a serious problem as he tries to be inconspicuous while providing the proper guidance for his singers.

3. A poorly prepared selection that demands excessive directing should never be used in public.

The training of every musician includes the study of a great deal of theory, sometimes of an impractical nature. The director must develop practical competence in this area, including a working knowledge of counterpoint, composition, and arranging—the tools of his profession. He must interpret the composer's wishes, and he cannot do so unless he understands the materials with which the composer works. Such a mundane matter as the correcting of misprints and errors demands considerable knowledge of theory. If he is to be an effective director he will find it necessary to do some composing and arranging. The matter of creating a hymn-anthem calls for an understanding of chord structure, voice leading, and other elements of basic harmony. Redistributing the parts of an SATB arrangement so that it can be sung by other combinations of voices, including TTBB, is not particularly difficult for one who understands such matters as the use of inversions, correct doubling of parts, and again, good voice leading. Any choir will respond well to music that has been written, arranged, or rearranged in terms of its strengths and weaknesses. The director must understand the theoretical implications of the music he uses in order to do justice to it, to his choir, and to himself.

Another simple but important task is arranging music to be used by children's choirs with other choirs, for the quantity of good multiple-choir music is rather limited. More important, perhaps, than the shortage of usable arrangements is the fact that no one understands the potentialities of a particular choir or combination of choirs as well as their director.

It may seem farfetched to expect the director to be able to play orchestra instruments, but it will be to his advantage if he has this ability. If he cannot play he should at the very least have an understanding of the various instruments and be able to write intelligently for them. He will be a more competent director when he uses instruments with his choir if he understands the possibilities and limitations of the instruments he is conducting.

We have heard of directors who did not like or understand good poetry and prose. It is doubtful that they were very effective in their chosen field because the interdependence of words and music in good choral literature is so complete that the two should be considered together, as director and choir attempt to recreate the ideas of composer and author.

If the foregoing list of qualifications of the choir director seems idealistic and impossible of attainment, one has only to compare the present situation with that in existence two generations ago. In 1901, Waldo Selden Pratt made the following general statement: "Forty years ago our churches were far less careful than now about the character of those to whom they entrusted their musical work, employing freely not only non-Christians, but persons of notoriously evil lives." [3]

Other writers of the time gave considerable attention to the problem of obtaining dedicated Christians to lead their music programs. While Pratt seemed to feel that conditions in 1901 were better than in previous years, he implied that there was still much room for improvement.

In many places are found leading music teachers who have skilfully manipulated the local choirs and their policy for their own professional aggrandizement, apparently regarding the churches . . . as fair game for the

[3] *Music Ministries,* p. 118.

59

cleverest hunter. In other cases we find that good musicians have grown weary of trying to preserve self-respect as choir managers, and hence have withdrawn from all active connection with church music.[4]

The years between 1900 and 1920 were not productive of much change in attitudes despite the efforts of a few outstanding leaders. However, their work showed results in the period between 1920 and 1935 as is implied by the following quotation, which is almost wistful in its expression of hope and determination.

As days go by and the new profession [the ministry of music] develops there will be courses in the colleges and departments in the seminaries and schools of religious education where suitable training can be secured. . . . If leaders in the church despair of finding directors thus fully equipped, conscious of a great Christian mission . . . technically competent to develop the musical gifts and endowments of the people, to train the voices of the children . . . and . . . to lead the people into communion and fellowship with their heavenly Father, then let them turn their attention to preparing such leadership for the future.[5]

Opportunities for obtaining the necessary training are more readily available today than they were thirty-five years ago, and some churches are making funds available for the employment of full- or part-time church musicians who have properly prepared themselves for this great profession.

The duties of the choir director are as many and varied as there are churches. They fall quite naturally into two categories, however—musical and administrative. While there is little to choose in terms of importance between the two, it might be ageed that a fine musician could succeed despite his poor administrative ability, but the converse is quite unlikely, and for that reason the musical duties are discussed first.

Obviously, he is responsible for directing the choirs of the church. Although in certain situations he may have paid or volunteer help, the principal reason for his existence is the choir program. He must supervise the promotion, organization, and use of the various choirs. Even more important, he must make careful preparation for every rehearsal so that

[4] *Ibid.*, pp. 83-84.
[5] Earl E. Harper, *Church Music and Worship* (New York: Abingdon Press, 1924), pp. 69 ff. Out of print. Used by permission.

he will know exactly what results he hopes to attain and the means he will use to attain them. It is not too much to say that the success of his whole program depends upon the way he plans and conducts his rehearsals. Let us hope that he is never one of the "directors who leave everything to the eleventh hour and then scramble." [6] His rehearsal might follow a plan similar to this:

TIME OF REHEARSAL: 7:00–8:45 P.M.

7:00–7:03	Opening worship
7:03–7:08	Familiar, vocally easy selection (or vocalises)
7:08–7:18	New anthem scheduled to be sung in four or five weeks
7:18–7:25	Hymns for the coming service
7:25–7:45	Anthem, or anthems, for the coming Sunday
7:45–7:55	Business meeting (if needed)
7:55–8:10	Anthem to be used in two weeks
8:10–8:20	Anthem to be used in three weeks
8:20–8:45	Oratorio or other major work, or, if needed, more work on Sunday's anthem
Dismissal	

The director should be careful to include selections that differ as to difficulty, key, style, and purpose in order that a high level of interest will be maintained throughout the rehearsal. He should also vary his own approach according to the demands of each composition.

It is quite unlikely that the director can or should attempt to follow any rehearsal schedule without change. He must make adjustments as needs arise. It is important, however, that he set up and study a plan so that he will be mentally and emotionally prepared to lead his choir effectively. The fact that he is ready and waiting when the first singer appears will have an uplifting effect upon the choir and will tend to make the group more conscious of the correct starting time. It goes without saying that rehearsals begin and end as announced. Over a period of years a choir tradition regarding promptness can be developed to the extent that the late-comer is a rarity, and not tolerated for long.

Affairs involving the director and the accompanist, such as tempo, balance, and interpretation must be settled before the rehearsal. In these

[6] Joseph N. Ashton, *Music in Worship* (Boston: Pilgrim Press, 1943), p. 175.

61

and all other matters there should be a firm understanding between these two leaders. When the accompanist is not a competent musician the director's task is made difficult indeed. He must patiently try to lead the accompanist to higher levels of attainment and search out ways to simplify the accompanist's responsibilities.

Quite often, the organist/pianist is superior to the director in training and ability. Wise is the director who recognizes his own limitations and has the good judgment to depend on his co-worker for assistance. Unfortunately such wisdom is rare. In addition to conferring regularly with his accompanist as he plans his rehearsal, the director must study every selection before he presents it to the choir. He should sing or play each part in order to discover problems that may appear. If he cannot play all parts together he should ask his accompanist to help him. "Besides selecting all the music beforehand, the director ought to make himself intimately familiar with it." [7] Federal L. Whittlesey believes in thorough preparation beyond the mastery of notes. He had this to say:

He must decide on the desired emotional tone and how to obtain it. He must study the anthem for its musical form and style. He should know about the composer and author. He must consider the anthem for its effect in the service. . . . If the director has complete mastery of the number, he can teach it in a relatively short time.[8]

The director should understand that his singers may be slow to accept music that is new and different; in fact, they may even show resentment toward him if he strays far from the conventional and the familiar. Despite their conservative viewpoint, he will find it possible to prepare the way for the friendly reception of almost any kind of good music, provided it is technically within the grasp of the choir. First of all, he must be sure that the choir has confidence in his good judgment. The members must know from past experience that he will not ask them to sing music of which they will be ashamed or which they will not ultimately come to appreciate. Then he must make an effort to relate the new music to something already familiar to them. He may tie text,

[7] *Ibid.*, p. 177. Used by permission.
[8] *A Comprehensive Program of Church Music* (Philadelphia: The Westminster Press, 1957), p. 109.

composer, selected portions, or general effect to past experiences. He should introduce those sections which are easiest and most immediately attainable, or others which are so unusual that they will demand the choir's attention. In rare instances he may find it helpful to play a good recording of the selection. Whatever devices are used, the director must plan his strategy carefully and be reconciled to slow progress and an occasional failure to obtain complete acceptance.

The physical setup for the rehearsal deserves more than the director's passing attention. While the choir should rehearse occasionally in the sanctuary in order to have the "feel" of the larger space, it is better to work most of the time in a room that is intended for rehearsal. Regular rehearsals in the sanctuary may cause the musicians to develop a careless attitude toward the worship service. Practicing in a room to which all essentials are easily accessible makes the rehearsal run more smoothly. The intimacy of a smaller room which has good acoustical properties creates a better study atmosphere, and individual members may find it easier to hear themselves in relation to the group than in the sanctuary.

The director should arrange seating in the rehearsal room as it is in the choir loft. Music in preparation should be kept in folders—one for each singer. By making available a storage cabinet that has as many compartments as there are choir members, the director can hold each singer responsible for his own folder and hymnal. A simple system of distribution and recovery will save time and confusion. Adequate provision should be made for the care and protection of coats, hats, bad-weather garments, purses, and other personal possessions. Correct lighting and ventilation are quite important because the quality of a choir's singing deteriorates rapidly if sufficient light and fresh air are not available. Robe and wrap cabinets should be well vented to prevent the accumulation of odors and possible mildewing of garments.

If at all possible the rehearsal room should be easily accessible to the choir loft. Weaving through rooms full of chairs or perhaps detouring through the furnace room or outside the building in order to approach the sanctuary may create an unfortunate attitude on the part of the choir as they prepare to assist in the creation of a worship atmosphere.

The Sunday morning pre-service rehearsal is almost as important as the weekday rehearsal because it provides a vocal, emotional, and spiritual warm-up for the service to follow. It is sometimes difficult to arrange because of space demands, or because so many singers have church-school obligations. It is important enough, however, to justify the making of sacrifices in other areas in order to have a few minutes for rehearsal and for moving the choir into the proper attitude. There must be, as a bare minimum, a prayer or some brief devotional period conducted by the minister, the director, or a member of the choir. The choir should understand and accept the responsibility for helping to lead the congregation from attitudes created by the strains and stresses of everyday life into an attitude of devotion and prayer; the singers must, themselves, make this transition before they leave the rehearsal area if they are to lead others. Ideally, there will also be time to examine the entire service, prepare for any changes or unusual situations, go through a stanza of each hymn, and review the anthem. Members who have regular commitments that will cause them to be late should be permitted to enter the choir room without criticism or comment.

Another major task that regularly confronts the director is the selection of materials appropriate for the musical needs of the church. The most obvious need is for anthems to be sung by the various choirs. It is at this point that directors may fail because of the time and effort needed to do the job effectively. With thousands of selections being published each year the director is constantly faced with the need to study, evaluate, and discard perhaps 98 per cent of the material that comes to his attention. The remaining 2, or at the most 5, per cent may be usable under certain circumstances.

While consideration should be given in selecting music to the limitations of the choir, this fact must be kept constantly in mind: good music need not be difficult and difficult music is not always good music. Constant and unremitting attention to the problem of choosing good music will make the task easier and more satisfying. The director will become familiar with the styles of composers and writers; he will discover that some publishers are quite reliable while others are less reliable; the appearance of certain names as arrangers, composers, authors, and publishers will come to have significant meaning. (See Chap. VIII, "The Choir's Music.")

A relatively old concept of the director's responsibilities is finally gaining acceptance—he should consider himself to be the musical leader of the entire church. "The people should learn to depend on their musical chief as the central source of authority and inspiration." [9] The increasing emphasis being place upon the total program of music creates opportunities for service never dreamed of a few years ago. The church school has long been a musical stepchild in many Protestant churches. Church leaders have finally awakened to the need for co-ordinating Christian education and music. A carefully planned program that starts in the nursery and extends throughout the whole life of the church can, within a very few years, produce congregations that will respond to church music more effectively than ever before. (See Chap. XI, "Music in Christian Education.")

The director should let it be known that he welcomes every opportunity to help in the church school and the men's, women's, and youth organizations, and other facets of church life. He can assist in the selection of music and musicians for special and regular events; he can prevent the purchase of doubtful song collections; he can make recommendations regarding the purchase of pianos, phonographs, and other musical equipment.

The choir director may be asked to speak at luncheons, study sessions, or worship services. He may teach short-term classes in hymnody and related subjects with which he is familiar. He may counsel with interested parties regarding music for weddings and funerals. His influence can easily become a strong force in the growth of the church.

Because the choir director is responsible for much that goes on before, during, and after the worship service and because many last-minute problems are apt to arise, he should have everything possible planned in advance; his energies and attention are thus reserved for unforeseen contingencies. He may wish to have a final conference with the minister, the organist, and others who are directly concerned with the service. During the service, he must be reconciled to the need for his remaining slightly aloof and somewhat apart. He cannot lose himself in worship to the extent that he is unable to attend to the mechanical factors that are his responsibility.

In co-operation with the minister and the music committee, the director should make every effort to develop leaders in various musical activities. He can encourage young people to study piano and organ;

[9] Pratt, *Music Ministries*, p. 144.

older youth who wish to do so should be given opportunities to study voice; the director may himself give private or class voice lessons; if he is capable of doing so, he may also give keyboard instruction to worthy persons. At all times he must be searching for talent that might otherwise lie undiscovered and unused.

Wherever there are adequate private teachers in the community, the director must be careful lest he be accused of taking students away from them. He should avoid the appearance of seeming to contradict their teaching, even though he is unable to accept it at face value. It is important that he maintain friendly ethical relations with all who are, or claim to be, his professional peers.

Last, but far from least, the director should give careful attention to his relations with local schools. A great deal can be gained by all concerned if a good working understanding is established with the musicians of the community. Conflicts involving rehearsal schedules, performance dates, and personnel can become quite serious unless some agreement is reached by everyone concerned. The avoiding of difficulties is important, but more important are the benefits obtained by a community-wide plan of co-operation. In those occasional communities where schools and churches work closely together, the music program has been strengthened and the whole community life broadened.

The director's administrative duties may take almost as much time as his musical duties. Just as the pastoral minister finds much of his time devoted to organization and administration, so the choir director must plan rehearsals, order music, keep records, work out promotional plans, integrate his program with that of the whole church, and supervise the one hundred and one tasks that go with the musical ministry. It is obvious that he must make good use of his time. Because his work is so general, covering such a wide variety of obligations and opportunities, the efficient director will accept the fact that he cannot do everything. It follows that he should delegate as much responsibility as possible to others. By doing so he will enrich the lives of persons who might not otherwise become involved in the activities of the church; he will train leaders and at the same time make the music program more effective. The choir member who accepts the responsibility of being librarian, secretary, or robe warden immediately places the choir high on the list of important things in his or her life.

66

The director should be effective in public relations. If proper financial support is to be forthcoming, the church and community must be kept informed about the music program—its contributions, its needs, and the opportunities it offers. Good public relations aid in bringing in the new talent that is needed for replacements and for growth. The director must work closely with the ministers and other members of the church staff. No one is so futile as the director who tries to function apart from everyone else. He will strengthen his program and that of the whole church if his planning is broadened to include the others. Certainly there must be close liaison with the director of Christian education, because music is part of the educative process. The director should lean heavily upon the music and education committees, and try to avoid leaving any member of the staff in ignorance of his plans.

There is much about the director's job that is pure routine. Robes need care; music must be mended, cataloged, distributed, and collected; pianos and organs must be kept tuned and repaired; hymnals need attention; letters should be written; bills must be paid; meetings must be attended. The list is endless, and these routine tasks sometimes interfere with the completion of a successful program of music.

The church musician is no different from any other professional person in his need for continuing growth. "Every director who enters into his work with a spirit of devotion and service to his church will strive to continue his personal and professional development in order to make that service more effective." [10]

There are many kinds of opportunities available for study. Church music conferences and workshops are common and effective. Colleges, universities, and seminaries offer church music courses and degrees. There are numerous publications, both books and periodicals, which are devoted partially or entirely to church music and related areas. Several denominational organizations for church musicians have been formed, such as the Fellowship of United Methodist Musicians, the Presbyterian Association of Musicians, and the Fellowship of American Baptist Musicians. Every church musician should belong to the Hymn Society of America. Such organizations as the National Association of

---

[10] Harry Robert Wilson and Jack Lawrence Lyall, *Building a Church Choir* (Minneapolis: Schmitt, Hall & McCreary Company, 1957), p. 28.

Teachers of Singing, the American Choral Foundation, the Music Teachers National Association, the Music Educators National Conference, the American Guild of Organists, and the Choristers Guild have much to offer. The American Musicological Society and the Music Library Association will be of value in specialized areas.

Why are certain directors less successful than others? Some are doomed because they lack the necessary musical abilities or because their training is inadequate. However, many excellent musicians are unable to make more than a small contribution to the church. Some are liabilities. Why? The answer may be found in the kind of life most serious music students are forced to lead. The attainment of musical skills is not conducive to the development of a well-rounded personality. The successful church musician is that fairly rare individual who has somehow maintained good contact with people and with God while promoting his musical growth. He has temperament without being temperamental. In brief, he is a sincere Christian, completely dedicated to his work, for which he is qualified by reason of his native talent and training. He is an excellent musician, but, even more important, he is a person of character who recognizes that his own personal development will affect the expansion of his church and its music program. He has accepted in all humility a great and challenging opportunity to serve God and man.

Recommended Professional Organizations

American Choral Directors Association,
Box 17736, Tampa, Florida 33612

American Choral Foundation,
130 West 56th Street, New York, New York 10019

American Guild of Organists (AGO),
630 Fifth Avenue, New York, New York 10020

American Musicological Society (AMS)
North Texas State University School of Music, Denton, Texas 76203

The Choristers Guild
Box 38188, Dallas, Texas 75238

Fellowship of United Methodist Musicians (FUMM)
Box 840, Nashville, Tennessee 37202

The Hymn Society of America (HSA)
475 Riverside Drive, New York, New York 10027

Music Educators National Conference (MENC)
1201 16th Street, NW, Washington, D.C. 20036

Music Library Association (MLA)
University of Michigan School of Music, Ann Arbor, Michigan 48104

Music Teachers National Association (MTNA)
1831 Carew Tower, Cincinnati, Ohio 45202

National Association of Teachers of Singing (NATS)
250 West 5th Street, New York, New York 10019

V

The Organist

IT IS EASY TO UNDERESTIMATE THE INFLUENCE OF THE ORGANIST ON A
service of worship and to assume that the choir director and the choir
are of greater importance. Yet at every turn the organist's presence is felt,
and taken for granted—in the hymns, the anthem and vocal accompaniments, the interludes, and in the organ solos. If his work is skillful
the congregation will be led to worship without being aware of the
organ or organist. On the other hand, the organist can be a disturbing,
destructive influence: if his music is never in the right place; if he noisily
arranges books and sets pistons during the prayer and scripture reading;
if his timing of interludes (silent as well as played) is poor; if his preludes,
offertories, and postludes are concert pieces played for his own glory and
gratification; if he forgets his responsibility is to lead others, and thereby
himself, to God. Such apparently small tasks as giving pitches, making
modulations, providing interludes and bridges, and similar items demand
skill and competence, and the mechanical factors in each item are successful to the degree that they are inconspicuous.

Willan Swainson approached the subject of the organist by stating:

Music is the tonal expression of feeling and related thought. Church music
is the expression of *devotional* feeling and thought—of the mind and spirit
of worship. The Church Musician's purpose, therefore, is not just to make
music in church, but to make music which in its thought and beauty and
emotional force is of the church.

. . . unless he is unreservedly prepared to use his powers and his musical
medium to beautify and intensify the expression of devotional feeling, his
cleverness simply becomes the measure of the mischief he can work. . . .

A musician may have the best imagination in the world, but in the end
that which he truly expresses will be what he has first impressed on his own
mind and character. The organist cannot put on artistry with his gown on

70

Sunday morning and throw it off at night. His kingdom of music is within him. His expression is the reflection first of what he is, and next of what he would be.[1]

While the technical demands made on an organist are great, the personal qualifications are often overlooked in the training and preparation of young students. A church has every right to expect that the organist be a good musician, but unless he is something more he can play havoc with a service of worship.

The first quality the organist must develop is self-discipline, for few instruments are as difficult to master as the organ. Discipline begins with the study of the piano—diligent practice of scales, arpeggios, and all forms of technique. Although he may think these drudgery, the prospective organist must discipline himself to master keyboard techniques, musical theory, and particularly sight-reading if he is to make adequate progress at the organ. Since the touch of the organ is different from that of the piano and a variety of releases is imperative to clean articulation, the organist must discipline himself to regular and critical practice, constantly listening to the music itself without being led astray by the beguiling tone colors of the instrument or by the sense of power which the sound of full organ gives.

A result of self-discipline is poise. The effective organist, through mastery of himself and the instrument, has a cool head in any emergency. Through the development of a fine technique he learns to sit quietly at the console, with no needless gyrations, no thumping of the pedals, no weaving or bobbing of the head. He directs attention to the music and away from himself and the instrument.

The successful organist is inquisitive. Many organists go through life without any clear idea as to the possibilities of the instrument they play. An organist should test every rank of pipes, playing scales and chords in every octave to determine the possible variations of scaling and sound. Every imaginable combination of stops should be tested, even those which at first thought seem improbable. Each mechanical device should be thoroughly explored for its maximum usefulness in making the organ

[1] *Manual of Church Praise* (The Church of Scotland Committee on Publications, 1932), pp. 190, 196. Used by permission of the Committee on Public Worship and Aids to Devotion, The Church of Scotland.

easier to play. The searching mind should also extend to hearing other organs and organists and to exploring unfamiliar literature.

A good organist is flexible and adaptable. No two organs are alike in design or tone, and the organist is expected to adjust registrations to make the most of the instrument at hand. In service playing he must rise to the occasion in any emergency. If the minister forgets a hymn, the choir bobbles the anthem, or the soloist skips a page, the organist is expected to cover the mistake so the service of worship does not suffer.

It is imperative that the organist evince an ability and willingness to co-operate. While he may enjoy or even prefer the solitude of practice, much of his time is spent working in collaboration with others. He must come to agreement with the director as to tempos, registration, and balance in the anthems. He must think of hymn singing as a co-operative venture with the congregation. He must work with soloists, even doing some coaching when necessary. The organist-recitalist who insists on being the star at all times at the expense of worship is not a suitable organist for the church.

Dependability is a major requirement for any organist, for he carries a heavy responsibility in the service. Accurate timing of the prelude determines whether the service moves according to schedule. (If the service is broadcast or telecast this matter is crucial.) The congregation depends on the organist to set the right hymn tempo; the director may leave the choice of the anthem tempo to the organist; the choir depends on him for support in the responses and anthems; and much of the movement and pacing of the service lies in his hands.

With such responsibility resting upon him, the organist must be emotionally mature. A display of anger at the console (with the tonal resources at hand for a weapon) is disastrous for worship. Although impatience with a congregation's singing may tempt an organist to dash madly ahead with a hymn tune, he must control such an impulse. The tendency to choose brilliant recital pieces for preludes and postludes can wreck the preparation for worship or erase all thoughts of the service as the congregation dashes madly for the exits to escape the aural onslaught. It may be great fun to change keys for every stanza of a hymn and to figure out delightfully different accompaniments for each, but unless a congregation understands what is happening hymn singing will be killed. It is easy for an organist to seize upon interludes

72

and modulations in the service as an opportunity to display the organ and his ability to improvise. If the congregation becomes aware of an intrusion of too much organ in the service, worship is impoverished. Yet there are times when the organist should let the organ be heard in its full grandeur, and imaginative use of materials may bring a moving spiritual moment. For example, Maleingreau's "Tumult in the Praetorium" may be played on Passion Sunday, with this program note:

In this organ piece the hearer can visualize the angry mob, by turns shouting and murmuring, the pomp of the Roman praetorium, and the Christ passing on His way to crucifixion. Finally the uproar dies away, and we seem to feel the whole earth relapse in awed hush at the overwhelming tragedy.

Followed by the choir singing "O sacred Head, now wounded," it can be an effective moment of worship. The emotionally mature organist constantly seeks a workable balance between aggressiveness and humility.

Above all, the organist must be a dedicated Christian—as much so as anyone else who assumes responsibility for leadership in worship. The organist must realize that even with a powerful instrument at hand, he is still primarily a servant of God's people. "An unchristian director of music, organist, or soloist is in the Christian Church as much an anomaly as an unchristian minister in the pulpit." [2]

While much attention has been given to personal qualifications, one cannot overlook or minimize the musical requirements for an organist. The first is a keyboard facility based on fine finger control and excellent co-ordination. The organist constantly plays several different lines with both hands and feet, adjusting swell shades, changing registration, and perhaps playing on several manuals simultaneously or in quick juxtaposition. With this agility must go musicianship and musical sensitivity since the organ is apt to be a machine rather than a musical instrument. Willan Swainson suggests that while the organ is often called the king of instruments it is in reality more like an elephant; yet it can be played with musical feeling if the organist has a keen ear for listening to the sounds he makes and adjusts his touch to create the musical forms which he has in his mental image. Keen listening goes beyond to the choice of stops and tone colors at several pitch levels. The art of

[2] Harper, *Church Music and Worship*, p. 72.

73

registration to a large degree is based on the artistic ability to combine suitable colors and pitches, and the organist must constantly develop the habit of critical listening.

The competently trained organist is thoroughly grounded in theory, ear training, harmony, counterpoint, form, canon and fugue, transposition, score reading, composition, improvisation, and musicology. The list of subjects is imposing, even forbidding, yet every one is vital at some time or other. The ability to "play by ear" should be developed through ear training, harmonic dictation, and transposition. Often the organist is called upon to play for group singing when no music or only the melody line is available.

His education should extend to the art of arranging piano or orchestral scores for organ, for many accompaniments are written with the piano in mind rather than the organ. All oratorios and cantatas have a piano reduction of the orchestral score beneath the voice parts, and these are seldom effective on the organ as printed. The organist must be an arranger, able to choose the basic thematic material, the fundamental harmonic movement, the best keyboard location, and the most appropriate organ tone to approximate the composer's intentions.

A knowledge of voice and vocal methods should also be a part of the training for every organist whether he directs a choir or not. An organist who understands vocal problems, "breathes with the singer," and is sensitive to vocal shadings and nuance makes a sympathetic accompanist. The ability to help a soloist with vocal problems is a great asset, and many organists are effective voice coaches. Since accompanying is one of the major responsibilities of the organist, he should certainly know something about the human voice.

Most organists give solo playing—prelude, offertory and postlude— the primary place in their scale of values, with accompanying choirs and soloists second and hymn playing last. We would make a plea for placing hymn playing first in importance. Playing hymns is an exceedingly difficult job, and the most important as far as the congregation is concerned. A service of worship may be held without any prelude or postlude, and there may be no choir, but hymns will be sung.

The first rule of hymn playing is that the organist is the leader of the congregation and not the follower. Leading does not mean dashing ahead and leaving the congregation straggling behind. The organist can never take the attitude, "I am the boss and the congregation will follow me or else!" The correct attitude is expressed in the revised proverb, "You can lead a horse to water, but why not make him thirsty?" Effective hymn leadership makes the people want to sing.

Willan Swainson says that the organist is concerned with the *Emotion*, the *Life*, and the *Shape* of a hymn tune. By Emotion he means inspiring the congregation to sing. Life involves recreating the vitality of the music, its energy and movement, by a sense of rhythmic drive and progression. Shape has to do with melodic outline, harmonic progression, the relation of phrases, and the scale of climaxes. He further indicates that the problem is complicated by the fact that every hymn presents an individual problem.

As a leader the organist directs his entire attention to making the hymn text come alive, and to clothing the music with beauty and vitality. Concert treatments, sentimental wallowings with slushy stops and full tremolo, decorations—arpeggios, glissandos, slides, rolling chords—are forbidden. Both hands should strike simultaneously and unless there is an overriding reason to do otherwise the pedal part should be played exactly as it is written (not played down in the bottom octave as is done by the "one-legged organist").

Obviously hymn playing calls for accuracy and the ability to play in all keys. Many hymns need to be transposed to lower keys for ease in singing, particularly when many men are present, and the skilled organist is able to transpose any hymn to any neighboring key. Accuracy in time values is also vastly important, for many organists fail to give full value to notes of long duration and to notes which are dotted. The pattern of a dotted quarter followed by an eighth is usually mistreated rhythmically, and even many fine players tend to rush patterns of eighth notes in 4/4 time. All rests should be given exact value, for they are the breath of music. Keeping a steady beat and feeling the pulse calls for practice with the metronome as well as the development of a variety of touches. A slightly non-legato touch is most helpful to a congregation in hymn singing, since the microscopic rests after each note prevent the organ tone from droning endlessly and give a rhythmic impulse to the note which follows.

Closely related to rhythmic accuracy is consistency. A congregation at best is self-conscious about its singing, and if there is any insecurity

75

created by uncertain stopping, tempo, beginnings of stanzas, or un-expected reharmonizations, what little confidence they have will be shaken and their hymn singing will deteriorate. Perhaps the most controversial problem is the amount of time to be allowed between stanzas. Some organists give an entire measure—either of silence, which becomes endless and unendurable, or of a sustained chord on a secondary manual. This strait-laced practice is often used where metrical processions are employed since the extra measure is needed to keep the choir on the correct foot at the beginning of each stanza. The insistence on a whole measure has the very great disadvantage of stopping the thought pattern of the hymn at the end of every stanza. The tune is present only as a vehicle to carry the text and to provide a unifying device for enabling the congregation to proceed together. Therefore any musical habit or mannerism which disturbs the flow of the text is to be avoided.

We are left with the question of how much time to allow between stanzas. The authors would recommend that it be just long enough to get a comfortable breath, for there is no exact, unvarying amount of time between stanzas applicable to all hymns. A hymn which ends on the third beat of a 4/4 measure presents a different problem from one which ends on the downbeat of a 4/4 measure. In "Joyful, joyful we adore Thee" (to the tune, "Hymn to Joy") the last half note should receive more than two beats, probably three; while "Holy, holy, holy" (to the tune, "Nicaea") will be held three beats with the congregation breathing during the fourth. If an organist is sensitive to the singing of the congregation and if he will sing the hymns himself, he will have little or no difficulty in deciding what is a comfortable breathing time between stanzas.

Whether the organist sings or not he must play the text rather than the tune. The tune usually associated with "O little town of Bethlehem" ("St. Louis," or "Redner") will sound quite wooden unless certain notes are dwelt upon momentarily where certain syllables are more important than those which precede them. For example, the syllable "Beth-" in the word "Bethlehem" must be given slightly more time than any other note in the first phrase. To exaggerate such a note will make a parody of any hymn tune, however, and a fine balance comes only with much soul searching as well as practice in singing while playing. Punctuation should be studied carefully, but the music should

76

not be overpunctuated. A comma is not necessarily a flashing red stop sign. There are two kinds of commas: (1) a comma which indicates a separation, or break in thought, calling either for a breath or an infinitesimal breaking of the vocal line; (2) a comma which merely calls for a slight leaning on the previous syllable, such as, "Be *still*, my soul."

Following the text mentally is of utmost importance since in most hymns not all of the text phrases coincide with the musical phrases. Many an organist has found himself playing an extra and needless chord at the beginning of the second stanza of "O come, all ye faithful" ("Sing, choirs of angels") which begins on the downbeat instead of the upbeat to the measure. In a hymn such as "Where cross the crowded ways of life" the organist, noting that the last two stanzas are one complete sentence, should reduce breathing time and plunge immediately into the final stanza so the congregation is carried along to the concluding thought and the climax of the hymn. Following the text will also prevent the embarrassment which many young organists have experienced of playing a fifth stanza for a four stanza hymn. Good hymn playing is primarily text playing.

The "Amen" presents a problem to many players. Some organists perfer to tie over the last note of the soprano line while others prefer to make a clean break. The only advantage of the former practice is that it gives the congregation a cue in case a hymn is to be abbreviated and stanzas omitted. More important than such a problem is the manner in which the "Amen" is played. It should move strictly in the rhythm of the hymn and be released cleanly on a downbeat feeling. The volume of the "Amen" should be the same as that of the hymn with little or no diminishing of the organ tone. "Amen," or "so be it," is an affirmation and should be positive in sound.

What about hymn tempos? First, let it be said that no two people will agree exactly, for there are too many factors which can alter a hymn tempo. The size of the building, the length of reverberation, the quality of the organ, the competency and placement of the choir (a rear balcony placement gets the organ and choir tone closer to the congregation and allows the tone to travel with the singing of the congregation rather than against it), the size of the congregation, the age grouping, and ratio of men to women can all affect the hymn tempo. For example, with older people the tempo will be slower than with a group of children. In a very resonant building the tempo can be more majestic than in a carpeted, dead room.

The correct tempo of any hymn, taking the previous factors into consideration, is finally decided after a study of the following points:

1. The music period from which the tune came and the style of the composition. There will always be tempo differences between plainsong, a chorale, a folk tune, or a hymn from the English cathedral school.

2. The phrase lengths as indicated by the metrical pattern. S.M. and C.M. and similar patterns having short phrases should be taken more deliberately to give them dignity and balance. Long patterns such as 10.10.10.10. must move more rapidly to make the phrases comfortable to sing on one breath.

3. The balance of long and short note values. Any hymn which ranges from whole notes down to eighth and sixteenth notes is difficult to pace because of the wide variety of rhythmic patterns. The shortest notes must sound easy and unhurried, while the longest must not feel too slow or draggy.

4. The harmonic idiom. Hymn tunes whose chords change harmonically with every beat must be played deliberately to allow each chord to establish its tonality clearly. Hymn tunes which change only infrequently, using only a few basic chords, can move with more rapidity.

5. Each hymn has its own tempo, for no two hymn tunes are alike. Only a conscientious study of the form and development of a tune will reveal its problems as well as its hidden beauties. And of course the words make each stanza a new problem.

6. If a hymn tune is musically weak the organist must attempt to make it sound as good as possible. Patterns of the dotted eighth and a sixteenth should be smoothed out toward the triplet pattern and the rhythm given as much stateliness and dignity as possible. An organist, despising such inferior music, may be tempted to overaccentuate the negative points in order to show his annoyance, but such a procedure is not the way to educate a congregation to better things. The congregational choir practice offers a better opportunity to work on the problem of raising appreciation levels.

A few other important suggestions are:

1. Play rhythmically and steadily, and work for the long phrase and

sweeping line. Many hymns with a 4/4 meter sound better and sing more easily in 2/2. (The tune "Duke Street" is an example.)

2. Do not ritard the end of any stanza except the last.

3. Open the expression shades and leave them open. Do not make the congregation seasick by pumping the swell shoe back and forth.

4. Work for general effects in registration and avoid sudden or unexpected changes in volume.

5. Avoid interludes between the last two stanzas unless you plan to modulate up to a new key to give a particularly long hymn a lift, or to improvise so that the choir may finish a processional or recessional smoothly and properly without having to repeat the first stanza.

6. If organ descants or free organ accompaniments are used, be sure the choir and congregation know what you are planning to do and are warned to sing the melody. Such alterations should be used sparingly, and possibly only for festival occasions.

The following technical principles will be of value only to the organist, but they represent an organized approach to hymn articulation which can be found only by searching through many books of instruction. In hymn playing:

1. Repeated notes in the soprano line are always broken to half of their unit of value. Thus two repeated quarter notes are played as an eighth note, an eighth note rest, and a quarter note. With a half note followed by two quarter notes, such as the beginning of "Fairest Lord Jesus," a dotted quarter note, an eighth note rest and two quarter notes would be played since the unit of value is a quarter note and not the half note. Care should be given to making the time values of the rests accurate, for most organists tend to hold the note too long and to cheat the rest. Since the only way to create accent and rhythmic stress is through the contrast of silence and sound, observance of rests and meticulous release of notes are of prime importance to clear, rhythmic playing.

2. Repeated notes in the bass line are broken on the same principle of the unit of value, but whether to break or not is determined by a study of rhythmic and harmonic design. Repeated notes over the bar line are always broken without exception because of the need for rhythmic impulse. In any given measure repeated notes are broken if doing so adds to the rhythmic quality of the hymn. In harmonically

79

static passages the rhythm is determined either by the change in chord or by some rhythmic characteristic inherent in the music. For instance, in the tune "Lancashire," often sung to "Lead on, O King Eternal," many measures should be played in the pedals as a dotted half note followed by a quarter, for this pattern creates the marching quality demanded. In the first measure of "Joyful, joyful we adore Thee" the question must be decided whether the pedal pattern is better played as two half notes or by a dotted half followed by a quarter. The first will give a smooth quality; the second will be closer to Beethoven's treatment in the symphony and will give a rhythmic drive which is infectious. In the third score the harmonic movement on the first and third beats would indicate two half notes as the best solution. It is impossible to go beyond these two general rules concerning harmony and rhythm, for no two hymns are identical in design.

3. Repeated notes in the alto and tenor may generally be tied together except where more rhythm is needed or clarity is necessary in the inner voices. If a congregation sings sluggishly, more and more detached playing becomes necessary, with all repeated notes and sometimes whole chords broken.

4. Beginnings and endings of phrases must be handled skillfully. An upbeat chord at the beginning of any hymn should be detached from the following chord to make it a rhythmic springboard which successfully launches the congregation. At the ends of phrases which are feminine, the minimum of broken notes and rhythm is the rule, and the ending should melt away instead of bump to a stop.

5. Touch is affected and partially determined by the acoustics, the way the congregations sings, and most important of all the form of the hymn. (Hymn patterns are discussed in Chap. X, "The Congregation.") The organist should study each hymn carefully to make the form clear to the people through his playing. "Praise to the Lord, the Almighty" ("Lobe den Herrn") is best played with the first four chords detached against a legato pedal. The first four notes of the third phrase should be similarly treated. The remainder of the hymn should be legato in keeping with the flowing scale passages.

The organist's responsibility to the congregation in hymn playing is primary, but he also has a responsibility to them in the way he plays the remainder of the service. Organ cues and preparation for such items as the "Doxology" or the "Gloria Patri" should be so definite and inspiring that the congregation feels the urge to rise and respond with vigor. The organ can bridge many gaps in the service, moving artistically from one section to another, and the organist's job is to make the service flow with smoothness and unobtrusiveness. If modulations and improvisations are used they should be skillfully done and kept within the framework of the service and in the musical style of the other service materials. If they are not skillful, silence is to be preferred. A few seconds' pause between two items is often the best modulation of all.

The organist also has positive relationships to other persons. For the director he serves as an accompanist, and he must be in musical agreement if he is to accompany well. There can be no quarrelling—particularly in public or in front of the choir—over tempos, phrasings, or interpretations. Blessed is the director who has an accompanist who can read his mind at rehearsal, give pitches quickly, locate the starting points, and firmly but unobtrusively undergird the choir. Less fortunate is the organist whose director is an inferior musician, unless the director knows his limitations and has the sense to turn to his organist for help. The organist must be very patient with his co-worker. He must make every effort to strengthen the director's relations with the choir and sometimes to protect him from his own weakness.

The organist should join co-operatively with the director and minister in planning worship services, choosing hymns, as well as suggesting appropriate organ literature for the service. To fulfill his part adequately the organist must know what is appropriate, recognizing that there is a difference between service and recital music. He should know that transcriptions of piano pieces, operatic arias and overtures, and even symphonic materials are not appropriate. He must know what the dominant mood of the service ending will be lest he ruin it by playing a loud toccata when a quiet chorale would be preferable. He will discover that a composition based on the closing hymn will do wonders to project the mood of the service beyond the church doors. The postlude may often add nothing to a service, but it can easily nullify all that is said and done. (A list of composers whose music should be studied is appended at the end of the chapter.)

The church organist must be patient with the choir and soloists, for it is easy to forget that amateur singers have not had the professional

81

training of the organist. Sympathetic co-operation and guidance will help bridge the gap. An organist should have the ability to play any combination of voice parts to assist the choir, and to transpose down any extremely high passages to make them easier during practice. There is also the question of balance of accompaniment to be considered, for the tendency of most accompanists is to play the piano too loudly as they attempt to drag the choir along. A light rhythmic accompaniment is preferable since it forces the singers to assume responsibility for pitch and for moving ahead. Often the piano should be silent so that the singers will gain confidence through unaccompanied singing.

At the organ there is the further problem of choosing the right tone colors to support the singers. Joseph W. Clokey suggests:

The accompanimental virtues are transparency, support, and reticence. An instrument which is to be used for accompanying singers must have these properties. It must have transparency, otherwise the singers will be covered up. It must have sufficient body to give support. Without support the singers lose confidence. It must have a certain reticence, otherwise it will draw attention away from the singers and therefore cease to be accompanimental.[3]

The organist also has a vital relation to the church school, for it is his duty to see that help is given to those who play hymns for the various groups. He cannot be everywhere at once, but he can hold hymn playing classes to improve the quality of playing throughout the church. It is particularly important that he find excellent musicians for the smaller children and that their playing be limited to the melody only, using a light, singing tone. It is his duty to check the pianos regularly and to see that they are kept in good tune and given no rough treatment.

For other organizations such as the men's club and the women's groups he should not try to do the entire job of accompanying. It is ridiculous to interrupt a busy schedule in order to play only the "Doxology" before a dinner meeting. The organist should seek to find and develop talent in the groups themselves and turn over the responsibilities to these persons. In each case the organist should make it clear to the program leaders that in all fairness to such volunteer help the

[3] In Every Corner Sing (New York: Morehouse-Barlow Company, 1945), p. 66. Used by permission.

hymns should be chosen far enough in advance for the pianists to have time for adequate preparation and practice.

The organist also has a tremendous responsibility for finding, encouraging, and guiding future leadership. Some communities have developed hymn-playing festivals in which all of the piano teachers train their students in the art of hymn playing. The organist could well be the organizer of such a program. He should encourage talented and qualified piano students to study the organ and assist in arranging practice time on the church organ. He should work closely with musicians and suggest ways of helping and encouraging such young people in the church.

One organist offers a free organ scholarship each year to any high-school student who is a member of the church family—the church, church school, or evening fellowship group. A subcommittee of the music committee handles the details and the judging, and in the spring auditions are held with the following piano requirements:

1. Play any major or minor scale in rhythms of one, two, three, and four octaves.
2. Sight read two or three hymns.
3. Play one of the Bach two-part inventions.
4. Play a piano solo of the student's own choice.

If no student has the piano background to meet the standards the scholarship is not given, for the committee feels that they should hold to a high standard. If there is a winner, the student receives an hour lesson each week during the academic school year and is assigned practice time. Much emphasis is placed on hymn playing, and the scholarship student is given the experience of playing for church-school chapel services as well as for the worship services of the evening youth group.

The organist is in a vital position to encourage talented young people to consider the vocation of church music and should be able to help guide in the choice of school and field of study. With the director and minister he should discover what scholarships and grants are available for students needing financial assistance.

The problem of wedding music is too often dropped into the lap of the organist, and he finds himself put on the spot when he insists that some request of the bride cannot be sung or played. It is the duty of the music committee, in co-operation with the minister and the organist, to draw up a definite policy concerning wedding music, and this report should be adopted as an official statement of the church. Then the organist will not be put in the embarrassing position of having to uphold standards alone. The church should collect and turn over a previously determined fee to the organist for his service at weddings.

Music for funerals also falls within the province of the organist, and again he is on the spot unless the minister takes some stand. Music played and sung at funerals should express the Christian faith and should avoid sentimental twaddle and tearful ditties. It is better not to ask what the "old favorites" of the deceased are, for their use only adds to the grief and sorrow of the family. A funeral is a triumphant service, if the Christian faith and hope mean anything at all, and should include the singing of congregational hymns such as "A mighty fortress is our God," "O God, our help in ages past," and "Love divine, all loves excelling." If hymns are not sung, it is preferable not to have a soloist or quartet but to limit the music to organ music and hymns of faith and confidence. *Music for Funerals*, published by the Seabury Press, is an excellent guide to the organist and minister in finding an answer to the musical problems of a funeral. (Incidentally, the church should encourage the return of the funeral service to the church sanctuary, since it rightfully belongs there. The usual mortuary setting and method of handling the service has led to many of the abuses which beset the funeral.)

In conclusion, we turn again to the words of Willan Swainson:

How can the organist communicate to his congregation the emotion, life, and shape of music? He will best do so by communicating these things in his own playing. No congregation can be compelled to artistry, but every congregation, according to the measure of its receptivity, can be unconsciously impelled. If the organist will only be sufficiently humble to proceed upon the assumption—it may not be altogether an assumption—that the main cause of unsatisfactory church music is not in the pew or the choir stalls, but in the organ chamber, if he will endeavor to make his playing a living expression of beauty and truth, of faith and hope and love, of courage and steadfastness, if he will relate all he does with the prevailing conditions of time and place, if he will cultivate the art of appropriateness, he will wake up one day to the joyful realisation that his congregation have begun to walk with him in the paths of artistic endeavour.[4]

[4] *Manual of Church Praise*, p. 196.

Suggested Organ Literature

A church organist should be familiar with music from all periods. The following composers are suggestive of the possible sources for organ music, and it is assumed that the organist would investigate the works of each name. It is also assumed that representative works from each composer would be used in church service playing. The list is far from comprehensive.

Pre-Bach composers
  Selections from "The Church Organist's Golden Treasury," Ed. Pfatteicher and Davison, 3 vols. Oliver Ditson.
  Selections from "Anthology of Early French Organ Music," Ed. Bonnet. H. W. Gray.
  Selections from "Historical Recital Series," Vol. I, Ed. Bonnet. G. Schirmer.
  Selections from "Alte Meister," several volumes in series. Ed. Straube. C. F. Peters.
Pachelbel—Collected works, several volumes. Bärenreiter.
Walther—Selected Choral Preludes. 2 vols. Concordia.
Buxtehude—Collected works. C. F. Peters.
Bach—Selections from "Orgelbüchlein"
  Some Preludes and Fugues beyond the level of the Eight Little Preludes and Fugues. Also Fantasies, Toccatas, Alla Breve, Canzona.
  Chorale Preludes from "Schübler Chorales," "Eighteen Great," and Volumes 6 and 7 of the Peters edition.
  Movements from the Trio Sonatas.
Couperin, F.—Pièces d'Orgue. Schott. Two Organ Masses. L'Oiseau Lyre.
d'Aquin—Noels. Mercury.
Mendelssohn—Six Sonatas.
Franck—Three Chorals. Durand.
  Selected Works. G. Schirmer.
Karg-Elert—Selected Chorale Preludes. E. B. Marks.
Brahms—Eleven Chorale Preludes. Mercury or H. W. Gray.
Vierne—Selections from "24 Pieces." 2 vols. Durand.

Selected works by the following composers:
Andriessen, Bairstow, Bingham, Clokey, Dupré, Edmundson, Harvey Grace, Hindemith, Howells, Jacobi, Jongen, Kee, Langlais, McKay, Messiaen, Peeters, Purvis, Pepping, Rowley, Reger, Schroeder, Sowerby, Tournemire, Titcomb, Van Hulse, Vogel, Oldroyd, R. Vaughan Williams, Willan, Whitlock, Widor, Charles Wood, Walcha.

VI

The Adult Choir

PROTESTANT CONGREGATIONS IN AMERICA HAVE NOT ALWAYS LOOKED TO choirs for musical leadership. At various times during the past three centuries, music of the church has been led by the pastor, a clerk-precentor whose responsibility it was to "line out the hymns," or by a quartet, the last named usually consisting of professional singers. A transition group made its appearance in certain areas; it is aptly described by Leonard Ellinwood in *The History of American Church Music:*

The infamous but popular "quartet choir" began to appear early in the nineteenth century. This term is descriptive of the volunteer chorus choir built around a quartet of strong solo voices which never blended with the ensemble, and for which frequent solo and duet passages were necessary, leaving a relatively small portion of the anthems for truly choral singing. . . .

Whatever their origins may have been, the quartet choirs, wherever they were maintained, soon degenerated into mere quartets of professional singers who were frequently more concerned with personal vainglory than with the worship of Almighty God. This fault became all the more apparent in liturgical churches, for the quartets could seldom achieve that impersonal association between music and liturgy which is the *sine qua non* of true worship.[1]

During the last fifty years a somewhat better understanding of the place of the choir has developed. The quartet and quartet-choir are—for all practical purposes—no longer with us and the basic principle of using a more or less select part of the congregation to serve as musical leaders of the congregation has been generally accepted.

Confusion is still rampant, however.

I assume that one hundred lay definitions of the choir would probably agree in substance, but the dictionary unexpectedly offers supplementary

[1] (New York: Morehouse-Barlow Company, 1953), pp. 73-74. Used by permission.

86

and suggestive information. "A choir," it says, "is an organized company of singers, especially in church." Disregarding the question as to whether *all* the members of any choir may accurately be described as "singers," my mind went on to the word "organized" and I decided to look it up also. An "organization," the dictionary informs us, is "any vitally or systematically organic whole; an association or society." The words "systematically organized whole" I find provocative. Those words imply integration, a fusion of the separate members, a corporate sense of responsibility, continuity, and a planned existence.[2]

He becomes even more pessimistic as he writes:

As the situation now exists, however, choir directors know from painful experience that the choir is a pretty constant abrasive; it often represents only such cohesion as is expressed in loyalty to the parish or to the choir-master; is easily distracted from attendance at rehearsals by the slightest lure of entertainment, and from service on Sunday by rain or snow, by too much heat or too much cold, by sports of sundry natures, by the radio, and by television. I sometimes wonder why the volunteer choir continues to function at all. Church choristers are, to my way of thinking, an unsung race of heroes and heroines. Superficially viewed, there is not much to command their loyalty. Has anyone ever inscribed on a tombstone the fact that this man or this woman conscientiously served his or her God through membership in the parish choir over many years? There is a deal of graveyard literature on the subject of husbands and wives who behaved themselves, and on piety in general; but that John and Mary, side by side, week in and week out, mounted to the choir loft and dutifully labored in the vocal vineyard—that, it would seem, represents no virtue at all.[3]

Long ago, Waldo Selden Pratt made a statement that is true today.

The chief cause of trouble about the choir is that its field and its aims are too vaguely defined in the minds of its members, its managers, and the public at large. . . . In default of some definite basis of principles, we shall find ourselves swayed hither and thither by chance impulses, bewildered by conflicting currents of hasty opinion, and occasionally swept completely off our feet. Happily for the general welfare of the subject, in all of our churches and among most musicians there is a far greater readiness for sound opinions

[2] Archibald T. Davison, *Church Music: Illusion and Reality* (Cambridge, Mass.: Harvard University Press, 1952), p. 47. Used by permission.
[3] *Ibid.*, pp. 47-48.

than some good people suppose. In this field, as in others, we may be sure that there is everywhere a large amount of diffused, latent commonsense and right feeling to which we may confidently appeal.[4]

This "diffused, latent commonsense" has pulled church music through many periods of doubt and uncertainty, and is the foundation upon which we wish to build our presentation of choir methods and materials. In the discussion to follow, basic principles applicable to churches of any size and condition will be discussed. It is not important whether a church has a music budget of fifty or five thousand dollars. It is, however, very important that the church's attitude toward and understanding of its choirs be correctly formulated and firmly established.

As a part of this understanding, it should be kept constantly in mind that the choir is a service organization whose members give freely of their time and talents. The term "volunteer choir" has unfortunate connotations, and its use should be discouraged. In the first place, one does not "volunteer" to attend church, to contribute to the budget, or to perform any other act which is less than the just return to God of a very small portion of all that he has given to us. When Jesus told the parable of the talents, he was making a statement of cause and effect. God gives us certain abilities which he expects us to use. If we fail to use them and by so doing fail to glorify him, we have sinned. It follows, then, that "in the musically mature church, the ministry of choir singing is now regarded as a privilege and a trust." [5]

In the second place, very few Protestant church choirs are professional in the sense that their singers are paid. The paying of soloists under certain special circumstances can perhaps be justified, but the entire choir must understand and approve. The practice of secretly paying some choir members is not only poor churchmanship but also is quite dangerous because choir morale will deteriorate rapidly if word of the situation were to get out. The paid singer may not have the attitude of dedication and service that is the foundation of every successful choir. In the long run, his is the greater loss because he is denied the privilege of giving freely of himself. However, it must not be inferred that the

[4] *Music Ministries.* Reprinted by permission of the publisher.
[5] Ruth Nininger, *Church Music Comes of Age* (New York: Carl Fischer, 1957), p. 13.

acceptance of pay automatically makes a singer any less dedicated than he would otherwise be.

"Volunteer" has an additional implication that is indeed unfortunate. Joseph Ashton aptly described the situation in the following statement:

The shortcomings and deficiencies of the choir are many times excused on the plea that it is volunteer and that therefore a respectable standard of excellence and efficiency for its purpose is not to be required. That its music is distressing and the service is rendered vapid is not duly regarded. Such a plea is, as a matter of fact, totally unworthy of the high function of a service of divine worship.[6]

Perhaps we can extend Davison's definition of a choir by listing a few of its characteristics. It is reasonably safe to say that a choir is:

1. A dedicated group of people who have joyfully accepted the opportunities provided by the choir for advancing the kingdom of God. "Ultimate human happiness probably results from creating something worthwhile, serving something besides one's self, and believing in something bigger than one's self. *Singing in a church choir is an adventure in human service.*" [7]

2. A leadership group in hymn singing and worship, functioning always as a part of the worshiping congregation.

3. A priestly group, whose primary purpose is to strengthen the act of worship by singing portions of the service which the congregation is unable to do quite so effectively.

4. An organization of people who consider that regular attendance at all choir activities is a vital part of their service to God.

5. A crusading force, striving always to make the worship service more beautiful and more valid.

6. A unifying force in the whole life of the church.

On the other hand, a choir is *not*:

1. A concert organization established for the purpose of displaying individually or collectively the operatic abilities of its members. Neither is it a display place for the director or organist with concert ambitions.

2. Maintained as an entertainment and social organization to which everyone who is anyone must belong. While the social life is important, it must never interfere with the real function of the choir.

[6] *Music in Worship*, p. 132. Used by permission.
[7] Wilson and Lyall, *Building a Church Choir*, p. 13.

3. A part-time group, holding the allegiance of its members on a basis of personal convenience, and accepting various flimsy excuses for their occasional attendance.

4. A group which one condescends to serve, thereby "laying up treasures in heaven."

5. An organization of persons who are pleased to help the director regularly or on special occasions.

6. An organization that increases in size, improves its attendance, and works with concentrated interest just before Christmas, Easter, and other "special" events, leaving the remaining services to get along as best they can.

7. A group of people who may attend rehearsal, and probably the morning service if an anthem is to be sung, or the choir featured in some other fashion.

8. An organization that offers opportunities for any kind of personal aggrandizement or for the display of temperament or jealousy.

Why do people belong to choirs? Directors may overlook the fact that it is sometimes highly inconvenient for laymen to fulfill the pressing demands of a good choir program. The service aspect has been suggested in preceding statements, and no one wishes to speak disparagingly of this phase of choir life. But despite his spirit of dedication and the attendant desire to serve, even the most consecrated choir member cannot be expected to remain enthusiastic unless he receives something more valuable than money in return. The effective choir can and should contribute much to the lives of its members.

1. The enriching experience provided by singing and hearing good music is perhaps the most obvious reward. In many communities there are few if any other such opportunities and it behooves the director to build his library and plan his rehearsals with this fact in mind.

2. A good choir rehearsal will give all the benefits of a voice class, provided the director takes into consideration the varying degrees of previous vocal training possessed by his singers. He can teach posture, support, diction, and many less obvious principles of good singing without seeming to do so. The fact that this learning is incidental will make it all the more effective.

3. Whether or not the rehearsal is opened and closed with a period of worship, a rewarding spiritual experience should be provided, often on

a level not attainable elsewhere. The sincere participation, in public or at rehearsal, in the singing of sacred music offers benefits that cannot be understood by persons who have never known such joy.

4. Membership in a choir must not depend upon social values, but it cannot be denied that such values should, and can, exist. Parties, teas, and other kinds of entertainment can make their contribution to the development of choir morale. However, there are other phases of social life that are far more important. Working together as a unit, ignoring individual differences and personal likes and dislikes for the greater good, and the growth of a tangible group personality—all contribute to the development of finer men and women.

The choir is often thought of as having as its reason for existence the preparation of anthems for performance each Sunday and the creation of services for Christmas, Easter, and other special occasions. Granted that these responsibilities are very real, and their fulfillment has significance in the life of the church, there is an increasing trend toward the thought that the choir is able to make other contributions of equal and perhaps greater significance. The actual meaning of the word "choir" will be found in these less obvious responsibilities.

The first task of the choir is to lead the congregation in worship. This leadership starts with the choir's first audible or visible activity at the beginning of the service and continues as long as the choir can be seen or heard. It includes the singing of hymns, responses, and anthems with or for the congregation and the praying of collective prayers and the reading of other collective items. It also includes an area that may seem at first thought to be no part of the choir's work, namely the pastoral prayers and the sermon. While the choir should at all times remain sufficiently aloof to keep the service moving, it must be one with the minister in all that he says and does. A noticeably wandering mind, a roving eye, or a wriggling body in the choir loft can interfere with the close communication that should exist between the minister and the congregation. The choir should not be the focus of worship, but should help to bring focus to the sense of worship.

Since the first responsibility of the choir is to make a positive contribution to the worship service, careful attention should be given to the apparently simple matter of getting into and out of the choir area. Perhaps the best procedure is to use a singing processional and recessional, provided the sanctuary is constructed in such a way that this is practical. If a processional does not seem advisable the choir should move quietly into and out of the chancel during the prelude and postlude, remembering that the service does not end until after each member is out of the sanctuary. It is even more effective if the choir is in place before the prelude starts. If they bow in silent prayer and listen to the prelude, the congregation is quite likely to follow their lead. Every attempt should be made to bring to life the beautiful words so aptly quoted by Halford E. Luccock:

For the artist who works in words, that sense of a reality which enters the mind and spirit from outside is expressed by Robert Louis Stevenson in a familiar purple passage in his letters—legitimately purple; for while purple is not to be splashed inadvisedly, but reverently and discreetly, nevertheless it is in God's spectrum. Recovering from a severe illness, he wrote to W. E. Henley:

"After this break in my work, beginning to return to it, as from light sleep, I wax exclamatory, as you see.

> Sursum Corda:
> Heave ahead:
> Here's luck.
> Art and Blue Heaven,
> April and God's Larks.
> Green reeds and the sky-scattering river.
> A stately music.
> Enter God. R. L. S.

"Aye, but you know, until a man can write that 'Enter God,' he has made no art!" [8]

There are many reasons why a processional is not always advisable, the type of architecture perhaps being the most obvious. "When the choir room is but a few steps from the chancel a sung processional becomes absurd. . . . Taking a circuitous route . . . is parading for the sake of a parade." [9] The manner in which the choir enters and leaves the choir loft should be determined by the physical structure of the church, and the requirements of the worship service. As with all other elements in the service, a processional can be justified only in terms of the positive contributions it makes to the service.

[8] *In the Minister's Workshop* (Nashville: Abingdon Press, 1944), p. 13.
[9] Clokey, *In Every Corner*, p. 45.

Because of doctrine or faith, certain churches maintain a pulpit center. Usually a processional is out of place in such a church. In others the aisles and entrances are so arranged that a logical processional cannot be worked out. The choir should be able to walk down a center aisle, two abreast, and directly into the choir area.

If a processional is used, it should be balanced by a recessional. However, neither has any value unless the participants understand the significance of this often mutilated act.

The processional solves the problem of getting a choir into its place without awkwardness. The entry of a choir is bound to attract attention, just at a time when the congregation ought to be settling down to a mood of meditation and prayer. The processional makes the choir's entry part of the worship itself, and not an interference with it. The psychological value is that the procession, since it involves drama and movement, heightens the atmosphere of expectation just at the beginning of a service, when such an atmosphere is of real importance in keying up the worshippers to the action in which they are about to take part. Care of course must be taken with the ensemble, step, tempo, and spacing of the entrants.[10]

There is much debate and little agreement about marching and nonmarching processionals. Advocates of the former maintain that its effectiveness and beauty are enhanced by the precision of the choir as they sing a hymn that is played with a metronomical beat. Others believe that the emphasis upon military precision is not conducive to worship. "If you have a processional . . . , make it as little like a march as possible. Swaying of hips and tramping of feet are out of place."[11] The marching processional has other liabilities.

1. It does not contribute to the creation of a true attitude of worship because it tends to be theatrical. The emphasis is placed upon mechanical factors. The music and words of the hymn are partially or entirely ignored as attention is given to keeping in step. The congregation may be more interested in seeing how many are out of step than in singing the hymn.

2. Many people find it difficult, if not impossible, to keep in step, and

[10] Devan, *Ascent to Zion*, p. 189. Used by permission of Mrs. Winifrede R. Devan.
[11] Clokey, *In Every Corner*, p. 45.

valuable rehearsal time is lost as the director struggles vainly with the mechanics of marching. Few sights are more ludicrous than that of a line in which one or two people zig as everyone else zags.

3. The number of hymns that can be used with a metrical processional is limited to those few that are duple meter and of such a nature that they can be sung at a marching tempo, with proper accents. Five sixths of the praise hymns that are appropriate for the opening of a service cannot be used.

4. The physical and mental requirements of playing an organ are such that very few organists can keep time with the precision of a metronome. In addition, the time lag in a long sanctuary is sufficient to break down any rapport that might otherwise exist among choir, congregation, and organist. It is physically and acoustically impossible to keep everyone precisely together. Because of the obstacles he is constantly trying to surmount, the organist may find it impossible to play musically.

We suggest that marching be eliminated and a comfortable walking pace be substituted so that attention can be given to singing the hymn. Each pair of singers should step together, with elbows slightly touching, and the hymnal carried high in one hand, supported by the other. Whether the hymnal is carried in the right hand or in the outside hand, uniformity is the goal. With bodies comfortably erect and eyes looking straight ahead over the hymnal the choir will find it easy to keep the agreed upon number of pews between couples. The elimination of swaying shoulders and hips and any suggestion of a "hesitation" step will result in a smooth flowing processional that will add to rather than detract from the beauty and effectiveness of the service.

Changing a choir from marching to walking is not difficult. It will be wise to practice the new way, perhaps for several weeks, before trying it in the service. The use of chorales and other nonmetrical hymns or hymns in ¾ time during the transition period will help to break the marching habit. I was needlessly concerned over my congregation's reaction to the change. Actually, few people were conscious of any change; one very intelligent, usually observant, member complimented the choir on its improved "marching."

Certain churches find it difficult to use a recessional because an invitation to membership is given during the final hymn. If such be the

94

case, the choir should remain quietly in place until after the benediction and response—if any—and then leave by side or back exits. Individual members should not rush out into the congregation. Because of the anticlimactic effect of ending in such a fashion we are of the opinion that, as mentioned before, the processional should be balanced by a recessional. The processional is symbolic of the onward going of the church, in which the immediate movement of worship is toward certain other symbols—the altar, the Bible, and the cross. The choir, as the leaders of the congregation, come out of the congregation during the early part of the service, and return to it at the close. Some churches carry this symbolism even further by having a baptismal font at the rear of the church. Thus the processional moves from the beginning Christian experience to its climax at the altar and the cross.

There is a narrow dividing line between a dramatic, effective processional and a spectacular flare of activity that jars the congregation out of the mood of worship into which a beautiful sanctuary and an appropriate organ prelude have led them. The church that uses several choirs for each service may unintentionally fall into procedures that are theatrical rather than worshipful. It is not unknown for the choirs to be announced by a fanfare, after which flag bearers lead them in a variety of fancy maneuverings until the congregation is reduced to the status of an admiring audience, all thoughts of worship forgotten.

Directors and organists who permit the choir to sing one or more stanzas of the processional and recessional alone are forgetting that the hymns belong to the congregation. The congregation should stand with the first note of the organ and sing all stanzas. The choir should move forward as the congregation stands so that they are in the sanctuary when the singing begins. The recessional should be so timed that the choir is in the nave for most of the hymn. Once they are out of the door they should not sing because the choir will get ahead of the congregation.

Sometimes the acoustical problems created by the time lag in long, narrow churches, make it advisable for the choir to enter by the shortest possible way, except on special occasions. Many Episcopal churches use the long aisle only on festival days. The congregation has a tendency to "drag" the hymn regardless of the tempo set by the organist, and as the distance between the choir and the organ chambers increases, the choir may tend to "drag" also. Two devices are effective in such a situation—a small antiphonal organ, placed where the choir can best hear it, or a speaker in the narthex with its microphone placed in the organ chambers.

A silent processional preceding or during the prelude can be quite effective. The time lag ceases to be a problem if the choir leads the entire hymn from the chancel. The introit, call to worship, or choral invocation may also be sung from the chancel with good results. If a silent processional is used, a recessional would perhaps be inappropriate in most services.

The second major task of the choir is to lead the whole church in the appreciation of better music and worship. Most congregations have been exposed to relatively little church music that is either good or sacred. The people who learn "Sunday school songs" of doubtful value during their childhood will carry the same level of understanding and appreciation into the sanctuary. The choir that accepts the challenge posed by this situation will take advantage of every opportunity to enrich the lives of young and old alike. Since most churchgoers resist any obvious effort to separate them from the music and poetry with which they are familiar, it is necessary to plan a deliberate and systematic program of education by enrichment. Consideration should be given to the level of understanding of the congregation that hears the choir every Sunday. The music and poetry must have some meaning for the people or they will be unable to make use of it, and these unused portions become stumbling blocks as choir and congregation move toward the attainment of higher levels of perception. It is not necessary to sing cheap or tawdry music in order to please the most inexperienced congregation. There is much that is good, simple, and easy to appreciate. By careful selection and programming over a period of years, it is possible to broaden the understanding of any congregation and to replace the poor material with more meaningful music.

Individual choir members can hasten the musical growth of the church by serving in the church school as teachers, pianists, music directors, and in other capacities. Others can serve on the committees or commissions that guide the church school. Still others can work with children's choirs and with choir parents. Wherever and however they serve, everyone should be working as part of a total plan that is established for the greater good of the whole church.

Third, the choir is a potential force for good in the whole community. Unfortunately, not every choir recognizes this responsibility. It is significant that the more community-minded choirs are almost invariably the best local church choirs. In some instances a large area can be strongly influenced by the missionary activities of a single choir. Ensembles, soloists, accompanists, and director can serve in small neighboring churches that have limited musical resources. The musician who has worked in one of the thousands of churches that lacks an adequate accompanist and/or director can appreciate the great lift that comes when these deficiencies are eliminated as a result of the generosity of a more fortunate church. It is difficult for us to realize that many churches have neither pianist nor instrument and that almost any program of music provided for them will be an improvement. Many choirs known to the writers could serve as parish resources for areas of thirty or more miles in diameter, sending out musical help to all who need it. The openhearted reception given to those who serve as leaders would be more than enough pay.

The immediate community can also benefit from the accomplishments of a choir that is generous with its time and talent. By calling upon the congregation and local schools, enough musicians may be found to provide excellent vocal and instrumental ensembles for a variety of community uses. In these days of strict church and school separation, any co-operation that can be worked out without creating antagonisms is all to the good. After the successful formation of vocal and instrumental ensembles, it will be a simple matter to organize a community-wide chorus and orchestra for the performance of works which could not be sung by the individual participating groups.

The interchange of ideas and the loaning of equipment and personnel will enrich the musical lives of all concerned. The choir that makes itself available for community ventures is usually a live, enthusiastic group, anxious to be challenged and looking for opportunities to serve.

While the opportunities provided by the regular morning service offer the challenge that keeps a choir functioning at its best, other activities provide the variety that transforms a good choir into a great choir. It is well for the church and community to see and hear the choir under varied circumstances, including some of an informal nature, in order to understand its true worth. Participation with the congrega-

97

tion in a hymn festival can supply satisfying experiences for all concerned. Adult and high-school choirs can occasionally sing for various church-school departments. But however active the choir may be, its leaders must keep in mind this important fact: it is an educational organization, influencing for good or bad those who hear it as well as those who sing in it. A choir should be much more than a twice-a-week group whose members are content to practice an hour each Thursday in order to sing an anthem each Sunday.

The effective choir is not something that just happens. It is the result of many hours of hard work and planning by many people, and is dependent for its success upon certain basic principles of attendance, discipline, and organization which must be understood by all concerned.

1. Attendance

New members should not be accepted, nor old members retained, unless they agree that their primary responsibility is to attend all of the activities of the choir except when kept away by a serious emergency, at which times the director will be notified. It is difficult to dispense with the services of the only good singer in a section—perhaps the only singer —despite his being tardy or absent whenever he wishes. However, the courageous director will find that choir morale builds quickly if all such occasional persons are eliminated and membership limited to those— however few—who are entirely dependable. Walter Samuel Swisher had this to say about attendance: "A dance or a motor trip has been known to decimate a choir. If the director has one-half of his choir at rehearsal and the other half at morning service, how can the singing be effective?" [12]

The choir that has a waiting list is fortunate. Attaining this delightful situation is no happenstance, but the result of careful planning and strict adherence to attendance regulations. If membership in the choir is limited to fewer singers than are available, and this number is increased only as the list of reserves increases, regular members will have an added incentive for maintaining a good attendance record. Reserves should attend rehearsals and be available to substitute for regular members who are excused from a choir presentation. It is not necessary to wait until the choir numbers forty or fifty before putting such a plan

[12] *Music in Worship* (Bryn Mawr, Pa.: Oliver Ditson Company, 1927), p. 73.

98

into effect. A regular, dependable choir of ten or fifteen is far superior to an uncertain group of thirty or forty. Good attendance alone gives no guarantee of a successful choir, but it provides the foundation upon which the whole choir structure is built. On the other hand, poor attendance is an almost certain guarantee of failure.

2. Discipline

Choir discipline is concerned with a great deal more than whispering, "horseplay," and such secondary matters. It involves the complete attitude of the choir and is directly concerned with the development of the spirit of dedication which must be present if the choir is to serve effectively.

The well-disciplined choir functions as a single unit whose value is much greater than the sum of its parts. Since the choir leads the congregation throughout the entire service, its members must make it habitual to do only those things which provide proper leadership. When the minister prays, the choir prays with him; when the minister preaches, the choir preaches too, with its collective facial expression, posture, and listening attitude. The choir that can eliminate personalities and become in the minds of the congregation a single entity has in all probability mastered the mechanics of worship. The matter of standing and sitting together is often an indication of the degree of unity. The average choir has two extremes—the jack-in-the-box who literally pops up out of his seat and looks around gleefully at his slower associates and the deliberate type who unfolds himself with great care. It is a simple matter for a member of the choir, the director, or the organist, to give the cue for rising. The well-disciplined choir stands and sits together, opens and closes hymnals and music folders together, watches the director carefully, holds its music in approximately the same way, and sits and stands with good posture. After some months of careful attention to these seemingly unimportant details, the choir will not only look better, but it will sing better because it is beginning to think as well as act as a unit.

The wearing of robes by the choir is accepted without comment in many Protestant churches today. Unfortunately, choirs are not always aware of the philosophy that justifies the purchase and maintenance of this expensive equipment. Robes have one basic value—they help to subdue the personal element and by doing so give the group the

99

appearance of unity. The wearing of earrings, flashy arm jewelry, "bare-foot" or other unusual shoes, and flamboyant hairdos restores the personal element and interferes with the attainment of this desired unity. A student at Garrett Theological Seminary described a situation that exists in all too many churches:

There were several women in the choir who put on a weekly show for the congregation. One was a rather large soprano who sat in the front row and wore some of the most unusual earrings I have ever seen. It must have been her hobby collecting them and I'm certain that she had more than fifty-two pairs because she never repeated in one year. They were big, and they always dangled way down and jiggled at the slightest movement. I know that the congregation was held spellbound by those dancing earrings many a time when Mrs. X was holding on to a long high note and vibrating all over.[13]

Youth choirs may wish to wear some kind of colorful but reasonably uniform outfits instead of conventional robes. This kind of apparel can be just as effective as robes provided it is in good taste and does not in any way emphasize the personal element or destroy the visual unity of the group. However, a flamboyant, commercialized, show-biz appearance should be avoided. A choir's role is in the realm of worship leadership rather than in concertizing and eye-catching entertainment.

Well-ordered rehearsals usually produce a well-disciplined choir. Music in folders, chairs in place, proper ventilation, a good well-tuned piano, good acoustics, all tend to eliminate disciplinary problems because distracting elements have been removed. Common courtesies should be observed by director, accompanist, and choir in order to maintain a healthy atmosphere. The singers should not be permitted to talk while any part of the choir is rehearsing. Proper posture should be maintained even in moments of repose and relaxation. No one should indulge in sarcastic comments, temperamental outbursts, and similar displays of bad manners and unchristian conduct. (See Chap. IV, "The Director.")

3. Organization

Some kind of choir organization and resultant delegation of authority will strengthen the choir by giving the members a greater part in determining its policies and shaping its growth. It may be advisable to

[13] Quoted by permission of the author.

have an elected governing body, sometimes called a cabinet or council. This group should be given actual responsibilities which may increase in number and significance as the choir grows and as the members show that they can accept added duties.

The cabinet may work with the director in determining matters of policy in relation to attendance, discipline, finances, social activities, and the like. Over-all promotion of the choir and its program is sometimes best handled by the cabinet, or by persons designated by it. A number of important tasks, such as the care and cataloging of music, the keeping of attendance records, and the care of robes can and should be assigned to choir members. Someone may be appointed to look after remembrances for members in times of family emergencies. Such an important but often forgotten item as arranging for a nursery attendant on choir practice nights may be handled by the choir.

The well-organized choir functions smoothly and efficiently when every member feels that he has an important contribution to make. The choir is, in a very real sense, a part of him and he a part of the choir. It is human nature to love and cherish the things for which sacrifices are made and to which a part of oneself is given, and singers are proud to participate in a group that expects the most of them. Paradoxically, this intense pride in and love for the choir sometimes creates problems. The singer who because of age or health has become a vocal liability may be a disturbing influence if he continues to sing and perhaps may disrupt the choir and congregation if he is dismissed. It is difficult for the man or woman who has given talent and time for thirty years to accept the limitations imposed by age. Friends of the singer may let their loyalty obscure the real problem, thereby reducing the situation to a personal matter. An understanding choir cabinet can often assist the director in solving this issue. Individual conferences with the person concerned may bring his quiet acceptance of the need to retire voluntarily. If, as a final resort, dismissal becomes necessary, it can be done more effectively by the cabinet, acting as the choir's representative, than by any single individual. Some choirs have an age limit for their members, thus establishing the machinery for avoiding trouble. For example, if fifty-five is the maximum age, the choir director is given the privilege of deciding, on the basis of a tryout, whether or not the member shall continue for another year and for each year thereafter.

The cabinet should work with the director and the music committee in establishing standards for admission of new members. If the choir is quite small and recruiting is a constant need, there is real danger that anyone and everyone will be begged to sing. Regardless of the choir's size, some system should be maintained that makes choir membership a prized possession. The choir must not become a tight clique of the musically elite, however. Great singers and talented musicians do not always make the best choir members. The person with an accurate voice, a good sense of pitch and rhythm, and an intense desire to serve is a far better candidate than the outstanding musician who is concerned with finding an opportunity to display his voice. Every old member should be interested in the addition of new singers. The choir through its cabinet may regularly evaluate its standards and counsel with the director in setting new ones. The director is, of course, charged with the responsibility of interpreting the standards and determining the status of all applicants.

The choir may or may not wish to have a constitution and bylaws. There are values in having the basic philosophy of the choir expressed in written form, especially if the final draft is the result of co-operative effort which includes director, organist, minister, music committee, as well as the choir. Other constitutions should perhaps be studied but each choir must work out its own in terms of the needs, responsibilities, resources, and opportunities of the church to which it will apply.

The benefits to be derived from the maintenance of an efficient choir organization are many and varied. However, one particular kind of benefit is very well described by a choir member in *Church Choral Service:*

This is a most amazing statement in view of the fact that four years ago this president had not the remotest idea of doing any singing other than congregational. . . . We have a choir of some thirty voices whose loyalty and dedication is something wonderful to behold. The voices range from the completely untrained, even practically unused, to four superb soloists. . . . Through participation we all became keenly aware and appreciative. An appreciative human being never remains static but grows, slowly but surely. This is especially true of all who experience the "togetherness" of those who gather to "make a joyful noise unto the Lord." [14]

[14] Laverne Palmer, "I Am a Choir President" (February, 1957).

102

The solution of problems related to attendance, discipline, and organization will not be complete unless the choir has access to a plentiful supply of good, singable music. In some respects, the building of a choir library is the director's most important task. Certainly it is a constant one. He is primarily responsible for determining what the choir sings, but the choir, minister, and congregation should have a concern in the matter.

Just as ministers sometimes select hymns entirely on the basis of their own likes and dislikes, so directors and organists tend to depend entirely too much upon their own standards in the evaluation of repertoire. The director must be the final authority, but he should not close his ears to suggestions that may serve as an indication of the direction in which he should move, and the speed with which he can safely travel. When certain well-worn anthems of doubtful quality are requested he should be able to substitute compositions that are similar in structure but of better quality.

A Midwestern choir director, who is also a successful public-school teacher, has said that he selects his new music in sets of four—one for the congregation, one for the minister, one for the choir, and one for the old man (himself). Over a period of years each category has moved up two steps so that the congregation understands music that had been a challenge for the choir, and the minister appreciates music originally understood only by the director. In the meantime, the choir and the director have moved ahead to even higher levels of attainment.

Perhaps this director was being a bit facetious when he described his plan; nevertheless, the philosophy contained in it is excellent. Everyone is given an opportuunity to feel completely at ease, and everyone is challenged. Such a procedure cannot be followed unless a great deal of time is given to repertoire study, and just as much time studying the needs and interests of the choir, the minister, and the congregation. (See Chap. VIII, "The Choir's Music.")

Mention is made elsewhere of the care of the library. Entirely too many churches have inadequate facilities for cataloging, repairing, and storing music. One person should be given the task of caring for the music. He may assign certain duties to others, but he alone has the over-all responsibility. If he follows certain basic procedures, he will save the choir a great deal of time and money.

1. Every copy of music should be stamped and numbered.

2. A file card, giving number of copies, composer, title, publisher and number, voice arrangements, and seasonal nature should be filled out for each selection. Other pertinent identifying material may be included. The card may contain space for recording the use made of the selection.

3. Damaged copies should be repaired with permanent music mending tape without delay.

4. Music not in use should be stored in durable envelopes, boxes, or folders which are plainly marked with the name of the composer, the title of the selection, and the arrangement of voices. A cross filing system will make it a simple matter to locate desired titles.

5. Music being studied should be kept in folders assigned to individual choir members.

There is a great deal of hard work connected with the proper functioning of a choir, and the singers may sometimes wonder whether or not their efforts are worthwhile. Their reward will not be found in words of praise or in public adulation, but in the deep satisfaction that comes from making a sincere contribution to the worship of God.

All must regard themselves equally as servants in their high calling; that they are unfitted for their position if they think the musical portion of the service is the most important of all, the rest being merely accessory to it. Nor is their leading of the praise to be directed towards impressing the congregation or attracting strangers to the church. Their joint work is to be in all humility an act of personal worship. It will attune the minds of others to their act of worship and must be devoted to the beautifying and dignifying of it. It will be a tender expression of glory and aspiration to the Lord of all, so that those present may not be found saying what fine music is to be heard here, but, rather, what an air of spirituality is over the service and how natural it is to worship in this holy place.[15]

[15] From the Ch. "The Choir and Choir Training," T. C. L. Pritchard [organist of Belhaven Church, Glasgow], in *Manual of Church Praise* (Edinburgh: The Church of Scotland Committee on Publications, 1932), p. 130. Used by permission of the Committee on Public Worship and Aids to Devotion, The Church of Scotland.

VII

Children's and Youth Choirs

CHILDREN'S AND YOUTH CHOIRS ARE ALMOST ENTIRELY A PRODUCT OF THE twentieth century. The use of boy sopranos and altos has been, of course, an accepted procedure for centuries, but the practice of using separate children's choirs was unknown until relatively recent times.

The movement actually started over sixty years ago in the First Presbyterian Church at Flemington, New Jersey. Elizabeth Van Fleet Vosseller, the founder, felt that the children of her church and community needed more music in their religious education than they were receiving in their Sunday school experience, so she started with a choir of four girls from the church. The history of this beginning is found in her book *The Use of a Children's Choir in the Church*.[1]

One of the first ministers to express himself in regard to the organization and use of graded choirs was Earl Enyeart Harper. In 1924 he said:

A single choir will not suffice in the organization of the church for religious education in music and worship. There must be such a series of choirs as shall care for the interests of all the people eligible to training, from the youngest to the oldest. . . .

The Sunday school supports the Junior and Intermediate choirs as part of its educational program, and has authority to use either or both of them in the Sunday-school session, or in special programs or services held under the auspices of the Sunday school.[2]

Harper's comments and recommendations are completely acceptable in terms of the philosophy expressed in the opening pages of our Chap. VI, "The Adult Choir." Unfortunately, in an effort to get on the "multiple-choir wagon" some church musicians and ministers have gone to

---

[1] Madeline D. Ingram, *Organizing and Directing Children's Choirs* (Nashville: Abingdon Press, 1959), p. 12.
[2] *Church Music and Worship*, pp. 132-33.

great extremes during the past thirty years. Christian educators have felt obligated to take a stand against the graded choir program when small children have been exploited. In certain denominations the situation has gotten almost out of hand because of an uneasy feeling among ministers and musicians that no music program is complete unless several choirs are maintained. If Brother Jones's church has six choirs, Brother Smith's must have seven.

It must not be inferred that we are opposed to the graded choir program. On the contrary, we believe that every child in the church school should have an opportunity to participate in a musical activity maintained on a level that will satisfy his musical, emotional, and spiritual needs, but musical activity planned and operated in close association with the church school. Almost any church that has a regular church school can benefit from the development of a children's choir. *Organizing and Directing Children's Choirs*, by Madeline Ingram, discussed the matter thoroughly in Chap. I, "Why Children's Choirs?" Whether the benefit to the child and the church is real or imagined will depend upon the goals and methods of the choir program and the uses made of the choirs. Some churches boast of "choirs" of nursery and kindergarten children. Others limit theirs to the junior age (nine-ten-eleven) and older. A careful examination of the purposes discussed in our Chap. VI, "The Adult Choir," will show that many groups of small children are not choirs in the true meaning of the word. Music for children below the junior age is discussed in Chap. XI, "Music in Christian Education."

The differences between primary and junior children are basically of degree rather than kind. However, these differences are important because the nine- to twelve-year-old brings to a peak of perfection all of the physical, mental, and emotional potentialities he showed when he entered the first grade. He is on the verge of the sometimes awkward, oftentimes painful, period called adolescence. For a short time he is master of all he surveys. He is an affectionate extrovert, capable of magnificent accomplishments in his own mind and actually able to succeed at many complicated tasks. He has developed characteristics that, for the first time in his life, enable him to be a real member of a real choir.

First of all, he is physically able to accept the demands of participation in regular rehearsals and worship services. Because his body does not demand unceasing movement, he can remain reasonably quiet for fairly long intervals of time. His voice and his ability to hear and reproduce tones have progressed to the extent that he can give and receive real musical stimulation from his singing.

Second, he is emotionally and mentally capable of understanding simple abstractions and symbols. Religion is becoming more than a fairy story to him. He is able to participate in worship with increasing perceptivity. He will accept the responsibilities of leadership, even to the extent of leading an adult congregation in true worship.

Third, he is developing social awareness. He is no longer a completely self-centered egotist, concerned only with those matters which affect him directly.

The junior and teen-ager, being good "joiners" and keen about all lively and lovely things, are ready to enter with comrades into choir activities even though they have had no taste of them earlier. These express and cement for them more effectively, their relationship with the religious community. Through the choir their desire to belong can be fulfilled.[3]

Materials to be used by the junior choir must be chosen with the maturity level of the children in mind. Texts and music should have meaning for them and at the same time be sufficiently difficult to challenge them and hold their interest. Simple two-part singing is not only possible but occasionally desirable; the major emphasis, however, should be upon unison singing with descants and rounds providing a natural transition from unison to part music. Most good hymnals contain a great deal of excellent worship material as well as hymns that are appropriate for junior choirs. Church-school literature is another dependable source of songs which may be used in church as well as church school. (See Chap. XI, "Music in Christian Education.")

We wish to insert a word of caution at this point. We believe that the tendency toward simplicity of materials for children has sometimes resulted in the use of texts and music that are valueless. We are inclined to give them a diet of musical pap and by so doing hold back development of understanding and appreciation.

[3] Edith Lovell Thomas, *Music in Christian Education* (Nashville: Abingdon Press, 1953), p. 107. Used by permission.

Educationally speaking, one should note how quick the younger ages are to appreciate and understand good music. These ages tend to approach all music with an open mind. . . . The names of Palestrina, Bach, and Handel are no longer the unique property of adults.[4]

The junior choir is an integral part of the church school; it follows logically that no child should be denied the privilege of choir membership. Directors must not succumb to the temptation to eliminate those who might be called "delayed singers." Even with the inclusion of children who do not sing well, the junior choir can be a musically effective organization.

Juniors may sing an anthem once or twice each month and participate in the activities of the church school whenever possible. They are sufficiently mature to substitute occasionally for the adult choir, singing all the responses and musical portions of the service and leading the congregation in worship. We doubt the advisability of using the junior choir every Sunday if their contribution to the service is limited to the singing of a single response. In the words of Madeline Ingram:

Heaven forbid that these choirs be given a "spot" in the service each Sunday just in order that they may feel necessary. . . . As choristers, theirs is an obligation to lead, . . . and they can easily learn that this is the function of a choir.[5]

Ruth K. Jacobs adds this thought:

Boys and girls like to feel that they are doing something worthwhile. You gain their allegiance by expecting the best they have to give. Give them every opportunity to perform publicly, but insist that they do no less than their best at every performance.[6]

Participation in a real choir has many values for the junior-age child. In addition to the social benefits gained by working with others for a common good, he develops habits of promptness, dependability, and courtesy. He learns much about the church, about worship, and about

[4] From *Steps Toward a Singing Church*, by Donald D. Kettring. Copyright 1948, by W. L. Jenkins. The Westminster Press. Used by permission.
[5] *Church Choral Service*, "Age Divisions" (May, 1957).
[6] *The Successful Children's Choir* (Chicago: FitzSimons, 1948).

108

God and Christ. Religion becomes real and personal to him. He discovers the meaning of reverence, and finds himself looking forward with gratifying anticipation to the morning worship service. A certain choir director was pleased to find that nineteen of the twenty-six children who joined the church at Easter time were members of her choir. Hers was not an unusual experience.

Under proper guidance the child will learn a great deal about singing and music in general. Good posture, correct diction, and easy tone production will be encouraged by the competent junior-choir director, who will also manage to do a great deal of incidental teaching of basic theory while the children are learning their many hymns and songs. The gains from the child's choir experience cannot be easily measured because they are often intangible and not immediately apparent.

What the children absorb unconsciously from their association with fine music, high ideals, and participation in public worship may have greater value than what we consciously teach them.[7]

It is only as the child grows through adolescence and young adulthood that we are able to see the full measure of his development in those areas that have been most affected by his participating in a junior choir. Edith Lovell Thomas said, "How a true ministry of music can be performed is hard to see without the educational training which an intelligent and systematic choir affords." [8]

The intermediate age (twelve-fourteen) is sometimes considered to be the most difficult and least rewarding age with which to work. These early adolescents in many respects resemble a drop of mercury. They are unstable, difficult to keep in one place physically, mentally, or emotionally, and impossible to confine with pressure. A group of early teen-agers seems to radiate insecurity and excitement, often giving the impression that an explosion is imminent. Despite these admitted liabilities, the intermediate choir can be a successful group, capable of leading an adult worship service with deep sincerity. Working with them can be one of life's most rewarding experiences, if they are permitted to use their abilities in a challenging manner. "The intermediate choir needs the

[7] Ibid., p. 8.
[8] Music in Christian Education, p. 107.

109

steadying influence of weekly service responsibilities and should have a routine place in one service each Sunday." [9]

Because of the difficulties associated with changing voices, many choir directors avoid using junior-high boys. Bell choirs provide an excellent, albeit expensive, outlet for these young men with uncertain vocal production. However, most educators are inclined to believe that boys should sing right through the period of voice change. Care must be taken to avoid any sign of strain. Music with parts arranged for changing voices is relatively easy to find. The good director can arrange his own when need arises. Boys who are silenced during this critical time may not be anxious to sing later. Some choirs use music especially written for the *cambiata* (or changing) voice, carefully planned to avoid extreme ranges and to keep a boy singing pleasurably. The local junior high choir director should be consulted about available sources of choral literature.

Another valuable supplementary activity for this and other age groups is the choric speech choir in which careful attention is given to word content, diction, and phrasing. By means of varying pitch and intensity the emotional implications of the text are revealed to both participant and listener. The speech choir has many of the same group benefits that are found in singing choirs.

Churches are rediscovering the beauty and value which choral reading can contribute to worship. Speech choirs are being added to Christian education programs, and singing choirs are including choral readings in their musical repertoires. The benefits derived by the cultivation of choral speech by a singing choir work in two directions. Where choral reading is thoroughly studied and prepared, the beauty of the resulting speech rests upon, among other things, the clarity of diction and purity of tone. The readers become aware of the meanings of words and their dependence on tone and diction for beautiful expression. This can only strengthen the use of words with meaningful expression in song. On the other hand, the cultivated tonal production and rhythmic expression of the singing choir lends beauty to choral speech.[10]

Some choir directors are finding that the boys' choir (grades four through eight or nine) provides the best answer to the misnamed boy

[9] Ingram, "Age Divisions."
[10] From *The Use of Music in Christian Education,* by Vivian S. Morsch. Copyright 1956, by W. L. Jenkins. The Westminster Press.

problem. Under intelligent guidance a voice can be led easily from soprano through the various levels of development until it begins to establish itself as a low tenor or light baritone. A serious difficulty faced by such an organization is the conflict with church-school departments. If a boys' choir is to be organized, church-school leaders who are concerned with the ages involved must be consulted and their help obtained in planning rehearsals and the use to be made of the choir. Space does not permit the detailed discussion of the boy's changing voice. Numerous books are available which cover the subject thoroughly. One of the best is Duncan McKenzie's *Training the Boy's Changing Voice*.[11] Others are listed in the bibliography.

So much attention has been given to the changing boy voice that the changing girl voice has been almost entirely ignored, even in the books just mentioned. Girls' voices *do* change, and the adjustment is often serious enough to deserve much consideration. The change is the same, although not so severe, as that occurring in boys. The singer of high sweet tones may find that her voice flows sluggishly and that the high notes become difficult to produce as she enters puberty. Unless she understands what is taking place, she will probably try to sing with the same high voice by using a great deal of force and strain. The result may be a damaged vocal mechanism, sometimes to the extent that the voice is permanently limited or completely lost. The answer is simple: easy, comfortable singing should be encouraged until the period of difficulty is past and the girl is completely "at home" with her new voice. Just as boys should be told well in advance of the change exactly what will occur and what to do about it, so should girls be forewarned and then helped through this critical time. Quite frankly, ignorance on the part of church and school musicians has caused many fine young singers to be deprived of the pleasure that singing could have brought to them.

If a boys' choir is organized, there should probably be both a junior and a junior-high girls' choir. It is not especially difficult to get fourth-grade and ninth-grade boys to work together; it is well-nigh impossible to do the same with girls. Recognition of this fact will save the director from almost certain disaster.

Some educators believe that disciplinary problems are much less

[11] New Brunswick, N. J.: Rutgers University Press, 1956.

evident if early adolescent boys and girls are separated during most rehearsals and public presentations. Others are of the opposite opinion, maintaining that discipline will take care of itself if the rehearsal is properly organized and the young people kept interested in their singing. Whichever view is held, there are certain basic facts that must be remembered if the choir is to be successful.

1. The intermediate wishes to be treated as a young adult. He needs to be given responsibilities; under careful, discreet guidance he is capable of great things.

2. The intermediate is a romanticist. Adventure, the world, the stars—the whole universe is his. He is a hero-worshiper. The boy-girl situation becomes a dominant, although sometimes hidden, motive.

3. The intermediate is interested in people. He likes to know the "how," "what," and "why" of human conduct.

4. Sarcasm is his deadly weapon. He will use it, but it must never be directed at the junior youth by an adult.

5. He wants to love and respect his teacher. He wants to be guided; he respects unprejudiced authority. He will figuratively die for someone in whom he believes.

6. He enjoys music and he wants to sing. Boys may, if not properly guided, disavow their love of music on grounds of its being "sissy."

7. He is interested in music that is colorful and rhythmic. Rich, exciting harmonies delight his ear. Accompaniments full of chords, arpeggios, and dissonances are pleasing to him. What he likes, he likes very much, and anything he dislikes becomes completely intolerable to him. There is no middle ground in his life.

Since his voice is in a time of rapid change the director should listen to each youth at least once a month, but not for the purpose of eliminating uncertain singers. These listening sessions may take place during rehearsal as the director walks casually among the young people. If a very close rapport exists between the director and his choir, occasional private sessions may prove advantageous. These informal, usually unplanned, auditions will enable the director to guide his singers better. He will anticipate the occurrence of strain and prevent the damaging of the vocal mechanism. Because his boys and girls sing freely and easily, their enjoyment is maintained at a constant high level.

We will admit that it is occasionally necessary to eliminate an inter-

112

mediate from the choir because of his inability to sing, but the occasion is so rare that for all practical purposes it does not exist. Extra care and attention will eventually free almost every young person from the emotional and physical limitations that keep him from singing.

The director who understands the intermediate's assets and liabilities can, with patient, unrelenting effort produce choirs whose music is beautiful and meaningful. In addition to the music he brings out of these young people, he will have the deep satisfaction of knowing that he has helped in the development of personalities that are a little more complete than they might have been without his efforts.

Mention should be made at this point of the extended-age choir (ages nine through thirteen or fourteen). Some churches maintain successful groups of this kind. The problems are numerous, but not insoluble. The children must first be made to understand that an unusually high level of co-operation and acceptance of responsibility will be expected of them because of the great differences that are certain to exist. No ordinary person can serve as director. He must possess great tact, understanding, firmness, and patience; he must have a lifesaving sense of humor. His knowledge of children and children's voices should be extensive, and he will himself need to be master of a large and varied repertoire, especially of hymns.

Extended-age choirs will depend upon the hymnal for most of their songs. Because some voices will be changed and others changing, a certain amount of simple part singing will be necessary. The older children will accept songs that the younger children like if such songs are properly introduced. The choir should learn a few selections that are chosen especially for the intermediates. The younger children will enjoy the occasional challenge of music that is a bit difficult for them to master.

With the right kind of inspired leadership, an extended-age choir can be of considerable usefulness to its members and to the church. However, such a choir should never be organized until there is a need for it, and until the right leader is available. Here, perhaps more than anyplace else, "keeping up with the Joneses" will be deadly.

The senior-high-school choir has musical potentialities that approach those of the adult choir. Students in the fifteen-to-eighteen age bracket are sufficiently mature to permit their accepting almost unlimited service responsibilities. While their voices do not yet have size, range, or quality equal to those of older persons, the freshness, life, and vitality of their singing compensate for other deficiencies. High-school students can sing almost any sacred music with real understanding. However, the director who knows the limitations of his young people will not permit them to abuse their voices with music that is technically beyond them. It is unwise to let them perform, except perhaps in a large chorus or with adults, anything as taxing as "The Hallelujah Chorus" from Handel's *Messiah.*

It is the limitations of high-school voices that are sometimes misunderstood by choral directors. For example, many a seventeen-year-old soprano can sing a high C or D easily, clearly, and with good tone. Her singing mechanism, however, including her abdominal muscles, is not equal to the task of learning and performing the "Mad Scene" from "Lucia" or the "Bell Song" from "Lakme." Many high-school girls can sing as low as alto F or E flat, but only one in thousands is anything more than a soprano with an extended lower range. The young baritone is often asked to growl a real bass part, and since the low voice seems to be a sign of manliness, he tries to oblige by depressing his larynx, pulling in his jaw, and shoving with all his might.

How many pictures have been printed of a young tenor reaching up with his head and neck for an elusive high tone? The situation exists often enough in real life to make it the cartoonist's model for "tenoritis," just as he uses the tucked-in chin and swelling of the throat to indicate a bass.

The capable high-school-choir director will never be guilty of the crimes just mentioned. His young people will sing easily, with correct posture, firm breath support, and good diction. No voice will strain beyond its comfortable limits. Sopranos will sing their high tones lightly, striving for accuracy and clarity; tenors will shift automatically to the falsetto for their high tones; altos and baritones will sing only those low notes that flow out easily—all others will be rewritten by the director. Better still, he will select music that is written in the range of high-school voices. A very serious vocal crime is committed by the director who leans heavily upon commercial recordings of an adult, professional choir as a teaching aid. Young people do themselves great harm when they try to imitate mature voices. The occasional use of recorded music is an

114

acceptable device if the young singers understand the limitations of their own voices.

The high-school choir must be given a position of regular responsibility if it is to realize its potential. Churches that have two or more morning services, and/or an evening service, find that this group can take over one of the services every Sunday. The young people will not only serve the church well, but will take great pride in doing their work effectively. They will be better men and women for having given of their time and talent.

In most respects, matters of discipline, attendance, and organization will be handled very much as for the adult choir. The difference will be in degree more than in kind. For example, the high-school choir should have a cabinet, but the director will need to exercise a bit more control —gentle but firm—than with adults. Young people respect and expect the firm, fair hand; they have no use for uncertainty or vacillation. At this age, not every young person is expected to "make" the choir. A certain amount of selectivity may be practiced; tryouts need not be a thing to be feared, and standards need be only as high as seems best for the whole group. Senior youth require frequent individual hearings, although not so often as do intermediates. Their voices are still growing, and they will profit from continuing guidance.

Further detailed information about choral groups for senior youth can be found in numerous books and publications, several of which are listed in the bibliography. An especially good source of information is The Journal of the Music Educators National Conference which contains dozens of fine articles on the vocal problems of youth.

Not many congregations are large enough to maintain a high-school choir. In most situations the adult choir accepts young people who have entered their ninth year of school, unless the community maintains a strict junior-senior division, in which case the dividing line is at the tenth year. High-school students can make a substantial contribution to the music of the church by singing with older people. It is true that difficulties sometimes develop because of age differences. Young people may be irritated by, and in turn, irritate, persons who are more mature and conservative. This situation can be avoided, however, if everyone, young and old, understands that individual differences and personality conflicts have no place in the life of a choir that has dedicated its collective time and talent to the service of Christ. One source of irritation, the excessive energy of adolescents, can be put to good use in the children's choir program. High-school girls often make successful directors and accompanists for junior children. Their own understanding of the meaning of choir participation will be enhanced by their accepting these responsibilities.

As mentioned in Chap. VI, "The Adult Choir," every member of the adult choir should be considered a potential children's choir worker. Many will have children of their own in the younger choirs. They may wish to organize a mothers' (or parents') auxiliary. Such an organization can provide considerable aid to the director if its activities and energies are properly supervised and controlled.

It seems almost impossible sometimes for busy organists and choir directors, especially those on part time salaries, to carry the full burden of these choirs themselves. It is for this reason that choir auxiliaries are organized.[12]

Choir mothers (and sometimes fathers) can handle many routine tasks for the directors, but they should at no time assume responsibilities that are not specifically delegated. They may care for robes and help with robing the children, keep attendance records, arrange social events, provide transportation, and generally relieve the director of many small duties. It should be emphasized that no two directors will profit alike from a choir auxiliary. Before the plans for an organization of parents are announced, the director, the music committee, and the minister should determine the responsibilities and limitations of the group in order that misunderstandings may be avoided.

A discussion of children's choirs has no end. The subject is vast, and growing every year as more ideas are investigated and more churches discover the values inherent in a well-balanced music program. Books have been written about the subject. A useful one, Madeline Ingram's *Organizing and Directing Children's Choirs* contains up-to-the-minute suggestions, and is based upon a thoroughly sound concept of music for children. Other fine books are listed in the bibliography.

The writers wish to emphasize one basic thought that is the foundation of their philosophy of children's choirs: participation in a children's

---

[12] Paul Jerome Miller, *Youth Choirs* (New York: Harold Flammer, Inc., 1953), p. 18.

choir must contribute to the child's musical and aesthetic development and at the same time add to his understanding of worship and the meaning of religion in his life.

To become mature Christians we grow little by little to love God and our neighbors with heart, mind, soul, and strength—Jesus' definition of what really matters. The building of these right relationships in emotion, thought, word, and action is powerfully helped or retarded by what and how we sing. For we put into song the feelings, ideas, imagination, and hopes which shape the persons we become. We make singing a direct means of connecting ourselves with others in fellowship as we take part in worship and celebrate occasions of high moment.[13]

Suggested Hymns for Junior Children

All creatures of our God and King
All glory, laud, and honor
All people that on earth do dwell
All praise to Thee, my God, this night
A mighty fortress is our God
Awake, awake to love and work

Blessed Jesus, at Thy Word (st. 1)
Book of books, our people's strength

Christ the Lord is risen today
Come, Thou almighty King
Come, ye thankful people, come

Day is dying in the west

Fairest Lord Jesus
Faith of our fathers! living still
For the beauty of the earth
From all that dwell below the skies

God is my strong salvation
God moves in a mysterious way (st. 1)

God that madest earth and heaven

Hark! the herald angels sing

Heralds of Christ, who bear the King's commands
He who would valiant be
Holy, holy, holy! Lord God Almighty
Hosanna, loud hosanna
How firm a foundation, ye saints of the Lord (st. 1)

In Christ there is no East or West
Infant holy, Infant lowly
In the bleak midwinter
I sing a song of the saints of God
I sing the mighty power of God
It came upon the midnight clear
It fell upon a summer's day
I think when I read that sweet story of old

[13] Thomas, *Music in Christian Education*, p. 67. Used by permission.

117

Joyful, joyful, we adore Thee
Joy to the world! the Lord is come

Let all the world in every corner sing
Let us with a gladsome mind
Lift up your heads, ye mighty gates

Men and children everywhere
My country, 'tis of thee

Now thank we all our God

O beautiful for spacious skies
O come, all ye faithful, joyful and triumphant
O come, O come, Immanuel
O God, our help in ages past
O little town of Bethlehem
O Master Workman of the race
Once in royal David's city
O Son of Man, Thou madest known
O Word of God incarnate (st. 1)
O worship the King, all glorious above

Praise God, from whom all blessings flow
Praise the Lord! ye heavens adore Him

Praise to the Lord, the Almighty, the King of creation

Rejoice, ye pure in heart
Remember all the people
Rise up, O men of God

Silent night, holy night
Sing praise to God who reigns above
Soldiers of Christ, arise

Take my life, and let it be
The first Noel
The God of Abraham praise
The Lord's my Shepherd, I'll not want
The strife is o'er
This is my Father's world

We gather together to ask the Lord's blessing
We give Thee but Thine own
We plow the fields and scatter
We would see Jesus; lo! His star is shining
When morning gilds the skies
Where cross the crowded ways

Suggested Hymns for Primary Children

All creatures of our God and King
All things bright and beautiful
Away in a manger, no crib for a bed

Fairest Lord Jesus
Father, lead me day by day
For the beauty of the earth

Infant holy, Infant lowly
In the bleak midwinter (st. 1, 4)
I think when I read that sweet story of old

Let all the world in every corner sing

Let us with a gladsome mind
Now thank we all our God (st. 1)

O come, all ye faithful, joyful and triumphant
Once in royal David's city

Rejoice, ye pure in heart

Silent night, holy night

Tell me the stories of Jesus
The shepherds had an angel
The wise may bring their learning
This is my Father's world

Anthems for Youth Choirs

Most of the unison to SATB listed at the close of Chap. VIII, "The Choir's Music," can be used with senior youth.

UNISON AND SA

A Child's Thanksgiving	Baynon	Oxford OCS 1138
A Prayer of St. Richard	White	Oxford E43
A Song of Praise	Thiman	(York) Banks & Son 1193
All glory, laud, and honor	Bach	E. C. Schirmer 870
All praise to God who reigns above	Lenel	Concordia 98-1142
All things	Lewis	Summy-Birchard 1629
And the best is love	Proulx	Augsburg 11-1639
Before the paling of the stars	Boda	Concordia 98-1566
Brother James' Air	Jacob	Oxford OCS166
Brothers	Lovelace	E. C. Kerby 90373-024
Christmas Dance of the Shepherds	Kodaly	Presser 312-40573
Christmas Hymn	Peeters	World Library of Sacred Music
Christmas Song	Holst	G. Schirmer 8119
Come, together let us sing	Bach	E. C. Schirmer 1001
Dear Christians, praise God	Kindermann	Concordia LD503
Down to earth	Lovelace	Hope AD1977
Easter flowers are blooming	Lovelace	Gray 2513
Feed my lambs	Sleeth	Fischer 7777
Gifts for the Christ Child	Catalan	Tracy Music Library
God, make my life a shining light	Lovelace	Flammer 86170
Green the weeping willow tree	Graham	Art Masters 179
I am the Good Shepherd	Matthews	Mercury MC460
I will sing new songs	Dvořák	G. Schirmer 8646
In Bethlehem	Shimmin	E. Arnold 625
In the dark of the night	Halter	Concordia 98-1661
Japanese Christmas Carol	Lee	Gray 2767
Jesus was born in Bethlehem	Marshall	C. Fischer 6946
Kindly spring again is here	Lovelace	J. Fischer 9019
Let all the world	Lang	Oxford E86
Let all things now living	Davis	E. C. Schirmer 1819
Lord and Savior, true and kind	Bach	Flammer 86162
Mary's Lullaby	Warner	Summy-Birchard 1611
Masters in this hall	Holst	Curwen 71656

119

My heart ever faithful	Bach	E. C. Schirmer 283
Now all the woods are sleeping	Davis	E. C. Schirmer 1567
O leave your sheep	Kitson	Novello 1633
O Savior sweet	Bach	Gray 198
Oh, I would sing of Mary's Child	Lovelace	Augsburg 1247
On Christmas Night	Vaughan Williams	Galaxy
Psalm 100	Roth	E. C. Kerby 81071
Psalm 150	Britten	Boosey & Hawkes 5584
Saw you never in the twilight	Lovelace	Gray 2553
Serenity	Ives	Associated Music A377
Seven Tunes for Twelve Psalms	Jerome	Choristers Guild A115
Simple Gifts	Copland	Boosey & Hawkes 1903
Sing to the Lord a joyful song	Hopson	Flammer FA5001
Thanks we give	Wood	Choristers Guild A122
The Cradle	arr. Hinton	Oxford U138
The Flute Carol	Couper	J. Fischer 8586
The Lord my Shepherd is	Lovelace	Augsburg 1284
The Shepherd	Brook	Oxford 149
The shepherds found Thee by night	Shaw	Novello SS1365
The sun is on the land and sea	Lovelace	Gray 3268
The wise may bring their learning	Mueller	C. Fischer 6302
Three Simple Melodies	Zimmermann	C. Fischer 7778
'Twas in the moon of wintertime	Willan	Harris 1589
Walk softly in springtime	Lovelace	Choristers Guild A108
When Christ was born of Mary	MacMahon	(York) Banks & Son 1353
Worship	Shaw, G.	Novello MT967

For Combined Choirs

A Festival Chime	Holst	Stainer & Bell
As it fell upon a night	Davis	Galaxy 1291
Boy Child of Mary	Lovelace	Choristers Guild A151
Christ the Lord hath risen	Lang	Novello MT 1044
Like as a father	Cherubini	Choristers Guild A156
Now thank we all our God	Bach	Gray 1497
Sanctus	Fauré	FitzSimons 2119
Stars lead us ever on	Gaul	Ditson 332-24320

The Easter Anthems	Shaw	Oxford A 68
The King of Love	Bairstow	Oxford A 46

COLLECTIONS

American Folk Hymns for Junior Choir	Lovelace, ed.	C. Fischer 7311
Anthems for the Junior Choir	(Books 1, 2, 3, and 4)	The Westminster Press
Anthems for Junior Choristers	Lovelace	Summy-Birchard
Five Settings of Texts by Thomas Tiplady	Lovelace	E. C. Kerby 6153C
Green Hill Anthem Book		E. C. Schirmer
The Belfry Book	Davis, ed.	Remick
The Little Church Choir Book	Lundquist, ed.	E. C. Schirmer
The Oxford Book of Carols		Oxford
Uncommon Christmas Carols	Cozens, ed.	Hall & McCreary
We Praise Thee	Willan, ed.	Concordia

(See bibliography for additional lists of music contained in books about choirs.)

VIII

The Choir's Music

In the service of worship the anthem is often an element of comedy, sometimes tragedy, and even at times a farce, judging from the bulletins that we review each year. This is more true of the anthems than it is of the organ music listed. Perhaps the fact that the organist pays for his own music, while the church pays for the anthems makes the average director less careful in choosing anthems. Perhaps if he had to buy them with his own money more care would be taken.

One has only to poke his nose into dusty choir room closets stacked with doggerel Victorian anthems and second- and third-rate collections of uninspired anthems spewed out monthly by the pound by musical hacks to get an inkling of the tragic situation in many choir libraries.

In the numerous seasonal brochures received by the writers each year listing choral and organ music, the organ lists reveal an attempt on the part of many organists to perform an extensive cross section of great literature and to keep up with the better new publications. But such is rarely the case with anthems. The choral lists indicate a rut—the same old war horses, chestnuts, and tear-jerkers used year after year, with very few lists indicating that the director has searched out the treasures of past ages or has sorted the wheat from the chaff in the contemporary harvest.

Why such a disparity? First and foremost we must say that organ teachers have done on the whole a better job than choral teachers and that organ graduates are more thoroughly prepared than choral conductors. Colleges, universities, and conservatories base their organ course of study on the standard literature, beginning with that musical giant, Johann Sebastian Bach. A study of the catalogues of music departments reveals that the course requires acquaintance with a wide variety of the best literature for the instrument. How many choral stu-

122

dents have ever seen more than two or three small works of Palestrina? How many know that Monteverdi wrote some beautiful works for the use of the church? To how many are Vittoria, Perti, di Lasso names from a textbook only? The absence of such composers from choral lists indicates that our church choir offerings are not up to the level of the organ literature performed. Choral classes in many schools tend to place the major emphasis on conducting patterns and techniques and include only a smattering of anthems for conducting purposes. Survey courses in sacred choral literature tend to be the exception rather than the rule.

A great deal of blame can also be laid to the lack of theological and liturgical training. Too many music schools grant degrees in church music without requiring any training in liturgy or religion, and their graduates cannot understand that there is a difference between the work of a church choir and a concert choir. Many schools "beef up" their music education course with a course or two in church music and call it a church music degree program; but while public-school music methods are helpful for their methodology, they are inadequate in interpreting the place, purpose, and choice of music for the church.

Perhaps part of the blame for poor anthems can be laid at the door of the multiple choir system. In the desire to get everyone into some choir—from the crier choir to the crypt choir—directors have grasped at any music handy. Youngsters are asked to sing cut-down adult anthems or massed choirs are asked to sing "souped-up" versions of old chestnuts, with a tidbit tossed here, now there, until a veritable Brunswick stew is the result. In dragging in the "cherubs"—a name which should be outlawed except in heaven, where it belongs—to be cute and sweet for doting parents, music which is completely unsuitable for worship has been foisted on congregations.

Another reason for poor anthems lies in the fact that the congregation, having arrived late after the prelude and having dashed out for Sunday dinner almost before the sound of the benediction has died, only has contact with the choral music of the service and therefore feels that it has a right to insist on having its fancy tickled. Many directors quail in the face of criticism of anything new or untried and take the line of least resistance—giving the congregation "what it wants." Yet the anthem is not primarily intended to please the congregation, and the

123

use of poor material cannot be defended since music should first of all be a worthy offering to God.

It would seem, then, that the blame eventually falls on the director. Writing in the *American Guild of Organists Quarterly*, Seth Bingham said:

Some have blamed the publishers for issuing so much "junk" (and who can deny it?) thereby discouraging serious composers from writing for the church. . . . We are also aware of certain publishers who deliberately traffic in the mediocre, the soporific, the slushy. And how do they manage to stay in business? Where do they get the stuff? Why, from the self-styled "composers" who concoct it. And who are these? Well, we're sorry, but many of them happen to be organists or choir directors. *But who decides what music to buy?* Here, friends we're very close to home. The organist or choirmaster who knowingly buys this trash and wishes it on his choir with the lame excuse "that's what the congregation wants," not only cheapens himself but incurs a heavier responsibility than that of the unscrupulous publisher. Neither of them can be legally prosecuted. But he who refuses to buy this pseudo-religious tripe strikes a blow against the "phony" publisher and in favor of the conscientious one.[1]

In defense the choir director may plead that it is difficult to see new music since the average local music store carries incomplete stock. Suppose the director goes to a music dealer and asks to see some anthems for his choir. When a stack of review material is brought to the counter, practically no screening of good and bad, easy or difficult has been done, and the stack is usually filled with the same old tired daisies which invite the game of "love me, love me not." Most end up "love me not." I once looked through some one thousand anthems at a music counter and found only five which deserved further consideration. A few dealers make available examination copies in packet form on approval, with much of the necessary winnowing already accomplished, but these are a minority. Many publishers will send examination copies of new publications on approval, but it is expected that orders will be placed in quantity for some of the anthems. Regardless of the difficulty of the problem, it is the duty of the director to see as much music as is possible

[1] July, 1957, p. 110. Used by permission.

if only for the sake of comparing the poor and good and for developing a sense of good taste and good judgment.

What are the qualities of a good anthem? The starting point is consideration of the text, although one would not guess this judging from texts heard in churches over the country. Many are nothing but maudlin sentimentality. Others are patently unsuited for singing; some are even an affront to religion. A recent publication uses a text which includes Santa Claus and his reindeer in the story of the birth of Christ at Bethlehem. If such secularization continues we may someday expect to hear, "Here comes Peter Cottontail hopping down the resurrection trail."

Consider also the spate of materials of late which might be called the ding-dong school, in which the choir sings "ding-dong" or other related bell sounds. Christmas bulletins each year are cluttered with these tin-tinnabulations. Consider also the anthem with humming instead of text. It is highly questionable whether humming can be defended in an anthem. Tone poems are best left to the organ, which is suited to un-worded sound; anthems are strictly vehicles for texts.

Consider, too, such a "classic" as Harry Rowe Shelley's setting of "Hark, hark! my soul." Because the music is sweet and sentimental, no one seems to have taken the trouble to look at the words. The impression is that of much singing by the angels, but the vagueness of total meaning is closely related to the greater vagueness of "Beautiful isle of somewhere." Contrast the sentimentality of such a text as "I walked today where Jesus walked" with the compelling call of "O Master, let me walk with Thee." Then too there are many texts of the "In the garden" type, which Henry Sloane Coffin, former president of Union Theological Seminary in New York, classified as blasphemous. Perhaps "My God and I," with its anthropomorphic presentation of God and its overfamiliarity (can you really imagine jesting and joking with the God of creation and our salvation?), belongs in this class. From these it is but a small step to the downright degradation of religion inherent in the jukebox songs such as, "Talk to the Man Upstairs," "He," "I Believe," "There Ain't No Flies on My Jesus," "Put Your Snout Under the Spout Where the Gospel Comes Out," or "Place-Kick Me, Jesus, Through the Goal Posts of Life."

To protect the sanctity of worship the Episcopal Church has decreed that only such texts may be used as come from the Holy Scriptures, the

Prayer Book, and the Hymnal. Such a decision would certainly seem to be safe, and yet there are some texts in the Bible which do not have too much to say to the present age. There are many passages which are even sub-Christian. The following texts from the psalms, which presumably were for singing, are hardly worth setting as anthems:

> O God, break the teeth in their mouths;
> tear out the fangs of the young lion, O Lord. (Ps. 58:6.)

> Happy shall he be who takes your little ones
> and dashes them against the rock! (Ps. 137:9.)

It is necessary to study the text of every anthem, even if it is scriptural, to determine if it is theologically acceptable, profound in its message, beautiful in its expression, and meaningful to the listener of today.

Nor are all prayers in the Prayer Book of equal quality—some are poor and others are unsuited for singing for reasons of peculiarities in form or language. Neither does inclusion of a text in any hymnal automatically ensure its suitability for an anthem setting.

While there is an element of safety in the rule of the Episcopal Church, there is also the danger that worthy texts of poets writing today may be excluded from use. Certainly the Holy Spirit did not cease to speak to men with the death of King David, or even Martin Luther and Charles Wesley. Poets as well as composers should be encouraged to present the Christian message in new and vital ways, and it is a director's duty and job to seek out the best new texts and to use them.

Studying the text is only the first step, for there are many ways to set a given text, and the director must decide which is the best. Among the technical considerations the first concerns text accents. Do they coincide with the musical accents? Next consider the rise and fall of the melodic line. Does the melody follow the contour of the words and thought progression so that the climax of each comes together? What about the rhythm? Does it derive naturally from the flow of the words or does it move in spurts and jerks? Does it carry the text along or does it force the text to fit its changeable moods? Does the rhythm have a long line or is it botched by trivial patterns? Is there a relation of text to rhythm and phrase length?

126

What about the length of the anthem? Is it long enough to cover the text and to give its fullest meaning? Or does the anthem wander on and on irrespective of the thought? It is at this point that many composers have difficulty. Having been taught various musical forms in instrumental music, they tend to try to force a set pattern on a text whether it fits or not, resulting in needless and senseless repetition of words and phrases for the music's sake. The musical length should be subservient to the text, and musical and textual development should coincide. There should be an economy and suitability of musical material—a long anthem is not necessarily a good one.

Neither is a difficult anthem automatically superior to an easier one, for difficulty is not synonymous with excellence, although some directors consistently attempt anthems beyond the ability of their choirs through such a mistaken belief. Perfection of interpretation and presentation is the goal rather than mere performance of difficult music. A simple anthem sensitively sung with unanimity of pitch, diction, tone, and rhythm is no small achievement and is a goal worthy of any choir. If difficult anthems are sung the congregation should not be aware of any problems but should sense only the underlying motive and thought.

Another consideration is the number of voice parts. There is a certain school of thought which considers eight-part music as the ultimate. For many years the market was flooded with padded works in which the duplication of parts was merely designed to give a lush sound. Today some radio and television choirs use much the same idiom with the addition of colorful chords and effects. In most music four voices is sufficient, but a careful study of the Golden Age of Polyphony and the nineteenth-century Russian school will reveal how to use extra voices effectively. The problem of voice lines raises the larger question of the harmonic structure of an anthem. It is a far cry from the incidental harmonic points of Palestrina to the involved chords of Sowerby, and yet each age has produced its own harmonic idioms, each with value. When an idiom is overworked into a harmonic cliché it loses freshness and value. Tin Pan Alley, which has recently invaded the field of religion and music for obviously commercial reasons, has made the added sixth unacceptable and has built its commercial success on harmonic clichés—too many of which have been borrowed by nondiscriminating composers. Rock and roll at its worst is often little more than the sense-

127

less repetition of a few chords and monotonous rhythmic patterns to the point of either boredom or near insanity. Unfortunately, some church music composers have chosen to follow the low road of trying to cash in on current musical fads and have produced a great deal of non-food music. If a child asks for bread, should you give him rock and roll?

In the area of melody there are also many clichés—chromatic swipes, leaps of a sixth, and others which are seen too frequently in the flood of anthems streaming from the presses. Composers would do well to return to a study of the modes of the Church and to a study of the wealth of melodic ideas in Gregorian chant.

The art of rhythm and the flexibility of plainsong seem to have been lost to many composers. Instead we find the rhythmic clichés of the dotted eighth followed by a sixteenth, the accompanimental chord repeated in triplets—"The Palms" by Jean-Baptiste Fauré, an example, is, unfortunately, widely used annually—or the deadly monotony of even note values. Even the excitement of syncopation soon disappears unless an occasional note falls on a strong pulse. Great choral works have always been built on vital rhythm, beauty of melody, and soundness of harmony.

There are three further tests to be made in choosing the choir's music. The first is suitability. Music used for sacred purposes is partially defined and limited by its appropriateness to special needs. A composition may be excellent music and fine for the concert hall but entirely unfit for church. Some works, such as Dubois' "Seven Last Words," Verdi's "Requiem," and Rossini's "Stabat Mater," while based on texts of the Church, are totally unsuited because of their operatic style. In none of them is the listener directed more to the words than to the music or more to the spiritual content than to the technique of the singers. In the appendix to Church Music: Illusion and Reality,[2] Archibald T. Davison illustrates the difference in suitability of several settings of the "Kyrie eleison," ranging from plainsong to the opera utterances of the nineteenth century. His book is a fruitful study of the qualities which separate appropriate from inappropriate, and every church musician will benefit from a study of his discussion and examples.

Suitability also refers one to a study of the acoustics of the church

[2] Cambridge, Mass.: Harvard University Press, 1952.

sanctuary. Organists as a rule are fairly sensitive to the acoustical properties of an auditorium and its effect upon organ tone. An edifice which has been acoustically mistreated with absorbent materials and buried alive under tons of draperies, carpets, and pew cushions offers problems to the organist, but it also offers serious problems to the choir. The glorious style of the sixteenth century is peculiarly ineffective and inappropriate in such a setting, for the masters of that century wrote long flowing lines which call for a cathedral setting in which the tones float and intertwine with one another. Without a "live" building an anthem of the polyphonic school is generally ineffective.

Suitability of the organ is also a consideration in the case of accompanied anthems. To attempt Gustav Holst's "Short Festival Te Deum" (Stainer and Bell) accompanied by most electronics is sheer folly, for the brilliance and support required are not available. Some excellent anthems must be laid on the shelf if the organ—or the organist—is not capable of carrying the load.

Suitability should also be thought of in terms of local usages and liturgical requirements. Even though an anthem be excellent, it still must be related to its use and placement in the service of worship. Is it appropriate to the season of the church year? Is it correlated with the sermon topic or general theme of the service? Does the text clash with nearby prayers or hymns? Does it duplicate or approximate too closely other texts in the service? Is its message clear and comprehensible? Is it worth singing? Across the country various denominations use all sorts and conditions of liturgies, some with strict requirements, but all with some definite pattern. Here the musician must follow the lead of the minister, but he should also make it a point to know as much about all liturgies as possible. Church music should be liturgically correct, but it should avoid the narrow confines and stifling quality of sectarianism.

Suitability also is partially controlled by the limitations of the choir. It is perhaps dangerous to mention this limitation, for all too many choir directors hide behind this excuse, knowingly or not. Many an excellent anthem is left untried, not because the choir is really incapable of singing it, but because the director is afraid to tackle it with the choir. Many works reveal themselves to be less difficult than they appear on the surface if one takes the trouble to analyze individual voice lines and balance problems. One should also face facts and not attempt works

129

beyond the choir—such as an anthem with divided tenor parts when the section consists of one high baritone.

Suitability also involves the congregation. How often one hears the complaint, "But my congregation won't like that anthem." Before berating the congregation too quickly, consider the following facts: an anthem which takes three minutes to sing may be in preparation for months before it is sung. The director spends hours studying the anthem to discover the composer's intentions. Then the choir may rehearse weekly for six or eight weeks before its presentation. The congregation is expected to absorb, to understand, to appreciate, and to accept on a fleeting hearing of three minutes what took months to prepare! This is patently impossible and unfair. The solution does not lie in bowing to any unfavorable reaction, but in repeating the anthem frequently. While too many new works a season can founder a congregation, a few new things repeated fairly often will do much to educate a congregation and to guide their growth in understanding and appreciation.

Percy Buck in *The Scope of Music*[3] suggests that there are three levels of appreciation. The first is crude appreciation in which chiefly the senses are concerned. This level is in evidence when members of the congregation either purr or growl at the anthem. The second is intelligent appreciation, and involves an element of comparison; the listener begins to prefer one anthem over another, and a choice is made on some basis of judgment. The third level is that of critical appreciation and calls for the maximum use of our powers of perception and discrimination. This level is not a plateau on which one can stop, however, for there is always something which leads us on from appreciation of something fine to something finer. Percy Buck said:

Only a fool will ever think the end of the road has been reached, for there is no end, and only conceit will allow anyone to think he has gone as far as he might have gone. And the going a little farther, which is possible to all of us, will not only result in an increase of our own enjoyment of life, but will also prevent that atrophy of our power of enjoyment which, as Darwin so pathetically lamented, may make our later years emotionless and grey.[4]

[3] New York: Oxford University Press, 1927.
[4] *Ibid.,* pp. 71-72.

So while we must consider the congregation in our thinking and planning we cannot let them be the final arbiter of decisions or choices. Yet any anthem should eventually communicate to the man in the pew.

Next, consider the quality of durability; an anthem should wear well with frequent repetition. One is often chagrined to discover that an anthem which seemed attractive at first glance loses its freshness after the first rehearsal. There must be many an anthem gathering dust in choir libraries because it never got past the first rehearsal successfully. Of course durability is not necessarily related either to newness or oldness. Sir Walford Davies in *Music and Worship* expressed it thus: "Music in aid of worship must be original in the two distinct senses of being something quite new and something so old that it has been there from the beginning." [5]

Closely related to durability is the element of imagination. An excellent anthem always elicits an enthusiastic response from choir members as its secrets are revealed to them, for they constantly find new beauty in it each time it is sung. A technical problem to be overcome, a new sense of the structure of the music, imaginative use of material, a breathtaking chord—these are but a few of the elements of a masterpiece.

Some people consider music only as entertainment, but they thereby relegate art to a place of relative unimportance. Great music is not an embellishment of life but a spiritual enrichment of it. It is a vital factor of expression, just as religion is a central, not a peripheral, matter. Alvin Schutmaat said:

We need the arts for stimulating and cultivating our religious imagination. The ability to see harmonies and relationships among people, things and events is surely God-given. There can be no love of one's neighbor without imagination, nor any love of God. How can a man grasp for himself the reality of Christ without a lively imagination? Pastors and teachers often fail to raise us to the heights of imagination which the gospel demands and prefer to reduce the gospel message [and we would add parenthetically, many anthems] to prosaic formulas. That is why we are often considered a people without visions, mysteries or dreams.[6]

A third characteristic of a good anthem is simplicity. This does not mean that a great anthem will necessarily be simple, but the motive

[5] (New York: The H. W. Gray Company, 1925), p. 31.
[6] *The Pulpit*, "Protestantism and Art" (January, 1957), p. 38.

back of it will be simplicity itself. The "Hallelujah Chorus" from *The Messiah* has complexities in the various voice lines, yet the fundamental material is not complicated, and the motive of rejoicing and adoration is simply and effectively projected. Simplicity has to do, then, with form and purpose.

Finally, is it too much to ask that an anthem have beauty? C. E. M. Joad expressed the divinity of beauty well when he suggested that goodness, beauty, and truth are three ways in which God reveals himself to man.[7] Beauty is a gift of God, and a work of art is a presentation in form of feeling that which the artist has experienced or received from God. In the best sense it is a presentation of his own catharsis. While there are many arguments as to what is beautiful, we are obliged to make an attempt to understand what the artist felt and is trying to express if we are to see the vision of beauty he experienced. For art always reaches our feelings *through* the understanding. Art is not an appeal *to* the understanding but aims at a goal whose only approach is *through* comprehension. Therefore the awareness of beauty in an anthem depends upon the inspiration of the composer, the insight of the conductor, the devotion of the choir to perfection, and the sympathetic understanding of the congregation.

The purpose of the anthem, then, is much more than entertainment or background music. In an article in *The Christian Century*[8] Warren H. Deem points out the dangers of using music as a vague background of noise—particularly in church, where much music today is pleasant but little more. Leonard Raver said:

Such music exists only on the most basic level: music to dance to, to read by, to eat with, and to talk to (or in spite of). It does not occupy us, it does not command the full attention of the mind and spirit of man.[9]

Worthy texts which can inspire the soul, enlighten the mind, and express the finest emotions of the congregation are the basis for the choir's music. To these texts must be added worthy musical settings in which melody, rhythm, harmony, and form serve to highlight, delineate, undergird, and set aglow the words. Any anthem used must be suitable

---

[7] *The Recovery of Belief* (London: Faber and Faber, Ltd., 1952), p. 212.
[8] "Muzak, Muzak, Everywhere!" (September 25, 1957), pp. 1132-33.
[9] *Organ Institute Quarterly*, 6, No. 4, 22.

for the purposes of worship, to the acoustics of the sanctuary, to the limitations of the choir and organ, to the liturgical requirements, and to the understanding and appreciation of the congregation. The best anthems will be durable, simple in motive, beautiful and worshipful, and will help us to return to the function of music which Martin Luther stated as

putting music upon the living and holy Word of God, therewith to sing, praise and honor the same, so that the beautiful ornament of music, brought back to its right use, may serve its blessed Maker and His Christian people.

Hymns Arranged as Anthems

The hymnal offers one of the richest and most inexpensive sources of anthem material. A hymn used as an anthem is an effective way of presenting it to the congregation with the view of having them sing the hymn at a later time. The following devices may be used to vary stanzas; the ways in which a hymn may be arranged are limited only by the imagination and musicianship of the director, the organist, and the choir. Certainly many commercial versions are less effective than arrangements made to fit a particular combination of voices.

1. SATB, with accompaniment either duplicating the voices or slightly embellished
2. SATB, without accompaniment
3. Other combinations (such as SAT, SAB, SSA) without accompaniment
4. All voices unison, with or without accompaniment
5. Men's voices in unison
6. Women's voices in unison
7. ATB sing the melody with S on a descant
8. SATB with S and T exchanging parts
9. SA or ST in duet form, using other voices to accompany or with instrumental accompaniment only
10. Unison with free organ accompaniment
11. Unison, with organ playing a hymn or choral prelude
12. SA, SAT, or SATB with solo voices for small ensemble effect
13. Various voice combinations with instrumental descant (flute, violin, trumpet)
14. Various voice combinations with organ descant (flute 4', flute 8', trumpet, oboe)

133

15. Antiphonal effects
16. Use of a canon, or round (Such tunes as "Gräfenburg," "Tallis' Canon," "Lasst Uns Erfreuen," "Foundation")
17. Congregation joining on selected stanzas, usually the last
18. Children's choirs on melody or descant, or singing the soprano part in combination with adult voices (SA or ST)
19. Organ interludes and key changes for variety
20. Change minor to major; major to minor.
21. Faux bourdon (reharmonizations in which the melody is given to the tenors, and sopranos have a new melody)
22. TTBB or SSA arrangements
23. Combine two or more of the above devices within the framework of one stanza.

Every choir library should contain representative works from the following groups of composers. This list is not definitive since many other composers have published fine music. The choir that knows the works of these men, however, will be better equipped to evaluate other writings.

PRE-EIGHTEENTH CENTURY

Jakob Arcadelt
Dietrich Buxtehude
William Byrd
Richard Farrant
Melchior Franck
Andrea Gabrieli
Giovanni Gabrieli
Orlando Gibbons
Jakob Handl
Hans Leo Hassler
Orlando di Lasso
Antonio Lotti
Johann Pachelbel
Giovanni Palestrina
Michael Praetorius
Henry Purcell
Heinrich Schütz
Thomas Tallis
Christopher Tye
Tomás Victoria

Melchior Vulpius
Adrian Willaert

EIGHTEENTH CENTURY

Johann Sebastian Bach
J. C. Bach
Maurice Greene
George Frederick Handel
Franz Joseph Haydn
Wolfgang Amadeus Mozart
Giovanni Pergolesi

NINETEENTH CENTURY

Thomas Attwood
Johannes Brahms
William Crotch
Anton Dvořák
Edward Elgar
César Franck
Felix Mendelssohn-Bartholdy
Camille Saint-Saëns
Franz Schubert
Samuel Sebastian Wesley

134

NINETEENTH CENTURY—RUSSIAN

Alexander Archangelsky	Alexander Katalsky
Anton Arensky	Alexander Kopyloff
Mily Balakireff	Alexis von Lvov
Dimitri Bortniansky	Sergei Rachmaninoff
Alexander Gretchaninoff	C. Schvedov
Michail Ippolitoff-Ivanoff	Peter Tschaikowsky
Vassili Kalinnikoff	Paul Tschesnokoff

Moderately Easy to Easy Anthems

Abbey	Sleep, sweet Jesus, sleep	Mercury MC 191
Anderson	Come, I pray Thee	Mills Music 60628
Bach	Awake, my soul, and sing ye	Wood 548
Berger	A rose touched by the sun's warm rays	Augsburg 953
————	The eyes of all wait	Augsburg 1264
Billings	A Virgin unspotted	Mercury 64
Brahms	Mary Magdalene	Gray 1747
————	The Hunter	E. C. Schirmer 1680
Brandon	The Word became flesh	E. C. Kerby 5201C
Burleigh	Behold that star	Ricordi 785
Buszin	Now sing we, now rejoice	Concordia 98-1189
Caldwell	A Lute Carol	Gray 2808
————	Tell us, shepherd maids	Gray 2358
Christian-sen, P.	Wondrous Love	Augsburg 1140
Clokey	A Canticle of Peace	Summy-Birchard 340
Coleman	Jesus, Lover of my soul	Oxford 42.135
Copes	For the bread	Abingdon 115
Curry	Tell out the news	Oxford X113
Davis	Come ye to Bethlehem	Galaxy 1996
————	Good folk who dwell on earth	Wood 731
————	Let all things now living	E. C. Schirmer 1819
————	Long hast thou stood (U. with Des.)	E. C. Schirmer 1765
Davison, arr.	Thy wisdom, Lord (SAB)	E. C. Schirmer 1703
Diemer	Praise ye the Lord	Flammer A5021
Distler	A Little Advent Music	Concordia 97-4707
Farrant	Call to remembrance	Bourne ES17
Fauré	Sanctus	FitzSimons 2119

135

Franck, J.	Father, thy Holy Spirit send	E. C. Schirmer 1687
Franck, M.	O Jesus, grant me hope	Schmitt, Hall & McCreary 1544
Friedell	Jesus so lowly	Gray 2018
Fryxell	Psalm 67	Gray 2337
Gaul	The March of the Wise Men	Gray 2384
_____	Stars lead us ever on	Ditson 15130
George	Ride on, ride on	Gray 1765
Gevaert	The sleep of the Child Jesus	Witmark 5W 2610
Gibbs	Sleep, Little King	Boosey & Hawkes 1899
Graham	Two Songs of Bethlehem	E. C. Kerby 80978
Halter	A Virgin most pure	Concordia CH79
Handel	Jesus, Sun of Life, my splendor	Concordia 98-1445
Haydn	Great and glorious	Wood 316
_____	In Thee, O Lord	Sam Fox PS103
Hill	The whole bright earth rejoices	Gray 1861
Holst	A Festival Chime	Galaxy FC8
_____	Christmas Day	Novello 983
_____	Let all mortal flesh	Galaxy FC5
Jacob	Brother James' Air (U. with Des.)	Oxford 44.047
Johnson	Thy blessings, Father	Galaxy 1026
Joubert	Torches	Novello MT 1316
Kitson	Jesu, grant me this, I pray	Oxford A 57
di Lasso	Lord, to Thee we turn	E. C. Schirmer 1124
Lenel	All praise to God (2 part)	Concordia 98-1142
Lotti	Surely He hath borne (SAB)	E. C. Schirmer 1124
Lovelace	A Gladsome Hymn of Praise (SAB)	Flammer D5001
_____	Breaking of the bread	Hope A430
_____	God is my strong salvation	E. C. Kerby 90478
_____	More SAB Anthems for the Church Year	Sacred Music Press
_____	SAB Anthems for the Church Year	Sacred Music Press
_____	Talk with us, Lord	Summy 1545
_____	What shall I render to my God	E. C. Kerby 90578
Lundquist	Of the Father's love begotten	Concordia 98-1227
Lvov	O Holy Jesu	G. Schirmer 4506
Marshall	Awake my heart	H. W. Gray 2515
_____	He comes to us	C. Fischer 6996
Matthews, H.	O'er Bethlehem's plains	Elkan Vogel 1048

136

Matthews, T.	The Lord is my Shepherd	FitzSimons 2137
Mendelssohn	Behold a star from Jacob shining	E. C. Schirmer 1683
Micheelsen	With high delight	Concordia 98-1942
Nagle	Joseph dearest, Joseph mine	Presser 21301
Niles	Jesus, Jesus, rest Your head	G. Schirmer 8302
————	The Little Lyking	G. Schirmer 10110
Oldroyd	Prayer to Jesus	Oxford 43.037
Pachelbel	Now thank we all our God	Brodt Music 524
Palestrina	Adoramus Te	G. Schirmer 6091
Peek	Now glad of heart	E. C. Kerby 80278
————	Righteous Joseph	E. C. Kerby 82078
Pfautsch	Sing praise to God	Summy-Birchard 5315
Posegate	God is with us	Flammer A5581
Praetorius	From heaven on high	G. Schirmer 9641
————	Shepherds Him their praises bringing	Concordia BA 16
desPres	The name of Jesus	Concordia CH 1095
Purcell	Thou knowest, Lord, the secrets of our hearts	Wood 209
Purvis	What strangers are these (U. with Des.)	Summy-Birchard 969
Ramsey	A Hymn of Brotherhood	Gray 1980
Ream	O, sleep, Baby Jesus	Hall & McCreary 1623
Reed	Rise up, O men of God	J. Fischer 8004
Roberton	I see His blood upon the rose (SSATB)	G. Schirmer 8597
————	Let all the world in every corner	G. Schirmer 8721
Rossello	Adoremus Te	G. Schirmer 8377
Roth	Christ our Passover	E. C. Kerby 6101C
Rowley	Praise	Oxford 42.031
Rutter	Shepherd's Pipe Carol	Oxford 81.133
Sampson	My song shall be always	Belwin Mills AP10
Schütz	Praise to Thee, Lord Jesus	Novello 1202
Scull	Rise up, O men of God	Novello MT 1140
Shaw, G.	Praise God in His holiness (SAB)	G. Schirmer 8574
Shaw, M.	With a voice of singing	Curwen 958103
Shaw, R.	O sons and daughters	G. Schirmer 9950
Shaw-Parker	Here, mid the ass and oxen mild	G. Schirmer 10186
————	I will arise	Lawson-Gould 905

	The Cherry Tree Carol	G. Schirmer 10170
Sowerby	Beneath the forms of outward rite	Abingdon 940
Stanton	Christ is the world's true light (U. with Des.)	Oxford 40.007
Suitor	Poverty	Abingdon 634
Tallis	If ye love Me	Oxford 42.601
Thatcher	Come, ye faithful (SAB)	Oxford 42.809
Thiman	A Hymn of Freedom	H. W. Gray 1683
————	A Hymn of Praise to the Creator	H. W. Gray 2290
————	Awake, awake to love and work	H. W. Gray 2411
————	Immortal, invisible	Novello 1140
————	O love of God (SAB)	Novello MT 1195
Thomson	My Shepherd will supply my need	Gray 2046
Titcomb	O love, how deep	Gray 2226
Tkach	To Thee we sing	Kjos 6501
Vaughan Williams	Come down, O Love Divine (arr. Dietterich)	Abingdon 241
————	O how amiable	Oxford 42.056
————	O taste and see	Oxford 43.909
————	The Old One Hundredth Psalm-Tune	Oxford 42.953
Vaughan Williams-Shaw	For all the saints	G. Schirmer 9908
Vulpius	Now God be praised	E. C. Schirmer 1693
————	The strife is o'er	Oxford 42.219
Wadeley	That God doth love the world (SAB)	Oxford 42.138
Weelkes	Let Thy merciful ears be open	Oxford 43.076
Wesley	The Word of the Lord endureth forever	Flammer 84412
Wetzler	He comes! He comes!	Art Masters 198
Whitten (arr.)	Shepherds come a-running	Choir Publications 30008
Willan	Christ whose glory	Concordia 2006
————	Sing to the Lord of harvest	Concordia 98-2013
————	Strengthen for service	C. F. Peters 6510
————	What is this lovely fragrance	Oxford 42.171
Williams, D. H.	Draw nigh to Jerusalem	Gray 2410
————	Lo! He comes with clouds descending	Gray 2350

138

Williams, R. E.	Let the people praise Thee	Schmitt, Hall & Mc-Creary 865
Wilson	To Bethlehem, singing	Boosey & Hawkes 5056
Yarrington	Calls to Praise and Prayer	Chantry Music Press
Young, C.	Be Thou my vision	Kjos 5254
Young, G.	Now let us all praise God	Galaxy 2108

More Difficult Anthems

Bach-Malin	O Jesu, King of glory	Wood 727
Bairstow	The King of love	Oxford 42.024
———	Though I speak with the tongues	Oxford 42.042
Berger	Extolled and hallowed be the name	J. Fischer 9591
———	Speak to one another in psalms	Augsburg 954
Bloch	Silent devotion and response	Broude
Boyce	All the ends of the earth	Novello 1229
Brahms	Create in me, O God	G. Schirmer 7504
———	O heart subdued	Novello 880
Casals	O vos omnes	Broude
Clokey	King of Kings	Summy-Birchard 2030
Coke-Jephcott	Surely the Lord is in this place	Gray 1974
Cousins	Glorious everlasting	Brodt 808
Distler	Lo, how a rose	Concordia 98-1925
Fleming (arr.)	His voice	Schmitt, Hall & Mc-Creary 8054
Franck	If God be for us	Marks 12781-7
Gardner	Brightest and best	Oxford 42.870
Gore	The Beatitudes	Chantry Press
Gottlieb	Shout for joy	World Library of Sacred Music CA2086
Graun-Buszin	Surely He hath borne our griefs	Concordia 98-1171
Gretchaninoff	Blessed is the man	J. Fischer 9902
Hassler	Cantate Domino	E. C. Schirmer 1262
Haydn	Evensong to God	Boosey & Hawkes 1824
Holst	Eternal Father	G. Schirmer 8510
———	Psalm 86	Augener (Galaxy)
———	Turn back, O man	Galaxy FC6
Hovhaness	Psalm 61	C. F. Peters 6255

Howells	A spotless rose	Stainer & Bell CCL 220
Ireland	Greater love hath no man	Galaxy CC146
di Lasso	Though deep has been my falling	G. Schirmer 8423
Leighton	Nativitie	C. Fischer 7734
Lovelace	Faces like mirrors	C. Fischer 7757
Manz	E'en so Lord Jesus, quickly come	Concordia 98-1054
Marshall	Good news	C. Fischer 7758
Niles	No room in the hotel (8 parts)	G. Schirmer 9981
Pachelbel	On God, and not on human trust	Concordia 98-1006
_____	Now thank we all our God	Brodt Music Co. 524
Petrich	Ah, holy Jesus	Oxford 94.317
Rickard	Gloria	Augsburg 11-9191
Schütz	Christ our blessed Savior	G. Schirmer 9657
_____	Who shall separate us	Chantry Press
Shaw, M.	The Easter Anthems	Oxford 42.045
Sowerby	Now there lightens upon us	Gray 1307
Thompson	The best of rooms	E. C. Schirmer 2672
_____	Glory to God in the highest	E. C. Schirmer 2470
_____	The Last Words of David	E. C. Schirmer 2294
Tye	Praise ye the Lord, ye children	Oxford 43.241
Vaughan Williams	Lord, Thou hast been our refuge	G. Schirmer 9720
Weaver	Epiphany Alleluias	Boosey & Hawkes 5683
Willan	Worthy art Thou	Concordia MS 1015
Williamson	Procession of Palms	G. Schirmer 11251
Wright, S.	Prayer of St. Francis	Witmark 5W 3446

Pop, Contemporary, and the Cutting Edge

Adler	Psalm 150	Choristers Guild A39
Avery and Marsh, arr. Pfautsch	Here we go a-caroling	Hope AG7105
_____	I wonder why	Hope AG7104
Britten	Festival Te Deum	Boosey & Hawkes
Diercks	Clap your hands	Abingdon APM-103
Felciano	Cosmic Festival (with electronic tape)	E. C. Schirmer 2938
_____	Pentecost Sunday (with electronic tape)	World Library of Sacred Music EMP1532-1

140

Joubert	Torches	Novello MT1316
Lahmer	It is good to give thanks (2 parts)	World Library of Sacred Music EMP1499-5
Lovelace	Christmas Gloria	Hope CF159
————	Every stone shall cry	Hope CH660
————	The psalm that swings	Hope CF146
Moe	Nunc Dimittis	Hope AG7113
Nystedt	De Profundis	Associated Music A499
Pelz	Good news	Art Masters 215
Pepping	Laud Him	Kjos 30
Pfautsch	Go and tell John	Hope CY3334
————	The new is old	Abingdon APM-855
————	Reconciliation	Abingdon APM-345
Poulenc	Videntes stellam	Salabert 12527
Rimmer	Sing we merrily	Novello MT 1443
Rohlig	O sing unto the Lord	Hope A431
Sleeth	Jazz Gloria	C. Fischer 7752
Suri	Smol Taon	Hope F948
Swann	Jubilate Domino (2 part)	Galaxy GMC2481

(See also a "Bibliographical Index of Music and Musicians" in Erik Routley's *Twentieth Century Church Music* [New York: Oxford University Press, 1964].)

More or Less Conventional with Instruments (SATB)

Blahnik	Easter Fanfare	E. C. Kerby 4378-942
Buxtehude	In dulci jubilo (SAB)	Concordia 98-1500
Diemer	Alleluia! Christ is risen	Flammer 84859
Erickson (arr.)	Love is come again	Art Masters 1206
Johnson (arr.)	The lone, wild bird	Augsburg 11-0524
————	Thy kingdom come	Augsburg ACL 11-1629
Moe	Fanfare and Choral Procession	Augsburg 11-9166
Pelz	Who shall abide (SAB)	Augsburg PS617
Pfautsch	Christian, dost thou see them	Abingdon APM-345
————	I'll praise my Maker	Abingdon APM-110
Proulx	My heart is full today	Augsburg 11-0645
Scandrett	Adam lay ibounden (U)	J. Fischer FE9849

141

Schroeder	In Bethlehem a wonder	Concordia 98-2063
	Now sing we, now rejoice	Concordia 98-2062
Sleeth	Jubilate Deo	Abingdon APM-885
Wood	Jubilate Deo	Augsburg 11-1603
Zimmerman	Psalm 100	Augsburg 11-0640

IX

The Soloist

THE SOLO PRESENTATION OF MUSIC BOASTS A LONG AND PROUD HISTORICAL background. The songs of Miriam, Deborah, Zacharias (Benedictus), Mary (Magnificat), and Simeon (Nunc Dimittis) as well as the personal utterances of David (such as Psalm 51) are solos, although many are now used corporately in chant form. The use of the cantor in the Jewish synagogue is an ancient tradition, and the responsorial singing of psalms called for a soloist answered by the congregation. Thus at least two uses of the solo can be defended on historical grounds—the utterance of a text which is personal in nature, and the use of a soloist in a liturgical pattern of solo and response.

The solo has been used to particularly good effect in cantatas and oratorios, and some of the finest literature available is to be found here. Bach's use of personal reaction to the story of Christ's passion, as found in the "St. Matthew" and "St. John" settings, is a valuable study for all church musicians.

Abuses of the solo have come from operatic tendencies wherein the text, or its method of setting, is unsuitable for solo presentation in church and the musical material is primarily designed to display the voice, as in such works as "The Seven Last Words" by Dubois, "Requiem" by Verdi, and "Stabat Mater" by Rossini. The English verse-anthem to some extent is unacceptable on the grounds that the solos were often added to display the talents of an available soloist and to entertain the royalty attending services. Perhaps the chief objection of the present day is to the low caliber of music which clothes so many solos heard in church.

The solo has gained too much prominence and has fallen into disrepute among worship leaders in this country through the influence of the solo quartet and through the tendency of many lazy directors to use the solo as an easy way out when the choir is not prepared to present an anthem. Particularly is the solo overworked in the summer when maintaining a choir may be difficult. In some cases voice teachers who also direct choirs use the solo as a means of presenting their students, and incidentally for recruiting more students who desire to perform before the public.

Many anthems include solo parts—some designed to show off available voices—and in almost every instance such anthems should either be avoided or else the passage should be sung by the entire section. Dudley Buck's "Festival Te Deum in E flat" is an example of the depths to which church music can stoop when the music is geared to fit the soloists rather than the needs of worship. In churches with soloists there is a tendency to expect each to perform in turn, and the congregation comes to feel they do not get their money's worth if a different soloist is not heard every Sunday. Such a situation can only lead to the misuse of music as entertainment and personal aggrandizement and should be vigorously and emphatically discouraged.

The chief complaint, however, against soloists is their propensity for "upstaging" the service. At a recent summer service a soloist came from the choir pew to the pulpit, faced the congregation, and sang "Ye now are sorrowful," from the "German Requiem" by Brahms, complete with gestures. I recently heard of a tenor in a Midwestern church who "gave his all" one Easter morning; after the ringing high note which closed the solo—the organist played from the high key copy—he received a rousing ovation and bowed deeply to the congregation!

If solos are to be permitted in church, the soloist must be like an actor on stage only in the sense that he makes us aware of the solo and not himself. The congregation should never be aware primarily of the singer as an intrusion but should be aware of the message of the song. This is a difficult task, but only in so far as the singer can succeed should solos be used.

Certain qualifications should be laid down in choosing a soloist. The first concerns the voice itself. A soloist must have a pleasing quality and be well trained; the service is no place for learning or practicing. Vocal problems must be solved at the studio so the mechanics of singing do not interfere with the important job of leading a congregation in worship. Good diction as well as musicianship should be expected of a singer. He who cannot keep accurate time and must have intervals pounded into his ear should not be expected or allowed to appear as a soloist at any worship service. All texts must be presented sympathetically as well as correctly—for singing is more than hitting the right notes and pronouncing the correct syllables. If a soloist does not rise above technical matters, he is not ready to assume the responsibility of singing for the whole choir.

Replacing the choir is a large responsibility that carries with it the necessity for humility and precludes any show or display. In a chancel the soloist must not turn to face the congregation but should stand facing the opposite singers. A robe should be worn by every soloist—including those at weddings—and no earrings, hair ribbons, jewelry, or corsages should be worn. If music is held it should be placed in a suitable folder, but a solo should preferably be memorized. Attention should be directed to the projection of the text and to the subjugation of personality.

Above all the soloist must lead a Christian life and have a desire to praise God worthily. A soloist can no more lead a congregation in worship when there is a doubt about his character and life than a preacher can move a congregation with his sermons if his personal life is questionable. Nor can there be any place for displays of temper—often miscalled temperament—jealousy, or bickering over who is to sing solos. Such unchristian attitudes are sufficient grounds to bar a soloist from singing for a worship service.

One of the gravest faults with the solo in church lies in the choice of so much unsuitable material. Where the philosophy is to use solos without regard to their suitability, the director often finds himself agreeing to the use of whatever solos are in the singer's repertoire. Many voice teachers tend to know very little about the sacred solo repertoire and encourage artistic and religious atrophy by suggesting the same threadbare junk to each succeeding generation of church singers.

The choice of an appropriate solo starts with the study of the text. There are many texts which are clearly unsuited for solo presentation and should be avoided. Passages designed for corporate use—such as the Lord's Prayer—are particularly inappropriate for solo presentation. The fact that a text is biblical is not adequate proof of its acceptability.

145

When a good solo text is found, then the harder test must be made as to the excellence of the musical setting. The melodic line should follow the contour of the words, the rhythmic stresses of the music should coincide with the accents of the words, and the harmonic idiom and entire musical style should heighten the effectiveness of the text. Developing the ability to recognize musical excellence can come only from the study of great solo literature of all eras, and every soloist must constantly search for the choicest old and new material. For a further discussion of this problem, see Chap. VIII, "The Choir's Music."

The best solo can be a misfit if it is not co-ordinated with specific liturgical, seasonal, and topical needs. Here is the real danger of the solo—it can be excellent music beautifully sung and still undermine the service of worship. "O for the wings of a dove" sung on Loyalty Sunday ("far away would I fly!") is hardly the best way to get a congregation to respond to a call for action. "It is enough," sung following a sermon is at best ludicrous unless the minister has preached about Elijah, and even then it is doubtful that any service should end on such a despairing note.

While the poorly chosen and poorly sung solo may be a capricious interruption or a disturbing irrelevancy, it is also capable of expressing more sharply than an anthem the personal emotions of the congregation. If the soloist sings with inspiration and dedication, and if the song is an excellent choice, appropriate for the singer, the time, and the place, the sacred solo can be a unique contribution in worshiping God and in speaking to the needs of the people.

Carl Halter has summarized the role of the solo well:

It is obviously not our purpose to suggest that the solo should be the basic special vocal song of the church. The congregation and the choir are still and must remain the principal vocal groups in worship. But it is foolish to restrict the possibilities of worship experiences in any direction for light or insufficient cause. The solo, judiciously and reverently prepared and sung, can contribute, as the history and experience of the Church abundantly reveal.[1]

[1] The Practice of Sacred Music (St. Louis, Mo.: Concordia Publishing House, 1955), p. 19.

146

Sacred Solos

Abbey	Sleep, sweet Jesus, sleep	Mercury	(M)
Bach	By waters of Babylon	Gray	(M)
————	God my Shepherd walks beside me	Gray	(H)
————	I follow with gladness	Paterson	(H)
————	My heart ever faithful	G. Schirmer	(LMH)
Bairstow	The Hostel	Stainer & Bell	(LH)
Banks	O brother man	Gray	(L)
Barber	Lord Jesus Christ	G. Schirmer	(H)
Barnes	The Gate of the Year	Chantry Music Press	(M)
Baumgartner	Behold, what manner of love	Concordia	(H)
————	He that dwelleth in the secret place of the Most High	Concordia	(H)
————	Lord, I have loved the habitation of Thy house	Concordia	(M)
Berlinski	Psalm 23	Mercury A335	(H, flute)
Bernstein	A Simple Song	G. Schirmer 47178	(M)
Bitgood	The greatest of these is love	Gray	(LM)
Blair	As the hart panteth	Gray	(H)
Boardman	Ancient Prayer	G. Schirmer	(M)
Bone and Fenton	The First Psalm	C. Fischer	(M)
Bowling	He shall be like a tree	R. D. Row	(HL)
Brahms	Four Scriptural Songs	G. Schirmer	(M)
Browning	The Beatitudes	C. Fischer	(HM)
Buxtehude	Lord, in Thee do I trust	Gray	(H)
————	My Jesus is my lasting joy	Gray	(H, 2 violins)
Cassler	Awake, awake, good people	Augsburg 11-722	(M, viola)
Charles	Incline Thine ear	G. Schirmer	(HL)
————	Psalm of Exaltation	G. Schirmer	(M)
Clokey	God is in everything	J. Fischer	(HL)
————	No lullaby need Mary sing	J. Fischer	(LH)
Cornelius	Six Christmas Songs	Boston	(LH)
Creston	Psalm 23	G. Schirmer	(HM)
Curran	Blessing	G. Schirmer	(H)
Davis	Trust in the Lord	Galaxy	(HM)
Dello Joio	A Christmas Carol	E. B. Marks 15209	(H)
————	The Holy Infant's Lullaby	Marks Music 15207	(M)
Diack	All in the April evening	Boosey & Hawkes	(M)

Diamond	The Shepherd Boy Sings	Southern Music	(M)
_____	Let nothing disturb thee	Associated	(M)
Dvořák	Biblical Songs (vols. 1 and 2)	N. Simrock-Associated	(LH)
Elmore and Read	Come, all ye who weary	J. Fischer	(M)
Franck	O Lord most holy	Boston	(LMH)
Freed	Psalm 8	Southern Music	(M)
Goode	Seven Sacred Solos	Abingdon APM-484	(M)
Gore	O sing unto the Lord a new song	J. Fischer	(M)
Greene	Seven Sacred Solos of the Early English School	Bosworth	(HL)
Hinchcliffe	Tranquillity	C. Fischer	(M)
Holst	Four Songs for Voice and Violin	J. & W. Chester No. 106	
_____	The Heart Worships	Stainer & Bell	(LM)
Hovhaness	Out of the depths	C. F. Peters 6045	(H)
Howells	Come sing and dance	Oxford 63.401	(H)
Humfrey	A Hymn to God the Father	Schott	(HL)
Humphreys	Put on the whole armor of God	Row	(HL)
Johnson	Ah, Jesus Lord, Thy love to me	Augsburg 11-724	(M)
_____	Lovely Child, Holy Child	Augsburg 11-727	(M)
_____	Sweet was the song the Virgin sang	Augsburg 11-0732	(H)
_____	When Jesus left His Father's throne	Augsburg 11-725	(M)
LeFleming	Five Psalms for Soprano and Choir	J. & W. Chester	(H)
	The Lord is my Shepherd (available only in *Five Psalms*)	J. & W. Chester	
Lehmann	No candle was there and no fire	Chappell	(HL)
Lekberg	I will lift up mine eyes	M.P.H.C.	(M)
_____	How long wilt Thou forget me, O Lord	M.P.H.C.	
Lovelace	Our Lady sat within her bower	J. Fischer 9479	(M)
_____	Star in the East	Galaxy	(L)
MacDermid	As the rain cometh down	Forster	(HL)
_____	Ninety-First Psalm	Forster	(HML)
MacGimsey	Think on these things	C. Fischer	(HM)
Malotte	The Beatitudes	G. Schirmer	(HL)
_____	The Twenty-Third Psalm	G. Schirmer	(HML)
Matthews	Emmaus	Oliver Ditson	(ML)

148

McAfee	Two Songs for Medium Voice	Abingdon APM-661	
Milford	Laus Deo	Novello	(H)
————	Love on my heart	Novello	(M)
Moe	The greatest of these is love	Augsburg 11-0702/3	(ML)
Niles	I wonder as I wander	G. Schirmer	(HL)
————	Our lovely Lady singing	C. Fischer	(M)
————	The Little Lyking	G. Schirmer 42872	(M)
————	Wayfaring Stranger	G. Schirmer 42667	(M)
Noble	Grieve not the Holy Spirit of God	Gray	(HL)
Nordoff	Lacrima Christi	Mercury S816	(M)
O'Connor-	Alleluia	Boosey & Hawkes	(HML)
Morris			
Pfautsch	Solos for the Church Year	Lawson-Gould	(HL)
Pinkham	Letters from St. Paul	E. C. Schirmer 142	(H)
————	Three songs from Ecclesiastes	E. C. Schirmer 128	(H)
————	Two Hymns	E. C. Schirmer 131	(H)
Purcell	Four Sacred Songs	International Music 1699	(H)
————	Three Divine Hymns	Boosey & Hawkes	(M)
Reger	The Virgin's Slumber Song	Associated	(LMH)
Roberton	All in the April evening	Curwen (G. Schirmer)	
Rogers, J.	Today, if ye will hear his voice	Schmidt	(HL)
Rogers, S.	New Testament Songs	Hope	(M)
McAfee,			
Burroughs			
Rorem	A Christmas Carol	Elkan Vogel 161-00056	(M)
————	Alleluia	Hargail Music Press H312	(H)
————	A Song of David (Psalm 120)	Associated 19469	(H)
Rowley	A Cycle of Three Mystical Songs	Boosey & Hawkes	(H)
Sanders	A Song of the Spirit	Galaxy	
Schreiber	St. Francis' Prayer	Mercury A381	(H)
Schroeder	I will lift up mine eyes	Gray	(H)
Schuetz	Five Sacred Songs	Concordia	(H)
————	Herzlich lieb hab' ich dich	Bomart	(Alto)
Scott	Come, ye blessed	G. Schirmer	(HL)
Sinzheimer	Blessed are those who fear the Lord	Concordia 97-4893	(M)
Sjolund	I beseech you to look	Word CS2444	(M)

149

Sowerby	Three Psalms
	  I. Hear my cry, O God
	  II. The Lord is my Shepherd
	  III. How long wilt Thou forget me
		Gray	(L)

_____	Three Psalms for Low Voice
	  I. O be joyful in the Lord
	  II. I will lift up mine eyes
	  III. Whoso dwelleth
		Gray	(L)

Stebbins	Come now, and let us reason together	Presser	(HM)
Thiman	Jesus, the very thought of Thee	Novello	(M)
_____	The God of love my Shepherd is	Novello	(HL)
_____	The Wilderness	Novello	(M)
_____	Thou wilt keep him in perfect peace	Gray	(M)
Van Dyke	In the beauty of holiness	Boosey & Hawkes	(HL)
Vaughan Williams	Five Mystical Songs	Stainer & Bell	(L)

_____	Seven Songs from Pilgrim's
	  Progress
	  II. The Song of the Pilgrim
	  VI. Bird's Song
	  VII. Woodcutter's Song
		Oxford	(M)

_____	The Song of the Leaves of Life	Oxford 62.206	(M)
Warlock	The First Mercy	Boosey & Hawkes H15844	(M)
Warner	Song of the Seven Lambs	Augsburg	(M)
Whikehart	O sing unto the Lord	Gray	(H)
Williams	Jesus, the very thought	J. Fischer 9271/2	(HL)
Yon	Christ Triumphant	J. Fischer	(H)
_____	Our Paschal Joy	J. Fischer	(LH)

(Many unison anthems make effective solos.)

See also listings in the following:

Espina, Noni. *Vocal Solos for Protestant Services*, 2nd ed. revised and enlarged. Published privately, Vita d'Arte, 1816 Cedar Avenue, Bronx, New York 10453, 1974.

Koopman, John. *Selected Sacred Solos in Modern Idiom*. Minneapolis: Augsburg Publishing House, 1965.

Siebel, Katherine. *Sacred Solos*. New York: The H. W. Gray Co., 1966.

Wedding Solos

Bach	God my Shepherd	Gray
———	My heart ever faithful	G. Schirmer
———	Like a shepherd, God doth guide us	Galaxy
———	Jesu, joy of man's desiring (use SATB, 2nd stanza)	E. C. Schirmer
Barnby	O Perfect Love	All hymnals
Baumgartner	Love is of God	Concordia 97-9327
Bender	Wedding Song	Concordia 97-4887
Bortniansky	Lord, grant Thy servants (SATB)	E. C. Schirmer
Bunjes, ed.	Wedding Blessings (solo collection)	Concordia SC19
Cassler	Three Wedding Solos	Augsburg 11-9498/9
Clokey	O Perfect Love (from *Wedding Suite*)	J. Fischer
Davies	God be in my head (SATB)	Novello
Distler	Three Sacred Concertos	Concordia 97-4925
Dvořák	God is my Shepherd (from *Biblical Songs*)	N. Simrock-Associated
Fetler	O Father, all creating	Concordia 97-9325
Franck	O Lord Most Holy	Boston
Fryxell	The Candelighting Hymn	Augustana Press 62-104
Jacob	Brother James' Air	Oxford
Lovelace	A Wedding Benediction	G. Schirmer
———	Jesus, stand beside them	Abingdon APM-158, APM-159
———	My beloved	Boston Music
———	Our Father by whose name	Abingdon APM-155, APM-156
———	O God of love	Augsburg 11-0734
———	O Savior most bounteous	Abingdon APM-153, APM-154
———	O ye who taste that love is sweet	Abingdon APM-157
Lovelace, ed.	Wedding Music for the Church Organist and Soloist	Abingdon APM-164
Lutkin	The Lord bless you and keep you	Summy-Birchard
Moe	The greatest of these is love	Augsburg 11-702
Nystedt	O Perfect Love	Augsburg 11-0735
Pelz	A Wedding Blessing	Augsburg 11-0736/7

151

Proulx	Beloved, let us love	Augsburg 11-0715
————	Nuptial Blessing	Augsburg 11-0731
Rider	Establish a House	Concordia 97-5133
Rowley	Here at Thine altar (SATB)	Novello
Sateren	In His care	Augsburg 11-0733
Sinzheimer	Blessed are those who fear the Lord	Concordia 97-4893
Sowerby	O Perfect Love	Gray
Thiman	The God of love my Shepherd is	Novello
Wetzler	Bless us, God of loving	Augsburg 11-0721
Wetzler, ed.	Five Wedding Songs (Dale Wood, Robt. Elmore, R. Wetzler, Leland Sateren, Jeffrey Rickard)	AMSI
Willan	O Perfect Love	Gray
————	Three Songs of Devotion	F. Harris Music Co.
Wood, ed.	Five Wedding Songs	Concordia

X

The Congregation

THE ARBITRARY DIVISION OF THE CHURCH INTO CLERGY AND LAITY HAS THE unfortunate effect of giving the congregation the mistaken idea that their responsibility to the church extends only to paying the bills and attending the Sunday morning service when convenient. The preacher is paid to pray for them, to preach at them, and to worry about worship. Too many church members have been allowed to forget one of the basic principles of the Reformation—the priesthood of all believers, with its insistence on the responsibility of each individual in spiritual matters. Every person must make his own response to the call of God, and no one else can take his place. Perhaps the unfortunate failure of congregations to treat worship as concerned with life and to take their part seriously accounts for the sad state of worship in many churches.

In the enactment of a service of worship the congregation is not the audience which pays to see a drama performed; rather, as Kierkegaarde suggests, God is the audience and we are the actors. Thus each person in the congregation has a personal part to play in the act of divine worship which no one else can assume. This role can be played to the full with heart, mind, and soul, or it can be played slovenly, without enthusiasm and without vital participation. The person who comes late, sits on the fringes, sings only occasionally, listens to the anthems halfheartedly or antagonistically, and sleeps during the sermon will contribute little and receive even less.

The primary congregational responsibility is hymn singing. Earl E. Harper pointed out that hymn singing is not only a responsibility but also a privilege.[1] "Sing unto the Lord a new song," "Let all the people praise thee," "Praise ye the Lord"—these are unqualified imperatives. A Christian congregation must sing because of what God has done for them in

---

[1] *Church Music and Worship*, p. 88.

Christ. It is their joyful duty, and if they fail in it they come under the judgment of Isaac Watts who wrote, "Let those refuse to sing who never knew our God." One often suspects that poor singing in many churches is due to the fact that the flesh is unwilling (to sing) because the spirit is weak. There can be no doubt as to our responsibility to praise God.

Hymn singing is also a privilege. In the early Christian church Paul encouraged singing as a means of praising God and of teaching and admonishing one another. But the Jewish schedule of services at various hours (see Acts 2:15; 10:9; and 3:1), which developed into more complicated offices with specified psalms and hymns, made it difficult for a workingman to drop his trade and come at all the appointed times. More and more the clergy took over the singing of hymns. In the fourth century the Council of Laodicea decreed: "Beside the psalm singers appointed thereto who mount the ambo and sing out of the book, no others shall sing in church." Carols of the Middle Ages grew up outside the church because the people wanted to sing and yet could not participate in the hymns of the liturgy. Indeed the Reformation gained much of its impetus and its strength from the desire to give back not only the Bible but also the hymns to the people. Singing hymns is a privilege which too many Protestants take all too lightly and thoughtlessly.

Many reasons for the poor state of congregational song in most churches arise from misconceptions as to the purpose and role of hymn singing. Improvement cannot be expected until these are frankly faced and discarded. Some ministers treat the sermon hymn as a "seventh inning stretch with sound effects" [2]—time to stand and open the windows for some fresh air. Others use hymns as time fillers. A sensitive director cringes when someone says, "Let's sing a few hymns after the fellowship dinner while the tables are being cleared." Hymns are often used indiscriminately as a part of fellowship or fun singing. Fun singing has its place, but interspersing hymns invites a flippant and thoughtless approach to hymn singing in worship. Some churches use hymns as a "come on," and "singspirations" and Sunday evening "old time gospel hymn sings" are advertised more as crowd getters than for what the

[2] Davison, *Church Music*, p. 74.

154

hymns have to say. Such events often degenerate into a request session; members of the congregation shout out favorite numbers from the floor and sing only one stanza of each song.

Hymns under the title of "the good old hymns" are often used as an escape from reality. It is easy to settle comfortably into the belief that "the old time religion is good enough for me" and to forget that God has not made his final revelation to any one person or any one generation. His Holy Spirit still moves among us to reveal new truth to those who will hear. While the psalms are a great body of hymn literature, imagine how poor would be our worship if the early church had stuck only to the good old hymns. There would be no song of Mary (Magnificat) and no song of Simeon (Nunc Dimittis). If nothing but the "good old hymns" had been allowed during the time of Martin Luther, perhaps there would have been no Reformation and certainly not "A mighty fortress is our God." With only the good old hymns in the Wesleyan revival there would have been none of Charles Wesley's 6,500 hymns. Who would wish to be without Harry Emerson Fosdick's great hymn of the present century, "God of grace and God of Glory"? To stick to nothing but the good old hymns—meaning the songs one learned as a child—is to stifle the Holy Spirit.

Hymns have also been used for psychological manipulation and for a type of hypnotism. Many of the camp-meeting songs with their meager ideas and constant repetition of a few phrases are hypnotic when led by an overly enthusiastic song leader and sung by a large gathering in a hot, crowded room. One is led to question the lasting value of such hymn singing, for the paucity of ideas and shallowness of such songs is poor fare for Christian growth. No doubt such songs were useful in the past when hymnals were sparse or nonexistent, most people were illiterate, few could read music, and churches were scarce; but it is hard to see how clinging to this type of song can "serve the present age." While Charles Wesley believed in the emotional and experiential value of hymn singing he insisted that the Christian faith be clearly evident in a hymn. The weak ideas and poor poetry of most so-called "gospel hymns" would surely bring a storm of protest from both John and Charles Wesley.

Erik Routley summed up the problem:

155

A hymn, then, is not really a good hymn until it has been well written, well chosen, and well sung. . . .

. . . the shame of hymn-singing is not ultimately in the hymn but in the singer.

In a word, where hymn-singing is a self-indulgence, it is thereby not a sacrifice; and where hymn-singing is community singing by a closed company, it is not a means of evangelism. I do not say that the singing of hymns for enjoyment is bad; I am saying only that if you are singing hymns for fun you need not expect to be thought advanced in Christian virtue for doing so.[3]

Effective congregational response depends in large measure upon establishing correct attitudes and goals in the mind of the congregation so they will know why they sing the faith that is within them. The primary reason for hymn singing is to offer praise and prayer to God. As the psalmist of old, we express our deepest desires and longings. We lift our hearts in thanksgiving; we confess our sins; we call upon God. At the same time we express our faith and witness to others—not only by what we sing but the way we sing. John Wesley was so profoundly impressed by the singing of the Moravians on the ship bound for America that he learned German in order to translate their hymns into English, thus enriching our hymnal. Hymns are also media for teaching truth. Most people establish more of their beliefs on hymns than on sermons, since words learned in rhyme in conjunction with a melody are easily remembered. Therefore what a congregation sings is of far-reaching consequence. Unfortunately many a congregation sings a theology entirely different from that of its denomination as preached by the minister, thereby creating confusion of thought and belief. Hymns can also be used to admonish one another—for example, "Rise up, O men of God," "O brother man, fold to thy heart thy brother," and "Awake, awake to love and work." Others may be prophetic in tone, expressing our deepest longings and finest dreams, such as "In Christ there is no East or West" or "These things shall be."

Another value in hymn singing lies in the life-sustaining quality of fine hymns through recall of meaningful phrases, stanzas, or even entire hymns. A final value lies in the ecumenical nature of hymns. Churches which can never agree on doctrine or liturgy join—whether knowingly or not—in singing hymns from all faiths. All major hymnals contain

[3] *Hymns and Human Life* (New York: Philosophical Library, 1952), pp. 299 ff.

hymns by Catholics, Unitarians, Universalists, Jews, Presbyterians, Quakers, Baptists, Episcopalians, Congregationalists, Methodists, and other denominational groups. Though we may disagree on many theological points, when we sing we dwell in unity. Truly the ecumenical spirit begins in hymn singing.

John Wesley was so concerned about vital and meaningful hymn singing that he listed several practical rules which help to improve the singing in any church if followed:

1. Learn these tunes before you learn any others; afterwards learn as many as you please.

2. Sing them exactly as they are printed here, without altering or mending them; otherwise, unlearn it as soon as you can.

3. Sing all. See that you join with the congregation as frequently as you can. Let not a slight degree of weakness or weariness hinder you. If it is a cross to you, take it up and you will find it a blessing.

4. Sing lustily and with good courage. Beware of singing as if you are half dead or half asleep; but lift up your voice with strength. Be no more afraid of your voice now, nor more ashamed of its being heard, than when you sing the songs of Satan.

5. Sing modestly. Do not bawl, so as to be heard above and distinct from the rest of the congregation—that you may not destroy the harmony—but strive to unite your voices together so as to make one clear melodious sound.

6. Sing in time. Whatever time is sung be sure to keep with it. Do not run before nor stay behind it; but attend close to the leading voices, and move therewith as exactly as you can; and take care not to sing too slow. This drawling way naturally steals on us all who are lazy; and it is high time to drive it out from among us, and sing all our tunes just as quick as we did at first.

7. Above all, sing spiritually. Have an eye to God in every word you sing. Aim at pleasing Him more than yourself, or any other creature. In order to do this, attend strictly to the sense of what you sing, and see that your heart is not carried away with the sound, but offered to God continually; so shall your singing be such as the Lord will approve here, and reward you when He cometh in the clouds of heaven.

The congregation has other responsibilities in the service beyond hymn singing, one of the most ancient being the conversation between minister and people:

157

MINISTER: The Lord be with you.
PEOPLE: And with thy spirit.
or:
MINISTER: Lift up your hearts!
PEOPLE: We lift them up unto the Lord.
or:
MINISTER: O Lord, open Thou our lips.
PEOPLE: And our mouth shall show forth Thy praise.
MINISTER: Praise ye the Lord.
PEOPLE: The Lord's name be praised.

These examples are typical of the versicle and response, and with some practice the congregation can learn simple musical settings, such as the "Choral Service" (festal and ferial) by Thomas Tallis. Such responsive types, related to the psalms and their parallelism, invite a responsive or antiphonal use. Whether the responses are said or sung, the congregation should join unanimously and wholeheartedly in their answers.

The Gloria Patri was originally a teaching hymn to combat the Arian heresy, but today is used as a response after the psalm to bring it into Christian focus. Doxologies—ascriptions of praise—as well as spoken or sung amens belong to the congregation. Other responses, before or after prayer or scripture, can be taught to a congregation. Joseph W. Clokey suggests that in the small church where a choir is not practical, the congregation can handle the entire musical parts of the service with a few congregational practices.[4] This will be discussed more fully later in this chapter. All responses which are taught to a congregation should be used, not with the idea of giving the people something to do, but with careful thought as to purpose, suitability, value, and meaning in the service.

The congregation also has a unique share in the anthem, although this share is often misunderstood. The choir does not present an anthem as an opportunity for display; they do not sing just for the fun of it; they do not sing to please the congregation. The anthem is first and foremost an offering to God—a gift of creative inspiration interpreted through vocal gifts, God-given to man. In a sense the choir makes an offering on

[4] Op. cit., pp. 50 ff.

158

behalf of the congregation in the anthem, and yet the congregation has the right to expect the anthem to speak to their needs and to express their praise. Therefore they should learn to listen attentively to the anthem. The text should be printed in the bulletin so the words which inspired the musical creation may be clear to the listener. New music often meets with resistance on the part of untrained listeners, but if a new anthem is repeated several times at reasonably close intervals the congregation's resistance will disappear as they become more familiar with its musical language. There are some anthems in which the congregation can share, thus adding to their understanding and to their sharing in the offering of praise. Many English composers have incorporated hymn tunes into anthems—for example, R. Vaughan Williams' "All people that on earth do dwell," Charles Wood's "O be joyful in the Lord," R. Vaughan Williams' "O how amiable are Thy dwellings." Lloyd Pfautsch's "The new is old" has a congregational response which may be printed in the bulletin, and Malcolm Williamson's "I will lift up mine eyes" has a simple refrain easily teachable to the congregation.

It is all well and good to say that the congregation ought to sing and appreciate good hymns and anthems, but it is a problem to find ways and means of training and helping a congregation to assume its rightful place in congregational praise. Joseph N. Ashton observed: "The congregation is the only musical group of serious purpose regularly attempting performance without rehearsing." [5] We would never expect a choir to sing without having studied and rehearsed an anthem—or the hymns —adequately, but we are inclined to call a congregation stupid or perverse when they rebel at singing a new hymn which they have never seen before, have heard only once as the organist gave out the tune, and even that lost in complex harmony and organ tone. The problem boils down to several factors:

1. It is nearly impossible for the congregation to do two things at once—read words and listen for the tune.

2. Hymn singing depends upon interest, which must be aroused by some means.

3. New hymns must be related to familiar hymns, scripture, or ideas —moving from the known to the unknown. Obviously what is required is

[5] *Music in Worship*, p. 94.

159

education and a pleasant learning experience, and the worship service is hardly the place for informal teaching.

When can a congregational practice be arranged, in an informal atmosphere which makes the learning experience less painful and even enjoyable? No two churches will decide on the same time and place, but the following have been found acceptable:

1. Fellowship or family night suppers. (Instead of a speaker, have a congregational choir practice.)
2. Prayer meeting. (Before or after.)
3. Sunday evening service. (Before or in place of the sermon.)
4. Ten or fifteen minutes prior to a service of worship. (Let the hymn practice take the place of the prelude. It may be better preparation for worship.)
5. At the close of a service.
6. Youth meetings.
7. Women's meetings.
8. Men's club.
9. Meeting of the church governing body.

Many opportunities are wasted in every church. Time spent singing ridiculous songs could better be spent teaching a congregation how to learn a new hymn or to sing an old one with new appreciation. One choir director was surprised but pleased when the program chairman of the Men's Club asked him to teach a new hymn each month to replace the service-club style of singing which always included "America" or "When Irish Eyes Are Smiling." Surely there are abundant opportunities if they are sought and utilized.

Once the group is gathered, the session should begin with some familiar hymn which the congregation does not sing well or sings carelessly and with little thought. Try "Faith of our fathers!" and note how the singers plow through the exclamation mark after the word "fathers!" and then breathe after "living still." Obviously the breath should come after "fathers!" and there should be no more pause until after the word "sword." Or begin with "Nearer, my God, to Thee" and stop the congregation after the first stanza to discover if they recognize the theme of the hymn. (Very few will know that it is not a funeral hymn but is actually about Jacob's dream.) "Break Thou the bread of life" can be introduced as a hymn about the Scriptures and not Com-

160

munion. "How firm a foundation" can be studied to discover that stanzas two to five are individual promises of God, each in quotation marks. "Praise God from whom all blessings flow" can be sung first in the familiar but stodgy meter of all quarter notes, and then taught in the original pattern of the Genevan Psalter, which is more rhythmically interesting and takes less time to sing.

After arousing the group to sing with their minds as well as their voices the congregation should be put through the paces of some vocal exercises such as are used with the choir. Emphasize sitting erect, correct and deep breathing, purity of vowel production, and clarity of consonants.

While interest is high and a vigorous physical response achieved, introduce a hymn which is new to the group. This can be done best by learning the tune first, since it is impossible to do two new things at once, and learning the tune is harder than reading the words. Break down the melody into short phrases and learn them in a planned and logical order on some easy sound such as "lah" or "loo." If a piano is used, play only the melody; however, a group will respond better to the vocal patterning of the leader—who should be able to sing.

For example, "All creatures of our God and King" is composed of only three patterns—a rising figure starting on the bottom line, a falling figure starting from the top space, and the "Alleluia" pattern of four notes starting either in the medium range or on the top space. Each pattern is always repeated except for the final "Alleluia" which is expanded rhythmically. Many hymns use an AABA pattern—that is, the first, second, and fourth lines are approximately the same melodic pattern with the variation falling in the third line. Examples are "Joyful, joyful, we adore Thee" (to the tune "Hymn to Joy") and "Immortal, invisible" (to the tune "Joanna"). "Praise to the Lord, the Almighty" (tune, "Lobe den Herrn") begins with a trumpetlike call based on the major triad and is followed by a pattern which can best be described as going down in the valley and up over the hill. The remainder of the hymn follows these two basic patterns.

Any hymn tune will reveal itself to be cast in tiny sections which can be learned in a variety of ways—taking each section in turn, mixing them around, combining like passages, contrasting sections—starting up or down, or even working from the end by learning the last phrase first. Descriptions and procedures should be as picturesque as possible so

161

the pattern is firmly fixed in the minds and ears of the singers. As the patterns are learned, musical perception and appreciation are improved, making the congregation better listeners as well as singers.

Once the melody is learned, it becomes a road which easily carries the traffic of the words. The music learning may be most informal, but when the words are introduced the approach should be that of serious thought as to the meaning and content of the text. Four approaches are effective —the biographical, the historical, the literary, and the spiritual. The biographical should be used only if information concerning the author makes the text more meaningful. Definitely to be avoided are the romantic fantasies and deathbed stories found in many books of "favorite hymn stories." Knowing something about John Greenleaf Whittier and Quakerism makes his hymns live in a unique way. The historical setting often makes a hymn come to life when the situation out of which it came is known. This is true of "A mighty fortress is our God" and the Reformation. Sometimes there is a literary pattern which holds a hymn together. For example, "Come, Thou, almighty King" is a Trinitarian pattern—the first stanza addressed to God, the second to Christ, and the third to the Holy Spirit, with the last stanza a summary. In "Ye servants of God" Charles Wesley used the ideas which close one stanza as the starting point for the next.[6]

Finally, the spiritual approach is always necessary, for every hymn has a spiritual basis which is the reason for writing the hymn and for singing it. Every hymn is a poetic statement of a personal spiritual encounter, universal in its truth and application, and suitable for use as a corporate expression of worship in singing. All devices for learning must be focused toward the spiritual end.

At the rehearsal the hymnal indexes—topical, authors, composers, scriptural, and metrical—should be explored and explained. It is not often realized that in most instances the music to which a hymn is sung was not written specifically for the poem it accompanies. Therefore, hymn editors face the privilege and problem of choosing a melody already written whose meter coincides with that of the poem, or of asking a composer to produce a melody for the text. Editors often do not agree on a given tune, and different hymnals may use different tunes for the same

[6] Further information may be found in the article "Hymn Patterns" by Carl F. Price in *Religion in Life* (Summer, 1947), pp. 431-42.

set of words. For example, most hymnals now include two or three different tunes ("Coronation," "Miles' Lane," and "Diadem") for the text "All hail the power of Jesus' Name." In other instances the hymnal may indicate by footnote an alternative tune to which a hymn may be sung if the printed tune is not particularly good or if the alternative tune is more familiar or was used in a previous edition.

The three most commonly used metrical patterns are C.M., S.M., and L.M. C.M. stands for Common Meter and merely means that in the four lines of poetry which make up each stanza the first line has eight syllables, the second six, the third eight, and the last six; or 8.6.8.6. S.M. is Short Meter and stands for 6.6.8.6. L.M. is Long Meter and is 8.8.8.8. A "D." following any of these, such as C.M.D., means that the pattern is doubled, or repeated—8.6.8.6.8.6.8.6. Beyond these basic patterns most commonly used, there are possible any number of metrical patterns, depending entirely on the wishes and ingenuity of the poet. There may be a 4.4.7.4.4.7.4.4.4.4.7., 7.6.7.6.D., 10.10.10.10., or 14.14.4.7.8. and dozens more. Some may have a "refrain" and some may be so unusual that they are lumped together under the catchall title "Irregular." Once the metrical index and the matter of matching tune and text is understood by the congregation there will be more willingness to sing substitute or alternative tunes.

During a single congregational practice many responses and several new hymns can be learned and much done to make a congregation more sensitive to the values of hymn singing and their responsibility in a service of worship.[7]

Another method of introducing hymns is the "hymn of the month" plan which many churches have used successfully. The first step is the organization of a committee including the minister, the director, the organist, some choir members, and musicians from the congregation; their first duty is to make a list of all hymns in present use. Next they should study the hymnal carefully and choose a group of hymns which should be learned or will be needed during the year, including a particularly large group of hymns suitable for praise and the opening of worship. If the hymns are to be used throughout the entire church school as well the texts should be studied for suitability for various age groups from the

[7] Further suggestions for conducting a congregational practice can be found in Ch. 9 of *Music and Worship* by Davies and Grace.

primary or junior age through adults. From this list should be chosen those most immediately needed. These hymns then should be studied carefully, gathering material from books on hymnody. Most denominations have handbooks for their hymnals which are indispensable to anyone teaching hymns. (A large selection of books on hymnody is listed in the bibliography.) Interesting information helpful in teaching the hymns should be mimeographed—material about the hymn, its author, its historical setting, music patterns, and textual patterns.

This material should then be placed in the hands of every person in the church who has anything whatsoever to do with the leadership of music or worship—choir directors, organists, pianists, song leaders in all departments of the church-school, church-school superintendent, devotional chairmen of the women's and men's groups, and all others who may have opportunity to introduce the hymn. These leaders should be encouraged to use the hymn at all possible meetings during the month— prayer meetings, church school, youth groups—everywhere.

On the first Sunday of the month the text should be printed in the bulletin or on a separate sheet of paper and the congregation urged to take it home to use in family devotions, perhaps memorizing one stanza each week. At this time the minister should make some statement concerning the hymn, indicating anything of interest which will encourage the acceptance of the hymn. The organist should also play the hymn tune at some point during the service.

On the second Sunday the hymn should be sung by the choir at an appropriate time—as an anthem, a call to worship, or a response, depending on the type of hymn. On the third Sunday it should be used in the service with the choir singing the first stanza in unison and the congregation joining on the remaining stanzas. On the fourth Sunday when the hymn is included again it will be sung with more assurance. From time to time during the following months the hymn should be repeated so it will become familiar.

Variety can be secured by using different procedures from month to month—using a soloist instead of the choir, using different types of hymns—but the basic idea is to continue introducing one new hymn each month and to make a definite plan for presentation and repetition.

In introducing hymns, everyone in a position of leadership must assume personal responsibility, beginning with the minister and including the director, the organist, the church-school leaders, the members of all the choirs, the church-school superintendent, and the music committee. If each person does his part enthusiastically, systematically, and carefully hymn singing can be improved in any church.

Once a congregation has become aware of its role in hymn singing a church may profitably use hymn services to further this interest. The three hymn services at the conclusion of this chapter have been used successfully and may serve as guides in planning other services on the following subjects:

Hymns based on Ps. 23
Hymn tunes by great composers
God in nature
The history of the church in hymns
Hymns of the centuries
The good old hymns (hymns of the early church)
Ecumenical hymns
Hymns by women
Hymns by Charles Wesley, or Isaac Watts, or any other single author
Life of Christ in hymns
Men of letters of the hymnal
Different names for God in the hymnal
American hymns
Hymns of the twentieth century

The Hymn Society of America suggests hymn festivals marking the anniversary of the birth or death of famous hymn writers each year. Suggested orders of worship are available at nominal cost. Recent hymn writers so honored have been Isaac Watts, Charles Wesley, John Green-leaf Whittier, Paul Gerhardt, and Horatius Bonar among many others. There is no limit to the variety of theme or treatment possible in hymn festivals, and they may be presented by a small group, an entire church, or a community.[8]

While a festival of hymns is an effective way to present hymns to a large gathering, the church musician should not overlook the opportunities of presenting hymns informally to small groups in the church. The women's guild will probably welcome a talk by the director for

[8] For further suggestions see *The Hymn Festival Movement in America*, by Reginald L. McAll, Paper No. XVI of the Hymn Society of America, 1951.

one of their programs during the year, thus presenting him an excellent chance to discuss the purposes of church music and the role of the congregation. There are opportunities in the church-school program for the director to talk to various departments on church music and to teach hymns. "How to introduce hymns" or "Choosing hymns suitable for children" could well be subjects for a talk before a meeting of the church-school teachers. Too often the various groups of the church hesitate to ask the busy director of music to help, and the director takes a hands-off policy for fear he will be accused of meddling. All should join hands in the common enterprise of making music in the church a ministry to every individual.

Perhaps the time is ripe for another "reformation." Choirs have again usurped the rights of the congregation, or the people have turned over their duties of singing to the choir by default. Director and organist either endure the congregation or treat them as musical ignoramuses whose low-brow tastes interfere with the musical program. It is time for the choir to realize that it is a part of the congregation, for the director to expend his energies in training and guiding the people, and for the congregation to assume its rightful role in music and worship.

Contemporary Hymnody
(A Selected Bibliography)

Alive and Singing. Richard Avery and Donald Marsh. Proclamation Productions, Port Jervis, New York.

Alleluia! Songbook for Inner City Parishes. Cooperative Recreation Service, Delaware, Ohio.

Anatomy of Pop. Various contributors. BBC Publications, London, England W1A 1AA, 1972.

A New Song. Concordia Publishing House, 1967.

A Time for Singing. Geneva Press, Philadelphia, Pennsylvania, 1970.

A Time to Sing. Hope Publishing Co., Carol Stream, Illinois, 60187, 1967.

Break Not the Circle. Fred Kaan and Doreen Potter. Agapé, Carol Stream, Illinois, 60187, 1975.

Contemporary Ecumenical Folk Songs. F. E. L. Publications, 1543 West Olympic Boulevard, Los Angeles, California 90015.

The Contemporary Hymn Book. David Yantis Publications.

Contemporary Worship: Hymns. Augsburg Publishing House, 1969.

Dunblane Praises No. 1 and No. 2. Scottish Churches' House, Dunblane, Perthshire, Scotland.

East Asia Christian Council Hymnal. Machi, Shibuya. Avaco, 22 Miderigaoka, Ku, Tokyo, Japan, 1964.

Ecumenical Praise. Austin C. Lovelace, Erik Routley, Alec Wyton, Carlton R. Young, editors. Agapé, Carol Stream, Illinois, 60187, 1976.

Eternal Light. Hymn tunes by Erik Routley. Carl Fischer, 1971.

Faith Folk and Clarity. Peter Smith, editor. Galliard/Galaxy, 1967, 1969.

Faith Folk and Festivity. Peter Smith, editor. Galliard/Galaxy, 1969.

Faith Folk and Nativity. Peter Smith, editor. Galliard/Galaxy, 1968.

The Genesis Songbook. Carlton R. Young, editor. Agapé, Carol Stream, Illinois, 60187, 1973.

Heavy Hymns. Ed Summerlin and Roger Ortmeyer. Agapé, Carol Stream, Illinois, 60187, 1972.

Hymnal for Young Christians. F. E. L. Publications, 1543 Olympic Boulevard, Los Angeles, California 90015. 1966, 1967, 1968.

Hymns for Now (Resources for Youth Ministry). The Lutheran Church, Missouri Synod, 210 North Broadway, St. Louis, Missouri 63102, 1969.

Hymns Hot and Carols Cool. Richard Avery and Donald Marsh. Proclamation Productions, Port Jervis, New York. 1967.

Jazz in the Church. Jim Minchin. Presbyterian Bookroom, 156 Collins Street, Melbourne 3000, Australia, 1964.

The Mission Singers Songbook. Abingdon Press, Nashville, Tennessee, 1971.

My Soapbox. Don Wyrtzen, compiler, Singspiration.

New Church Praise. St. Andrew's Press, Edinburgh, Scotland.

New Life. Galliard/Galaxy, 1972.

New Orbit. Galliard/Galaxy, 1972.

New Songs. Congregational Church, Redhill, England, 1962.

New Songs for the Church, Books 1 and 2. Barrett-Ayres and Erik Routley. Galliard/Galaxy, 1969.

New Songs of Asian Cities. East Asia Christian Conference. Tainan Theological College, 115 East Gate Road, Tainan, Taiwan.

Now. Hope Publishing Co., Carol Stream, Illinois, 60187, 1969.

Pilgrim Praise. Fred Kaan. Galliard/Galaxy, 1972.

Reaching Out in Love. Mary Collins. 197 Melrose Street, Rochester, New York.

Rock Music. William J. Schafer. Augsburg Publishing House, 1972.

Sing! Ronald Beasley and Douglas Galbraith. Church of Scotland Offices, 121 George Street, Edinburgh 2, Scotland.

Sing a New Song. St. Catherine's Home, Andheri, Bombay 400058, India.
Sing a New Song to the Lord. Kevin Mayhew, editor. Mayhew-McCrimmin (Galaxy Music Corp.).
Sing! Hymnal for Youth and Adults. R. Harold Terry, editor. Fortress Press, Philadelphia, Pennsylvania, 1970.
Sing True. Colin Hodgetts. Religious Education Press, Headington Hill Hall, Oxford, England, 1969.
Sixteen Hymns and Processionals. Malcolm Williamson. Agapé, Carol Stream, Illinois 60187, 1975.
Songbook for Saints and Sinners. Carlton R. Young, editor. Agapé, Carol Stream, Illinois, 60187, 1971.
Songs for Celebration. Kent Schneider, editor. Center for Contemporary Celebration, Room 1600, 116 South Michigan Avenue, Chicago, Illinois, 1969.
Songs for the Seventies. Galliard/Galaxy, 1972.
Songs for Today. John Ylvisaker, editor. Youth Department, American Lutheran Church, 422 South Fifth Street, Minneapolis, Minnesota, 1964.
Songs for Worship. Joint Board of Christian Education of Australia and New Zealand, 147 Collins Street, Melbourne 3000, Australia, 1968.
Songs from Notting Hill. Geoffrey Ainger and Ian Calvert. Notting Hill Methodist Church, Lancaster Road, West 11, London, England.
Songs from the Square. Brian Frost. 27 Slipsatch Road, Reigate, Surrey, England.
Songs of Faith. Joint Board of Christian Education of Australia and New Zealand, 144 Collins Street, Melbourne 3000, Australia, 1968.
Songs of Sydney Carter in the Present Tense (Books 1, 2, and 3). Sydney Carter. Galliard/Galaxy, 1969.
Songs of the Spiritual Movement. Ecumenical Institute, Chicago, Illinois, 1967.
Twelve Folksongs and Spirituals. David N. Johnson, editor. Augsburg Publishing House, 1968.
20th Century Hymns. Church Light Music Group. Josef Weinberger, 10-16 Rathbone Street, London, England (or G. Schirmer).
Workers Quarterly . . . Hymns for Now. Walther League. 875 North Dearborn Street, Chicago, Illinois 60610, 1967.
Worship for Today, An Ecumenical Service. Daniel Moe. Carl Fischer, 1968.
Young Peoples Folk Hymnal. World Library of Sacred Music, Cincinnati, Ohio.

XI

Music in Christian Education

Religious education is the process in which the Church seeks to confront each person with the will of God as seen in Jesus Christ and interpreted in the Bible and Christian history; to set the problems of life in the context of what this means; to invite each one to accept Jesus Christ as heart and head of life and to identify himself with the Church which bears His name.[1]

WORSHIP IS DESCRIBED IN THE FIRST CHAPTER AS THE TOTAL RESPONSE OF man to the call of God in the God-man confrontation. Therefore Christian education is primarily concerned with worship and in its teaching must urge: "Let this mind be in you, which was also in Christ Jesus." (Phil. 2:5 K.J.V.) In guiding persons to confront God and his will for their lives,

a Christian education program furnishes the atmosphere, experiences, and training that should lead to the acceptance of Christ as the Lord of life and should foster continual Christian growth. A well-administered program of Christian music should also do this, and if it does, it is, to a high degree, Christian education.[2]

Christian education is primarily concerned with worship in its most comprehensive sense of helping the individual to hear God's call and to respond in complete love and obedience.

The importance of music to Christian education is highlighted in two words—expression and impression. In worship, music is an auxiliary, fortifying, and sublimating kind of communication, often more expressive than speech in giving form and substance to the feelings. At the same time Paul recognized the impressive value of hymns and spiritual songs to

[1] Harold A. Bosley, a statement prepared for the Commission on Education, First Methodist Church, Evanston, Illinois, May, 1959.
[2] From *The Use of Music in Christian Education*, by Vivian S. Morsch. Copyright 1956, by W. L. Jenkins. The Westminster Press.

169

teach and to admonish. Music which is well chosen, with both expressive and impressive values in mind, can play an important role in the development of Christian personality.

Yet the use of music in the church-school program is marked by a serious lack of understanding, agreement, and co-operation between Christian educators and musicians, existing from the highest echelons of professional leadership to the song leader and the class teacher.

The training of a musician who specializes in church music is so crowded with courses in the techniques of music that little time is left to consider the principles of educational psychology, much less the relation of music to the teaching program of the church, thereby causing many directors to think of their jobs as teaching music instead of persons. Anthems are often chosen for their musical stimulus with little or no thought as to the theological, poetic, or educational value of the text. In the practical field the music director is apt to think the program of the church revolves around his choirs and finds it difficult to understand why the church school is disturbed when the children are dragged from their classes to attend a choir rehearsal or to sing for a special service.

On the other hand many Christian educators tend to become so involved in the maze of educational methodology that they overlook the fact that music is more than a tool for teaching and that music used for worship may have a different viewpoint, purpose, and value than that used for education. The educator may be so concerned about the textual content that he fails to see that there is a theological basis for beauty in music. This blindness often leads to delegating music solely to the role of teaching.

The picture is further complicated by the fact that the choir director or organist is usually occupied with preparations for the service of worship on Sunday morning and is either unable to help with the church school or is not inclined to do so because of inadequate knowledge and training. So the teaching of hymns and music is usually left in the hands of the individual teachers. Unfortunately, the volunteer teachers in most churches have had only minimum training in the field of Christian education and none at all in music. As a result songs are chosen by individual caprice on the basis of favoritism and familiarity instead of excellence and suitability.

In attempting to integrate music more thoroughly into the curriculum,

170

both church and public schools have increasingly adopted the policy of asking the classroom teacher to handle every subject, including music, instead of calling in a specialized person for a specified period of music training. While the theory may be good, in practice most teachers are inadequately trained to make music attractive to children and to give thorough and proper guidance in correct singing habits and competent handling of musical materials and symbols.

A practical solution to the problem is to find, train, and use choir members—adult or high school—or other persons with musical training as auxiliary teachers in each class or department, working closely with the other personnel in teaching and using music in the classrooms. A light, high woman's voice is preferable for vocal patterning of songs for young children, but men can help with the older classes, particularly with boys. These helpers should have a preparatory period of training under both the director of music and the director of the church school. The musician should help them come to understand what good music is, what is appropriate for each age group, and how best to use music effectively and to teach new songs and hymns. The educator should interpret to the musicians the philosophy of Christian education, accepted educational principles and procedures, and integration of music with the curriculum by use of rhythm, songs, hymns, musical games, et cetera. In a large church such a program could well be developed by a staff member known as the supervisor of church music, working in close co-operation with the music and education departments.

This type of approach has the advantage of making music an integral part of the teaching process and at the same time of adequately preparing the children in the techniques of music under skilled leadership so their response in other settings and in moments of spontaneous worship may be more meaningful. Often attempts at "bringing in a song naturally" at a moment of worship fail because the song is not familiar, is not presented in an interesting or effective way, or is a poor choice due to the teacher's poor musical judgment.

Perhaps a brief review of the historical development of hymns and music for children may help to bring to focus some of the problems which face the church school. One of the earliest books for children was *Divine and Moral Songs* published by Isaac Watts in 1720, and the tone was more moralistic than divine. One of the most widely quoted items is:

Let dogs delight to bark and bite,
For God hath made them so;
Let bears and lions growl and fight,
For 'tis their nature, too.

But, children, you should never let
Such angry passions rise;
Your little hands were never made
To tear each other's eyes.

However, in all fairness we must admit that the following hymn by Watts for children is a gem:

I sing the almighty power of God
That made the mountains rise;
That spread the flowing seas abroad,
And built the lofty skies.

His hand is my perpetual guard,
He keeps me with his eye;
Why should I then forget the Lord,
Who is forever nigh?

In America the moralistic song flourished in examples such as "Wicked Polly," who, in her deathbed warning to others, catalogues all her wicked ways which now send her to the fiery pits of hell.

The next group of hymn writers were of the "little lamb school." They thought of children as sweet little lambs, and all their examples exude sweetness and light, figuratively patting the little lamb on his head in a patronizing way and talking down to the child. Two things a child despises are to be thought of as little and to be talked down to as an inferior.

The next generation was of the "lollipop school" whose philosophy was to keep the children happy with musical pacifiers. This was the age of the jingly chorus since children "love bright tunes"—according to the theory of that day. "Brighten the corner where you are" is a choice example of this category. Perhaps few of the songs are downright harmful, but nourishment found in "lollipops" is most inadequate spiritual food.

In the last generation the emphasis has been on the teaching possibilities of hymns—the period of the graded curriculum with songs manufactured to fit a particular lesson unit or to achieve a specific goal or response. On the whole this material is better than much that went before, but generally musical settings sound contrived and aesthetic values often take a back seat to pedagogy.

To put the use of hymns in Christian education in proper perspective, let us return in our thinking to the four categories of hymns—praise and prayer, teaching, admonishing, and prophesying. The teaching emphasis is important and valuable, admonishing one another is perhaps better left to the older age level, and prophetic hymns belong to the age of youth where ideals lead to action. However, the vast majority of hymns are primarily devotional in nature, designed to praise God, to thank him, to pray to him, to sing about him and his wonderful acts. Singing a hymn of worship to God can be an end in itself without any need to teach or admonish. Training to take one's place in the Christian faith and tradition should include a liberal study of the hymns of the Church, graded according to developmental levels, but taken in the main from the standard hymnal of the church. There is no reason or excuse for having a "Sunday-school songbook" unrelated to the church hymnal.

If music in the church school is to have meaning and value it must be selected and used in the light of the theological foundations of Christian education. A primary principle is that the main function of the Christian is worship with heart, mind, body, and spirit. God is a spirit and we are to worship him in spirit and in truth. Worship has to do with the creative and continuing relation between God and man and with the community of the faithful which is both redemptive and sustaining in that relation. God has made us free to choose, but he is constantly seeking us and working his acts of redemption if we will turn to him. Another chief principle of Christ's ministry was that teaching is centered in the needs of persons. Though ideas and doctrines attempt to put in verbal form what is observed, the chief concern is always the new life in Christ. Feeding an individual mere facts, doctrines, dogmas, and catechisms is ineffective in terms of the goals of Christian education and sometimes is invalid unless the feeding results in growth in the Christian life. Songs such as "I'm but a stranger here" and similar "longing to go to heaven to be with Jesus" hymns do little to meet the

173

needs of any normal child who much prefers to enjoy this, his Father's world.

A third principle is that Christ's teaching is based on the worth of the individual. God created man in his own image; he has made him a little lower than the angels; each person is important and is the concern of God. The lost sheep figure of speech is certainly better than that of man as a worm. Each person has been given the privilege of choosing what he shall do and how he shall respond to God, although man is made responsible for the consequences of his choice. A decision for Christ which is manipulated by psychological and social pressures—many revival conversions are in this category—is open to question. A decision must come willingly from the individual if it is valid; the final choice must be made voluntarily in free faith by the individual in response to God's seeking, redemptive love.

A fourth emphasis of Christ's teaching was on the kingdom of God— a fellowship of love in which Christ is Lord and King. While each individual is important and has his unique relation to God to fulfill, group relations and interactions are basic to learning and to the Christian life. We are our brother's keeper, and we are dependent upon one another as parts of the Body of Christ. Each part of the body has a unique function but depends upon the interaction of all the other parts through the bidding of the Head, or the mind of Christ. Individually we commune with God, but at all times we take our place in the redemptive, worshiping community that is the Church—a community not only here and now, but related to the great procession of saints of all generations.

Christian education is possible because of the God-given powers and possibilities for growth, change, and decision inherent in every person. Since God has created man a free creature with the power to make decisions and act upon them, it is the function of the Christian educator to create opportunities for right choices and right decisions. It is obvious that a child should not be placed in the position of having to make a choice for which he is not prepared. (This point will be elaborated in the discussion of the choir program as related to Christian education.)

Christian education is possible because God has given us the power to grow and develop physically, intellectually, socially, and spiritually. The church school must be concerned with the total development of the individual.

174

Christian education is also possible because God not only created us with the power to grow and change, but he continues to act in guiding and purifying those who will accept continuing revelations of his Holy Spirit. In every child there is the power to imagine and to create—two of the most powerful aids to education. Within every man there is the latent urge to seek what is ultimately real, good, true, beautiful, and holy.

The end result of Christian education depends entirely on the child's response to God in faith and love. All that the teacher can do is to give opportunities for right decisions and for right responses so the child comes to accept God completely. The teacher can only encourage and foster these decisions and attempt to remove the barriers to a free faith response to God's love. The ability to change, to grow, to decide is God-given, and the teacher's role is to guide, encourage, and motivate.

In the learning process there are four actions which take place in some degree:

1. Learning takes place by exploration—discovering facts, sorting and organizing, and analyzing them in relation to what is already known.

2. The learner discovers meanings and values of his new experience or discovery.

3. The meaning of the new experience is related to the individual's self.

4. The learner assumes personal responsibility for future action.

These processes can be illustrated by an experience of every child at an early age. A child having touched other objects touches a stove and discovers by a burned finger that it is hot. He then knows that it is unwise to touch a hot stove if he does not wish to burn his finger again. Therefore he will not touch the stove again soon, but eventually will learn that it is useful for heating and cooking.

The four processes can be summarized in these words:

Information through exploration

Interpretation

Participation (or appropriation)

Evaluation (or commitment)

In each of these four areas music can contribute richly to growth and to the development of Christian character. It can give information—basic beliefs are learned through the singing of biblical texts and paraphrases or

175

poems inspired either by the Scriptures or the Holy Spirit. The church hymnal is also a resource book for the study of the history of the Church and the development of its beliefs. The table of contents reveals an outline of what we believe about God, Christ, the Holy Spirit, faith, prayer, the Lord's Supper, among other things.

What do we believe about the nature of God? Hymns can be chosen to present the Trinity as the doctrine of the living God—God as creator and sovereign sustainer, Jesus as love made incarnate, and the Holy Spirit renewing, inspiring, guiding, and teaching still. What do we believe about the nature of man? The hymnal can help teach that man is finite but that he can be in tune with the infinite, that he can rise above himself and repent of his wrong actions. What do we believe about God's work? The hymnal leads us to believe in a creative, provident, revealing, redeeming, and sanctifying God.

The hymnal is our heritage of great thought and creativity of all ages. Evelyn Underhill pointed out:

History does not exhort us or explain to us, but exhibits living specimens to us, and these specimens witness again and again to the fact that a compelling power does exist in the world—little understood, even by those who are inspired by it—which presses men to transcend their material limitations and mental conflicts, and live a new creative life of harmony, freedom and joy.[3]

A hymn can do more than give information; it can give interpretation through the texts and music. The use of music through hymn singing can help to create right attitudes for Christian living. Again Evelyn Underhill is helpful in her insights:

We see therefore that St. Paul's admonition, "Whatsoever things are pure, whatsoever things are lovely, whatsoever things be of good report, think on these things" is a piece of practical advice of which the importance can hardly be exaggerated; for it deals with the conditions under which man makes his own mentality.

. . . How necessary it is to put hopeful, manly constructive conceptions before those whom we try to help or instruct; constantly suggesting to them not

[3] *The Life of the Spirit* (New York: E. P. Dutton & Company, 1922), pp. 138-39. Used by permission of E. P. Dutton & Company and Methuen & Company, Ltd.

the weak and sinful things that they are, but the living and radiant things which they can become.[4]

Personal enrichment and appropriation can come from the music experience, for new physical skills are gained along with cultural, intellectual, musical, social, and spiritual values. The arts are one of man's most useful and meaningful ways of carrying on the God-man conversation. Yet Earl E. Harper said:

Evidently, there are Christian leaders who feel, and also churches, and even church schools, that the Christian religion has no responsibility in the realm of art. Their attitude bespeaks a belief on their part that men may not only be suffered to lose their lives aesthetically and still be spiritually saved, but that the Christian Church may at one and the same time be an active agent of damning them aesthetically and saving them spiritually.[5]

The value of the arts as a means of participation and appropriation is vital in the total experience.

Through the assumption of creative and artistic responsibility the child develops a sense of stewardship and commitment—of time, talent, and self. Each singing experience can be a time of rededication, recommitment, and renewal, each worship service another opportunity to make a decision for the Christian life. The re-creation of music can become a creative moment of great importance.

In every age group the same four kinds of opportunities—information, interpretation, appropriation, and commitment—are given for learning, and the only difference is in the adjustment to the developmental level through choice of specific and graded activities, type of content and vocabulary which will have meaning to the particular age, and limitation of the scope of activities. It is obvious that in no one season can all of the available music possibly be sung by a group of children; therefore the teacher and musician, consciously or unconsciously, are choosing specific texts and music which become the raw material of the learning process. It would seem clear then that they should choose that which is most worthy and valuable to the total development of the child and that which will move him from the known to the unknown.

[4] Ibid., pp. 136 ff.
[5] Church Music and Worship, p. 25. Used by permission.

In choosing music it is imperative that the musician integrate his material and approach with the curriculum used for the child in the church school. In the area of content and vocabulary the director should co-operate by avoiding texts which are theologically unacceptable to the church or confusing to the child, but at the same time he should not be forced to serve musical pablum when meat is called for. Many texts which the child cannot completely understand at the moment can be partially explained and then left to germinate as his wisdom increases and he is able to interpret and appropriate the fuller meaning.

Granting, then, that music has a part to play, what are the criteria for choosing materials, either for the church-school classroom experience or for a choir program? Let us consider the text first by asking the following questions:

1. Is the information to be sung true? Are there any concepts which are false or which may have to be unlearned later?

2. Can the vocabulary be explained and made meaningful to the specific age group for which it is chosen? Does the language properly convey the ideas? Does it avoid meaningless repetition of trite phrases?

3. Is the text beautiful and does it stretch the imagination and creative powers of the child?

4. Does the text have lasting value or will it be eventually discarded as irrelevant? Is the concept large and challenging?

5. Is it the best possible expression of Christian truth?

6. Will the children grow into it instead of out of it? Does it avoid a patronizing or talking-down-to-the-child approach?

7. Is it a foundation on which other learning can be built?

8. Does the text foster the spirit of reverence and worship?

9. Are the texts chosen from the church hymnal insofar as is possible? (Children should be able to feel at home in the worship services of the total church through participation in the hymns which are sung.)

10. Could the time spent learning a given text be used to better advantage in some other activity?

11. Is the text consistent with the theological position of the church and is it in agreement with the church-school literature?

These eleven points can be summed up by saying that a text should have theological integrity, aesthetic discrimination, and evangelical effectiveness.

178

The following questions should be asked about the musical setting:

1. Is the melodic line beautiful, singable, and in the vocal range of the children who are to sing it?

2. Does the melody fit the text and add something to it? Is the product of melody and text greater than the sum of the parts?

3. Does the music have lasting value?

4. Is there any danger of its being parodied? Is it free from secular association?

5. Is there rhythmic vitality and variety?

6. Is the harmonic structure sound?

7. Is the music chiefly drawn from the church hymnal, or, if it is an anthem, is it suitable for use in worship?

There is a real danger in underestimating the ability of children to learn great music. While the small child should be given short songs with limited range, most children from the primary age up can learn almost any melody. Ditties and jingly choruses are poor fare, for children are capable of learning the very best music, often more easily and rapidly than adults.

While hymns are the backbone of music in Christian education, music has a unique place in two other areas—music activities and choirs. By music activities is meant the use of musical games, rhythms, actions, instruments, recordings, et cetera.[6] We believe the music experience of the very small child should be a part of the curriculum in the Sunday morning class where the child gets the "feel" of music—a sense of rhythm, the feel of the head voice, and physical response when listening to music. Individual children will respond differently, but getting them to respond is an important goal.

Music lends charm to what is done, not as a separate element, but as an integral part of the entire experience of the nursery class day. We discover how it connects each with the others and speaks to individuals with many voices. Count on the sensitiveness of children wherever music and motion are present, for they are only waiting for help to release the songs inside them. How closely music and life are related! All have the power to fulfill them-

---

[6] A discussion of music experiences in the various age groups of the church school is to be found in Music in Christian Education by Edith Lovell Thomas and in Ch. 10 of The Use of Music in Christian Education by Vivian Morsch.

selves as children of God every time they sing for joy in harmony with all creation. . . .

Beethoven confided in a friend the purpose of one of his sacred choral compositions: "It was my chief aim to awaken and to render lasting religious feeling in the singers as in the listener." Are these not outcomes which the Christian teacher desires? [7]

As children are able to use music with more skill, music sessions—not choir rehearsals—may be arranged as an extension of the church-school program for children through the second or third grades, meeting either on Sunday morning or during the week. These classes should emphasize ear training, vocal patterns, tone matching, and rhythmic games, and may begin to teach some of the musical symbols of pitch and rhythm. Here the songs suggested in the curriculum may be taught along with additional related and integrated materials. Such groups should be thought of as an extension of the church-school class session and as a training period for choir membership. Opportunities for group singing can be found in class worship moments, sharing sessions, and pageants. These extended sessions are designed mainly to foster confidence and a sense of sharing in each child and have the advantage of providing time for individual musical help and guidance at an age where it is most needed. The purpose should not be preparation for public performance.

While the subject of choirs for children and youth is discussed in Chap. VII, "Children's and Youth Choirs," such choirs of necessity are related to Christian education at the four points of information through exploration, interpretation, participation, and commitment. In a fine choir program there is constant exploration of new materials and new skills, but always based on the ability of the child to relate these to what he already knows. As each hymn, song, or anthem is learned there must be interpretation of text and music; musical patterns and words must be clear to the child if he is to re-create them with meaning. As hymns and anthems are sung as a part of a worship service the child participates in the life of the Christian community and appropriates personal and spiritual values from the text, the music, and the worship service.

A sense of responsibility, loyalty to the choir and church, punctuality,

[7] Thomas, *Music in Christian Education*, p. 83. Used by permission.

courtesy toward others, industry, and dependability are among the foundations of a good choir. These qualities are based on self-discipline, self-control, and a right attitude toward the group. The choir experience offers opportunity for such training in a larger degree than almost any other activity in Christian education.

The choir also offers participation and identification in the group experience. There are usually too few opportunities for most children to share in the work of the church and to feel that they have a contribution to make. The choir gives the child a sense of belonging to the "community of the faithful"; through singing participation in the service of worship he feels himself a part of the worshiping congregation.

There is today an uneasy feeling among Protestant churches that no music program is complete unless several choirs are maintained. In fact, the trend toward large numbers of choirs has become so pronounced that a re-evaluation is perhaps in order.

The entire children's choir program should be planned and operated in close association with the church school. The choirs must be considered as a part of the Christian education program as well as a part of worship leadership, not something outside of and unrelated to the other church activities for children. If a program operates as something apart it should be carefully examined and brought into proper place as quickly as possible.

A serious question which has troubled many Christian educators and should be faced more honestly and thoughtfully by church musicians is at what age a choir program should begin. We believe that since a choir's chief function is the leadership of worship, involving the ability to take complete responsibility for the leading of a service—including hymns, responses, chants, anthems—choirs should begin at the age of decision. By decision is meant the ability of the child to decide on his own whether the choir will have meaning to him and whether he can offer something to it. This would probably be the junior age in most churches, although it is possible that a choir could be successful with the third-grade group in some instances. Below this level the child is too young to have a comfortable place in public worship or to fit himself into the discipline of a group experience. When "cherub and angel" choirs are paraded before doting parents many people think it cute for a small boy to wave at his mother in the congregation, but this individualistic action is not natural in worship and indicates that very small children are not ready to organize into groups responsible for worship leadership. It is likewise bad educational psychology to use any choir group for show by having them parade to the steps of the chancel or to the pulpit platform to sing their "special." A choir should only be used where it becomes a part of the total worshiping congregation and a responsible agent in worship leadership. Choir directors are often forced into exploitation of children's choirs by ministers who use them as a means of getting the parents to attend church. A choir experience under such circumstances fosters the unfortunate and mistaken idea that music is an attraction and entertainment, and the children develop a wrong and unwholesome attitude toward worship.

The value of the group experience has been mentioned before but should be re-emphasized here. When a child is able to fit into a group and to make his personal contribution to it, a choir is possible. Only as each individual can subordinate his ego to the greater identity of the group can fine singing occur. Yet excellent workmanship and sincere effort on the part of the group is spiritually rewarding to each individual. The director should never allow a choir to sing unless it is adequately prepared, for a poor presentation is demoralizing to the group and is not good Christian education.

To avoid conflicts in schedules and loyalties, choir groupings and rehearsals should be related to the age groupings of the church school wherever possible, and the music materials should be integrated and correlated with the curriculum of each group. This does not mean that the choir music should be limited to the suggestions of the curriculum, but that it should grow out of it and tie into it at all possible points and become an enrichment of the total educational program.

It cannot be emphasized too strongly that music in all areas of the church life should be educationally and aesthetically sound—in the church school as well as in the choir. Too often one finds the choir singing fine hymns and anthems while the church school feeds the same children doggerel. Regardless of where the blame lies, the director of music must consider it his duty to train leadership in the field of church music and to give help in putting a correct philosophy to work. This can be done through guidance in the teacher-training sessions, where the teachers should be led to understand the place of music in teaching and

182

the characteristics of good church music, and be given practical help in evaluating material and methods of presentation to children. Such help should extend to the accompanists as well as song leaders and teachers. The successful use of music in Christian education depends upon skillful use of materials and methods by all leaders in guiding each person to the perfect worship which is the goal of all Christian endeavor. To this task the church musician and Christian educator are called in a spirit of co-operation and consecration.

In conclusion, music can play an important role in the growth of Christian personality at each level of development if the requirements of theological fitness are observed in choosing material that meets the needs of individuals at each level; if it recognizes the worth of each person as a child of God and encourages him to be worthy of the dignity of man's highest capabilities; if it develops in the individual a sense of Christian fellowship as sons of God, if it guides him to oneness with God and service to man in true worship; and if it preaches, teaches, witnesses, and heals through the power of music as well as text. To be educationally sound, only such music will be used as can be accepted and used by the child in honesty at his own level of development; that helps him to grow physically, intellectually, aesthetically, socially, and spiritually; that is constantly redeemed by the Holy Spirit, urging the individual on in an imaginative and creative search for what is ultimately true, beautiful, and holy; and that helps the individual to make right choices and decisions leading to the complete and perfect acceptance of God with heart, mind, and soul.

XII

The Worship Committee

THE DISCUSSION TO THIS POINT HAS BEEN CONCERNED WITH VARIOUS individuals and groups who share responsibility for music in the church—the minister, the music committee, the director, the organist and pianists, the soloist, the choirs, the church-school teachers, and the congregation. Yet there is one important factor lacking—a synthesis of divergent interests and activities. The minister may be enthusiastic in his leadership, the director well trained, the organist skillful, the choirs proficient, the church-school leaders musically alert, and the congregation responsive, but music can still fail to attain its true goal if there is no guiding force to direct the worship life of the church.

Since worship is the central focus of the church, the logical group to implement the program is a worship committee. Such a council is vital in the large, well-organized church and is of equal importance in the small church. Co-ordination of effort and correlation of planning are essential in both.

The worship committee's first concern is with the spiritual life and the ordering of divine service. At the same time it should relate itself to the worship program of the church school and to family life, including the development of future leadership for the church. The arts—drama, architecture, choric speech, painting, music festivals, rhythmic choir, poetry—would logically come under its domain.

The following diagram is a suggested way of organizing such a worship committee. Every church should make adjustments to fit local needs; however, the basic outline is capable of use in any size church.

It is logical to suggest that the minister, as spiritual head, serve as chairman. In large churches the last five sections should be expanded into full groups as subcommittees of the worship committee; in smaller churches one person may be sufficient for each.

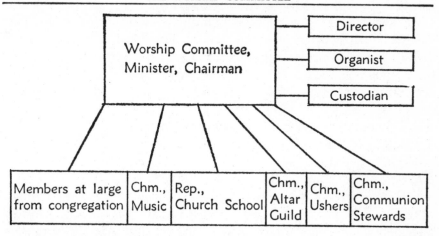

The worship committee's concern is primarily with two areas: physical properties and personnel problems. In considering the former, a basic question must be answered. What is the physical environment in which the minister, the musicians, and the congregation work and worship? Sometimes it is of such a nature that a worship atmosphere is quite difficult to establish. Other churches are so constructed that they seem almost to worship without any help from man.

The church building has more effect upon the vital life of a parish than many of its members would probably realize. . . . The beauty of the setting for worship sets the tone for worship. . . . If the setting . . . invites reverent quietness and attitude of listening, then music is better able to perform its ministry.[1]

The size and shape of the sanctuary will influence the movement and form of the service. A small area permits—even demands—an intimacy that cannot exist in a large area. In terms of space the service of worship might be compared to a painting: on the one hand, a tiny, exquisite miniature painted with small strokes, containing one or two featured items; on the other hand, a huge oil landscape, painted with bold strokes, containing many features which combine to tell one story.

Certain types of rectangular auditorium construction, with overhang-

[1] From *Steps Toward a Singing Church*, by Donald D. Kettring. Copyright 1948 by W. L. Jenkins. The Westminster Press. Used by permission.

ing balconies that extend partially or entirely along three sides, facilitate the use of several choirs in a single service. Their over-all inefficiency and lack of beauty, however, more than outweigh this one advantage. The adult choir in this situation is usually seated facing the congregation; the members "will have to undergo careful training in choral demeanor and procedure, but so prominently are many of our choir lofts placed that some visual distraction from worship is inevitable." [2]

One might assume that buildings constructed in recent years would reflect the attention that has been given to the placement of choir areas, organs, and pulpits. Such is often the case, but unfortunately there are other instances when one wonders what, if anything, was in the minds of those in charge of "assembling" certain edifices. For example, consider a recently built modified Gothic sanctuary that has a beautiful divided chancel. The organ console is outside the chancel, by the lectern. The organist can see but a small part of the choir, and can see the director only when he stands quite conspicuously at the front of the chancel.

Choirs have been elevated far above the "pulpit platform," tucked away at one side or another, and generally placed in situations that make the creation of a worship atmosphere quite difficult. It is often possible to rebuild a poorly arranged altar and chancel area without the expenditure of a large sum of money. The benefits of such action can be immediate and great, but competent counsel should be obtained if serious errors are to be avoided. Each situation will pose its own problems and demand special solutions. Ideally, the chancel should be easily accessible, sufficiently roomy, a good mixing chamber for sound, and so constructed that the organist, director, and choir can function as a unit without being placed in a conspicuous position.

The ancient balcony arrangement, with choir and organ at the rear or side of the sanctuary is receiving considerable attention for several reasons: it removes the musicians from the position of visual prominence; it brings the tone closer to the congregation and thus provides better leadership in congregational singing; the choir can be seated so that blend and balance are improved; the director need not worry about being obvious and he can therefore conduct more freely and effectively. At least one church has found membership in the choir increased since the

[2] *Ibid.*, p. 33.

choir moved to the balcony where it is no longer in the public eye.

There are certain disadvantages of the balcony choir loft: the choir may feel itself to be set apart from the congregation and somewhat "out of the picture" to the extent that discipline can become lax. It is much easier for members to arrive later or leave early, benefits of visual leadership are lost, and the pageantry provided by robed choirs is eliminated from the service.

There is considerable disagreement about the values of the divided chancel. Historically, it has as much justification as has the balcony choir loft. Numerous liturgical and architectural reasons justify the divided chancel, especially in the church that places the altar, the cross, or the communion table at the center of worship. The choir is thus located in "the most intimately consecrated part of the building. . . . The chancel location of the choir minimizes the tendency to regard the music of the church merely as 'music in the church' and the church musicians as performers." [3]

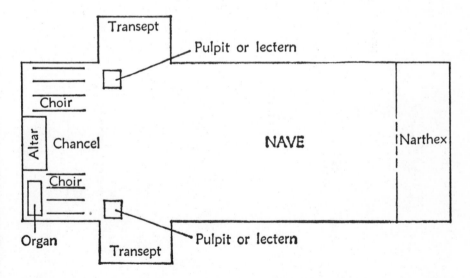

Musically, the divided chancel poses real problems. The fact that the chancel was originally designed for two choirs and antiphonal psalm

[3] Ashton, *Music in Worship*, p. 218.

singing gives an indication of the difficulties faced by today's choir. Because it is somewhat scattered, the choir may have such a feeling of insecurity that singing is constrained. This feeling will disappear in time, however, if the chancel is a good mixing chamber. The most vexing difficulty is to find a favorable spot for the director to stand. Certainly he should not stand in the center. The device most often used is a mirror placed at one side of the chancel, with the organist or director at the other side so that half of the choir sees the director in the mirror.

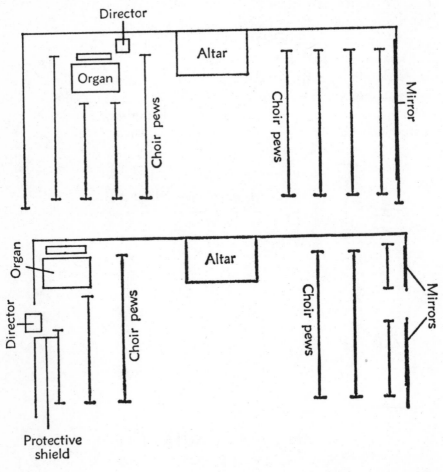

The American Guild of Organists is to be commended for its studies of organ and choir placement and general architectural problems in relation to music and worship. The materials contained in *The Contemporary American Organ*,[4] and in an article, "Acoustics in Churches" [5] are deserving of careful attention. (Also see *Architecture and the Church*, a bibliography by Herbert W. Johe,[6] and various articles in issues of *The American Organist*.)

Every effort should be made to provide the musicians with the best possible physical situation. It is not too much to say that a good choir can be severely handicapped and a fine organ made well-nigh impotent by improper placement. "Many organs are, in fact, buried at birth. . . . Care should be taken to relate the organ to the choir, placing it so as to give the choir a maximum of support with a minimum of instrumental covering." [7]

The acoustical properties of the sanctuary, and for that matter, of the entire church building, are not often given sufficient consideration. Some are too "live" in the sense that irregular or too-long sustained reverberations cause distortion of sounds. Far more are too "dead" for the effective enhancing of musical sounds. There is long standing disagreement between ministers and musicians over the amount of resonance and reverberation needed for speaking and singing. In a sound-proofed sanctuary that is sometimes considered ideal for speaking "the effect will perhaps be tonally depressing and the music will lack the 'bloom' of overtones and resonance." [8]

Many new kinds of building materials are used today, some of which have unknown acoustical properties. It has been found by bitter experience that certain types of brick are much too sound absorbent, while other glazed clay products are almost completely nonabsorbent. Those in charge of construction or remodeling should be very sure that the materials being considered have the desired qualities and properties for the enhancement of sound. The installation of an amplifying system may solve certain problems, while creating others. A good sound engineer should be consulted and various types of equipment given a thorough trial before permanent installation is made. The organist and choir

[4] William H. Barnes (Glen Rock, N.J.: J. Fischer & Bros., 1959, 7th edition).
[5] American Guild of Organists Quarterly (January, 1957).
[6] New York: National Council of Churches, 1958.
[7] Ashton, *Music in Worship*, p. 219.
[8] Kettring, *Singing Church*, p. 31.

189

director will be able to offer suggestions that might be just as valuable as those given by the engineers.

The minister, the musicians, and the worship committee will do well to give careful attention to the acoustical characteristics of the sanctuary in planning the structure of the service, the kind of music to be used by the choir and organist, the selection of hymns, and even the style of sermon delivery. To ignore the science of sound is to court disaster. A resounding Gothic nave will not lend itself to an informal, chatty kind of service. On the other hand, a drab, muffled auditorium is not friendly to a strict liturgical service.

Lighting problems, unlike acoustical problems, can often be solved with relative ease. A dim, dull sanctuary or choir loft is depressing indeed, but it need not be tolerated for long. Modern lighting fixtures and methods can make any church bright and cheerful. The ability to read hymns and the bulletins without eye strain is sufficient justification for the cost of better lighting. In some churches modern devices are used to highlight special areas during the worship service. Dimmers and spots give added emphasis to the cross, the altar, the pulpit, or the choir loft. There is danger, however, that these devices be used to the extent that the service becomes theatrical instead of worshipful. As with all other mechanical factors, lighting effects are good only insofar as they contribute to the worship movement without themselves becoming conspicuous.

An attractive, plainly worded bulletin eliminates the necessity for announcements and instructions and can also add to the atmosphere of worship. To be most effective, a bulletin should be a work of art. Beautiful but inexpensive covers can be obtained from several church publishing concerns. Many churches prefer to print their own covers, using a picture of the sanctuary or some devotional material. An effective cover should be balanced with an equally effective interior. The service portion should be neatly and carefully laid out and all instructions so plainly stated that a visitor can follow them with ease. Its arrangement should indicate the various movements of worship—praise, adoration, confession, illumination, and consecration—and there should be evidence of orderly and logical development. The back page can be used for giving information about the hymns, texts of the anthems, announcements, personnel of the church, or other pertinent material.

It would be interesting to discover how many inattentive, sleepy-eyed parishioners could be made more alert by proper ventilation and heat control. There is little excuse for permitting stuffy air to nullify the work of an excellent minister and choir. Often a simple readjustment of airflow will improve the situation. In other instances new equipment may be needed. Some congregations believe they cannot afford to purchase an air-conditioning unit for cooling as well as for heating. However, it has been found that this kind of investment has often resulted in increased attendance and the larger offerings have more than repaid the cost.

Church seats or pews are an item of equipment that should be the concern of the worship committee. The congregation should not be asked to sit in noisy, uncomfortable pews. "Most church goers do not become aware of sense of touch unless the pews are backbreaking or the kneelers uncomfortable." [9] The singers are especially deserving of consideration; their seats should be quiet, comfortable, and conducive to good yet unrestrained posture. The arrangement should be such that the choir can see the director easily and plainly. Adequate storage space should be provided for hymnals and music folders.

Mention has been made previously of choir robes. A drab, colorless sanctuary can be brightened by the use of color in robes, altar and pulpit cloths, and in other ways. Materials, however, should not be gaudy or in bad taste. Colors symbolic of the church year are appearing in an increasing number of Protestant churches. Stoles of various shapes and styles are sometimes used by choirs; but since the stole has ecclesiastical significance and is usually thought of as belonging to the clergy, the choir might better be limited to a collar or some similar type of ornamentation. Whatever and however color is used in the worship service, it should not be conspicuous in its own right. Its value is determined by the contribution it makes to the atmosphere of worship.

While much thought and attention must be given to physical environment and equipment, a major portion of the worship committee's energy will of necessity be devoted to personnel whose actions in the service may help or hinder worship. The ushers have an excellent opportunity to

[9] Clokey, *In Every Corner*, p. 21.

strengthen the service, if they serve quietly, efficiently, and inconspic-
uously.

There's more to being an usher than wearing a white carnation. No one
wants to be dragged or prodded to a pew, have an usher lick his thumb to
deal out programs, or dull one's senses with a combination of hoarse whis-
pers, bright plaid vest, and pungent after-shave lotion.[10]

A friendly greeting outside the sanctuary will establish a feeling of
warmth and may help to eliminate the loud talking and laughing that
frequently continue throughout the playing of the prelude. Because the
attitude of the ushers may be assumed by the congregation, it is of the
utmost importance that they understand the requirements of their work.
Ushers should be chosen for their quiet efficiency, dependability, and
willingness to serve. Regular training sessions should be planned by the
minister and worship committee to discuss the problems of ushering
and methods for solving them. All too often a single person has the task
of rounding up a crew just before service each Sunday morning. It is
unfortunate that few ushers have been given a complete understanding
of the significance of their assignment and the effect of their actions
upon a service of worship.

The work of the altar guild is usually taken for granted; yet the appearance of the altar, altar cloth or hangings, flowers, and other adornments
of beauty mean much to the physical setting for worship. The condition
of the candles is no small matter to many persons—unmatched, unevenly
burned, and askew, they can be a distraction. Candlelighters with wax
wicks are not expensive and their use is more esthetically satisfying than
the striking of a match on the bottom of the shoe—or the seat of the
trousers—to light the candles. In many churches boys and girls, usually
around junior or junior-high age, are used singly or in pairs to light the
candles. These "acolytes" should be trained to walk slowly and in an
orderly prescribed route to and from the altar; the time for lighting and
snuffing candles must be clearly established so that all is done decently
and systematically.

The custodian is another person who is taken for granted in almost
every church. Working behind the scenes, he is noticed only if he does

[10] *Together,* "Church Ushers" (September, 1959), p. 21.

not fulfill his obligations. The church that is served by a conscientious, dedicated custodian is fortunate. A clean building with all equipment in place is an asset that cannot be evaluated in terms of money. In addition to his other duties, the custodian should work closely with the ushers in controlling heat, light, and ventilation. He can see that hymnals are properly distributed, the choir loft correctly arranged, rehearsal rooms set up as the director desires, the loudspeaker system correctly turned on and adjusted, and do innumerable things that will make the whole church program function smoothly and efficiently.

The attitude of the congregation regarding the worship service is also a concern of the worship committee; yet little consideration is given to this matter since it is taken for granted that all is well if a congregation is present. A congregation rehearsal (see Chap. X, "The Congregation") could be used for the study of significant aspects of worship and of the manner in which the various elements contribute to worship. If a change is to be made in the order of service, the congregation should be given instructions in advance of the change. It is important that the people have a feeling of complete confidence in and understanding of their service.

Certain other problems can be discussed with the congregation, especially those concerned with the attitude shown during the early portions of the service. A noisy congregation is slow to enter into the spirit of worship. A late arriving congregation is even slower in more than the physical sense. A certain minister habitually enters the sanctuary with the organist and remains kneeling in an attitude of prayer throughout the playing of the prelude. The congregation appreciates the significance of his act, and now participates with him in this period of meditation. The atmosphere thus created cannot help but discourage the perennial latecomer.

A very frank discussion with the congregation of the disturbances created by late arrivals will usually bring some improvement of this unfortunate custom. Interrupting the service to seat people is a tacit admission of defeat, and an acceptance of a situation which should not exist. The problem of late-comers can be solved by a concerted effort on the part of everyone concerned, including the congregation.

The ultimate concern of the worship committee is relating worship in its broadest and all-encompassing sense to the total life of the church. It must work for the highest caliber of music possible for the services of worship through the choir program under skilled and dedicated leadership, but it must also work for a music program that touches the lives of all members of the church, evangelizes by proclaiming the "good news" through every medium of communication and art, and lifts the spiritual level till the entire congregation is educated in worship—to know the best, to love the best, and to give its best.

The worship committee can best serve the church by a regular, continuing self-examination of the worship, musical, and educational life of the church. The church must constantly strive to make its music program one which draws all persons into active participation, helping them to grow spiritually through the use of worthy, enriching, creative music which undergirds faith and life and summons a Christian response to the call of God to worship and service.

No longer can the church afford to look upon music as a delightful ornament and worship as a pleasant interlude at eleven o'clock each Sunday morning. Even as worship is inextricably woven into the warp and woof of living, so church music which is vital and spiritual will be seen by minister, musician, and layman as an integral design in the whole cloth which is life. "For to worship is to quicken the conscience by the holiness of God, to feed the mind with the truth of God, to purge the imagination by the beauty of God, to open up the heart to the love of God, to devote the will to the purpose of God." [11]

> Grant us wisdom,
> Grant us courage,
> Serving Thee whom we adore.[12]

[11] William Temple, The Hope of a New World (New York: The Macmillan Company, 1941), p. 30.
[12] Harry E. Fosdick. Used by permission of the author.

XIII

Contemporary Music and Worship

THE ONLY CERTAINTY TODAY IN WORSHIP AND MUSIC IS CHANGE, AND THAT what is changed will also change. When Vatican II opened the way to experimentation and innovation in the Catholic Church, many Protestants jumped on the bandwagon or tried to lead the procession. For Catholics it meant replacing the venerable language of the Mass with a variety of local tongues, replacing excellent choirs with song leaders and amateurs, and throwing out chant and polyphony for mariachi bands and guitars. Carl Schalk, in a paper delivered at a consultation on sacred music at Perkins School of Theology in Dallas, Texas, in the spring of 1973 said it "has resulted in over a decade of dramatic, spectacular, shocking, presumptuous, often impudent changes in worship and church music."

How can one describe what has happened? Activism, enthusiasm, ecumenism, humanism, pietism, revivalism, pluralism, mysticism, and nonverbalism are a few suggestive words.

For the activists, worship did not take place unless every one was doing something vigorously. Everything had to be "relevant"—a verbalism that has been abused beyond redemption. Few stopped to ask if the actions were suitable or understandable. Enthusiasm was more important than understanding. Because standard hymnals were thought to be too confining, "disposable" collections of relevant texts were mimeographed in great numbers, with current protest tunes often providing a rousing vehicle for the texts. Every service was supposed to be a "happening," but many were nothing more than an unholy hullabaloo. The "in" word was "celebration," but it is dubious that a rock-and-roll band, dancing in the aisles, parading banners, and releasing balloons is a completely adequate expression of the true meaning of that word.

For others worship has gone the route of ecumenism. If only we can get everyone to agree on the same order of worship, the same language

195

for the Lord's Prayer, then all problems will be solved. Yet the Lutherans are not in agreement with the new materials of the Inter-Lutheran Commission on Worship, there have been thunderous rejections of the new version of the Lord's Prayer as suggested by the International Consultation on English Texts (ICET), and the Consultation on Church Union (COCU) has met with strong resistance from many denominations.

Humanism had its day with emphasis on the ability of man to do all things by himself. The theologians even aided the cause by announcing the death of God—an announcement which seems to have been a bit premature. The emphasis on "doing your own thing" is an invitation to emphasize man's genius and to overlook his dependence on God. The solo singer with guitar created songs that were largely personal rather than corporate, and the emphasis in combos was on solo ornamentation and improvisation rather than on corporate responsibility and response.

Pietism, with its exaggerated emphasis on personal feelings, and a pseudo-piety has re-emerged in many churches and is best illustrated by the Jesus movement. Carrying a Bible to the football game has come to mean "being religious," and everyone who doesn't attend a Bible study (where pat answers are given to questions no one is asking) or wear a flamboyant religious medal is not considered to be a "newborn Christian." The judgmental quality of such false Christianity is truly frightening and is a perversion of the openness and love which Christ taught and lived. "Honk your horn if you love Jesus!" is a subtle form of judgmental pietism.

Revivalism has revived or continued with a new Madison-Avenue touch, but with the same approach as the nineteenth century and emotional exploitation as the theme. The so-called music dramas (which usually tell it like it never was) are designed to work primarily on the emotions.

Pluralism takes the form of the multimedia presentation in which all the senses are bombarded simultaneously. Sometimes there is unity of purpose, but often there is little more than a confusion of tongues, sounds, sights, and symbols that does not edify the mind nor clarify the spirit. Such sideshows tend to emphasize the medium and to overlook the message. James F. White wisely points out "Simply using Christian symbols as part of the *decor* does not baptize a bacchanal. . . . We need

196

to be clear about the message itself before we seek new media for it. Experimentation which begins by taking a theological shortcut can be thrilling, but it may do more tearing down than building up of the community of faith." [1]

Mysticism has had a tremendous surge with its emphasis on personal intuition of truth. There is no social concern for others, only a vague feeling of being at one with the "Soul of the Divine." Gibran's thoughts, while interesting and well written, are not a substitute for the Christian gospel or Christian worship.

Of all the "isms" the one with the most possibilities is nonverbalism. Protestants since the time of the Reformation have perhaps relied too heavily on the spoken and written word. The invention of printing made the eye the most important member of the body for seeing the truth, but since only the clergy were literate they made their appeals through the ear for understanding the written word. However, we should not overlook the fact that it was the medieval church that instituted many of the nonverbal forms which we are now rediscovering. The use of stained-glass windows for storytelling, the use of the miracle and mystery plays, processions, candles, instrumental music, incense, actions in the Mass, the use of special robes and vestments are only some of the nonverbal elements which were used effectively. Today TV has increased our sense of involvement—you are there. The spoken word is heightened by visual effects, color, and sound. Churches are discovering that banners, building design, colored slides, movies, dance, textile art, bulletin cover art, and other artistic forms are valid means of expressing the gospel in ways to appeal to all the senses.

One of the unfortunate side effects of this emphasis has been the deemphasis on preaching. Great exposition of the Word is hard to find in most churches today, yet the spoken word continues to be one of the most important means of communication. Neither the spoken word nor the visual presentation is more Christian than the other, but the church should be open to considering the use of any and all art-forms which express Christian truth—not just "art" itself. The possibilities of using art-forms is almost limitless, but James W. White warns, "If the art forms become simply toys that we enjoy playing with, they can be

[1] *New Forms of Worship:* (Nashville: Abingdon, 1971), p. 39.

197

demonic and destructive. And it is very likely that this is what will happen if we do not think through the pastoral, theological, and historical norms of Christian worship." [2]

These three words—"pastoral," "theological," and "historical"—are the clue to bringing sense out of our period of experimentation, some of it helpful but much confusing and divisive. All experimentation runs the danger of subjective pietism if the leaders do not have a solid foundation based on a knowledge of the past experiences of Christian worship. Or worse still, churches may be split if they are forcibly confronted with outlandish experiments that make no sense because they are not understood. It is easy for a leader (either pastor or musician) to become arrogant in forcing change on a congregation and soundly condemning them for not appreciating what he is doing "for their own good."

The word *minister* means "to serve," and a minister's first duty is pastoral—to know his congregation, to accept them as they are, and to serve them by leading them in love. In his ministry he must be concerned both with the emotions and the intellect. In these days of being contemporary it is easier to go to the low road of emotional titillation through the use of gimmicks than it is to take the high road of purely academic and intellectual stimulation.

But Christian worship is neither one nor the other. Containing elements of both, it must be concerned with theological integrity and scriptural fidelity. In the final analysis worship is a reminder of the acts of God as he has revealed these to man. His ultimate revelation of himself was in his Jesus Christ, and the theme of that revelation is love. If this is not reflected in what happens in worship, then no amount of experimental forms can make up for the barrenness of content. The goal of worship is to glorify God and to make man holy. Neither is exclusive, and worship which forgets man and his need to be changed, while it adores God with beauty, is empty and meaningless. True worship leads to right living. When Amos writes the words of God,

> I hate, I despise your feasts,
> and I take no delight in your
> solemn assemblies. . . .

[2] *Ibid.*, p. 148.

198

Take away from me the noise of your songs;
 to the melody of your harps I will not listen.
But let justice roll down like waters,
 and righteousness like an ever flowing stream. (5:21, 23, 24)

he is not saying that God hates worship or music, but merely that neither is a substitute for right living.

A great deal of experimentation in worship today is done under the false assumption that it is new, something never tried before. Many of the mistakes being made today were made before, and if worship leaders were knowledgeable of their church history they could avoid these errors. Hegel wrote, "The only thing we learn from history is that we learn nothing from history," but Santayana was much wiser when he said, "Those who cannot remember the past are condemned to repeat it." If one studies the past he will be amazed to find how much continuity there is in worship patterns, and yet how adaptable and flexible the church has been from age to age. Today it is possible to find churches with a silver chalice for communion using paper-cup music for the liturgy.

Again James F. White's comments concerning experimentation without an historical perspective are apropos:

We are convinced that experimentation in worship in ignorance of . . . givens of Christian worship is just as risky as trying to expound Christian doctrine without a knowledge of the Scriptures. It may be more sporting that way, but the score is not apt to be high. The result is all too often sentimentality and triviality no matter how much fun it all was. Entertainment is not the only function of Christian worship. . . .

Conservatism [therefore] is the only sound basis of radical renewal and development of Christian worship.[3]

Often there is no doubting the sincerity of those who attempt far-out patterns, but sincerity is not enough. Unless there is a pastoral concern for all people, theological integrity based on the Scriptures, and an historical understanding coupled with excellence and craftsmanship, the congregation will not be edified nor God glorified.

As Carl Schalk said in his address at Perkins,

[3] *Ibid.*, pp. 60, 79.

199

Experimentation and innovation to be successful, must be worthy and worthwhile; it must possess an integrity and durability which will enable a congregation to grow into a new rite, hymn, liturgical text, or practice and find it significant and truly meaningful over a long period of time; it must be done thoughtfully and with proper regard for what is helpful, useful, and possible at the congregational level.

Such change will be gradual, but in the end may be the most radical and effective of all.

Thus far we have been speaking primarily of the experiments and innovations in the realm of worship. At the same time there has been a revolution taking place in music. But with changes boiling all around, some churches are still singing themselves gently downhill with Victorian hymns and threadbare gospel songs while the world has been jet propelled into scientific and musical experiments almost past imagining fifty years ago. It is no longer reasonable or possible to argue about the differences between sacred and secular music as Archibald Davison presented them in *Protestant Church Music in America* in 1933.

While some people still think that strumming a guitar or adding string bass and drums to an anthem is *avant garde*, other more substantial experiments have been taking place. The twelve-tone technique and serial composition may be found in anthems, solos, and organ music. Richard Felciano's "Double Alleluia for Pentecost" (World Library of Sacred Music, No. EMP-1532-1) with its accompanying electronic tape is already a standard item in the choral repertoire. Choric speech is included in sung pieces by many composers. The Moog synthesizer has been used for improvisation in a Jewish Sabbath service. Aleatoric (or chance) music may be heard in a few places. Rhythmic movement is increasingly popular. When done with real artistry and good taste, this kind of religious expression is quite effective. It can be an honest statement of worship. While it is the responsibility of every church musician to keep abreast of what is going on in the experimental field (and even to try writing in new styles), it is important that certain matters be kept in mind as he tries to find out how to choose new material, how to teach it to the choir, and how to make it understandable to the congregation.

First, change for change's sake is pure brashness and is indefensible. It is easy for a church musician—or minister—to become a faddist, accepting any current popular movement as the ultimate answer in church life. Some choir directors are still grinding out one music drama after another because the fad is still popular, even though the musical, intellectual, and theological content in most is nil. Church choirs easily fall into the trap of having to top last year's show.

The advertising business is geared to pushing fads, whether in music styles or clothing. Long collars for men that look like drooping breasts on ancient aboriginal women, super wide ties which look like baby bibs, women's hemlines moving up and down like a Yo-Yo through mini, midi, and maxi—all are proof of the ability to manipulate styles and taste through promoting fads. There is nothing of permanent value to be gained by changing just to be different, and we should beware of swallowing every new and exotic musical development just because it is new and different.

But there is an opposite trap for church musicians—the tendency to reject anything new because it is unfamiliar. Many directors are unwilling to do the study necessary to understand a new idiom, to develop a methodology that will communicate it to the choir, and to lay the necessary educational groundwork to make it understandable and acceptable to the congregation. A good director can teach a choir anything that he can completely analyze. If he will not make the effort, he may be stifling the work of the Holy Spirit by his intransigence.

Still another danger for the church musician is the temptation to ride the "now" train only. In our attempt to be hep and with-it, we have allowed our adulation of youthfulness to lead us into the dangerous heresy that there is only the now. A now considered apart from a knowledge and wise understanding of the past is dangerous. Civilization is possible only through the accumulation of knowledge and construction on the past through a growing process of absorption and refinement. Christianity and Judaism are basically revealed religions, inconceivable apart from the knowledge of continued study of the Scriptures. Church music cannot afford to divorce itself from the past. The flowers of today and tomorrow always have their roots in yesterday.

One of the disturbing signs of our culture is the demand for instant gratification and for freedom from discipline. We live in a push-button society where we expect to have the TV come on instantly, and to learn how to play the piano or guitar in ten easy lessons or less. Instead of mastering an instrument, we are content to repeat endlessly a few chords and fragments of tunes which are just as impoverished as the gospel songs of the 1890s we delight in maligning. The philosophy is to do your own thing, even if it is done badly. It is high time that we return to the philosophy that artistry is a matter of moral responsibility. When Bach wrote on his music "Soli Deo Gloria," he was recognizing his responsibility to be a good steward of the musical gift with which he was endowed by God. The kingdom of God is not advanced by careless, thoughtless music whose only aim is to please the crowds and to make a fortune for the composer. Nor is sincerity enough. Some of the worst drivel foisted on the church is written by very sincere, but unartistic and undisciplined people. There is no substitute for artistic integrity, which can only come through submission to the disciplines necessary to free oneself to become a revealer of the truth.

The next danger might be called the transfiguration syndrome, the mistake Peter made at the Transfiguration on the mount. "Lord, this was a great experience! Let's build a temple and stay here and keep repeating the experience." As Erik Routley points out, the church has a melancholy habit of digging itself in at any given point where pleasant sensation has been associated with religion and saying, "That was good: let's have it again." This helps to explain why congregations like to cling to the good old songs, because they are trying to relive some past heart-warming experience related to some favorite. It also helps to explain how churches get into the rut of singing nothing but Handel's *Messiah* every Christmas. We are now falling into the same trap with the guitar. Because a youth service with guitars or a rock band was exciting, we must have guitars for everything.

A word of warning should be made about the misuse of the term "folk music." Myron Braun in an editorial in *Music Ministry*, February 1973, writes:

We are always amused, if we can maintain our sense of humor, when someone says, "I am using some contemporary music in my church," by which he means one of the now fashionable "mod" or "pop" songs accompanied by guitar or combo. (Our sense of humor is further strained when this music is called *folk* music. We presumed that the origin of folk music was lost in antiquity, that it grew up among the *folk* and that no

202

composer is identifiable. But here is music with a very specific composer's name on it, a very definite copyright date guarding it, and a high royalty for its duplication.)

True folk music is that which has a universal quality that is recognizable by almost everyone as speaking the true feelings and emotions of the listener. A lot of so-called modern music is really commercialized junk written with clichés which hint at folk music but contain nothing of the true spirit. Some songs, such as "They'll know we are Christians by our love," are good imitations, and some have enough universal appeal to last for a while. But there is always the suspicion that the Church, in appropriating the so-called folk idiom, has taken the easy way out, and instead of facing the problems of vital contemporary church music, has accepted watered-down versions of the real thing. Ed Summerlin has suggested, "We are going nowhere by replacing our old clichés with different ones. 'Joy is like the rain' is like an updated 'In the Garden.' "

There are two other things which might be added about "folk music." There is always the danger of widening the generation gap through polarizing a congregation into those who dig it and those who hate it. Creating a jazz or rock or folk service for the young people, and another for the old folks is hardly the way to build up the body of Christ, which is the Church. Any music worthy of the Church must be usable by the whole Church. Real liturgical music—that is, the work of the congregation—must be capable of gaining and retaining meaning after repeated use.

After these preliminary observations, are there any principles that can help to guide the church musician as he chooses contemporary music for the worship of all God's people?

1. All church music should have the ability to speak to the entire congregation. If the music is divisive, if most of the people do not understand what is happening, if it does not have meaning to most, then it is probably improper and wrong.

2. Church music should bring a sense of personal involvement, of spontaneous expression, and joyous celebration in the liturgy of the people. It is equally bad to bore people with poor music as the church has often done and to put them into shock with experimental sounds with which they can find no personal involvement. Worship is cele-

203

bration only when those present can identify (either immediately or eventually) with the actions and sounds which transpire.

3. Church music should edify the congregation; it should give them spiritual food. Christ said, "Feed my lambs"; but many greedy opportunistic contemporary pop composers translate this, "Fleece the lambs." This is a day of many nonfoods—fancy prepared foods with attractive appearance and intriguing taste, but no food value. The Church is dealing with food and drink which satisfies. To offer nonspiritual food is indefensible.

4. Church music should communicate and express a sense of awe and wonder in the presence of the Divine. It should lead our thoughts toward God rather than toward ourselves. Any self-righteous, holier-than-thou expressions such as those in "The bells of hell go tingalingaling for you but not for me," popular during World War I, must go.

5. All music should be chosen as carefully as any other liturgical materials so that it proclaims God's power and purpose in our lives and guides us to respond. It must be corporately useful, expressing and strengthening the unity of the congregation as it worships together.

6. The texts of church music must be sound teaching. Not every song that gives a warm feeling contains sound doctrine. God's truth is not usually found in texts or tunes which are directed at the lowest common denominator. Joseph Clokey had a good word of advice in *In Every Corner Sing*. "The purpose of worship is to elevate, not to degrade. The quality of the music used should be above rather than below the cultural level of the congregation. If the music seems to be 'over your head' the best plan is to raise your head." [4]

7. Church music should be primarily concerned with the mind of Christ rather than "blowing the mind." Christ humbled himself and became obedient unto death, even the death on the cross; but humility is not often a mark of music heard in church these days, and not enough composers are willing to make the sacrifice of time, energy, and talent to produce music which shines with clarity and glory.

8. We should keep open to any new style, for there is nothing sacred about any particular style or period of music-making. There is either good or bad music, appropriate or inappropriate music. Erik Routley

[4] *In Every Corner*, pp. 20, 21.

suggests that bad music is created by incompetence, slovenliness, insensitivity, personal pride, or egocentricity. Such music is an offense to God—not because it is secular, but because it is bad. But we must also beware of worshiping "good music." There are some choir directors who worship at the feet of Bach rather than God. For others "God" is Palestrina, Brahms, Sowerby, or Messiaen.

9. The test of the validity of church music must be what it has always been: the experience of Christians worshiping. If the temple is filled with smoke, who is to say that the music is wrong? But if the temple is filled with stagnant, dull, stupefying sounds how can the music be right?

10. All music chosen and performed must be prepared with a zeal for perfection on the part of the performers. The most difficult music or style can have a chance of being understood only if the music is given as perfect a presentation as is possible. Under no circumstances should a director force a choir to try to perform music which is completely beyond its capabilities. Simple music done well is far superior to difficult music badly mangled.

11. Education of the congregation is equally as important as education of the choir. Through written and spoken words they need to be guided to an understanding of what a new piece is trying to say. If they know something about the different style and understand what the piece is supposed to do and say in the service, the congregation will tend to be more open and receptive.

12. The church musician above all must be a communicator. If he is only interested in exotic and ecstatic utterances he will not be understood. But if he is a prophet and priest, communicating the love of God through love of people, no matter what music is chosen it will not be a matter of entertainment, of dazzlement, of confusion, but of involvement of the whole community in a total response to God.

This is a day when it is easy to fall into the trap of "Can you top this?" dashing from orgy to orgy of sound and experience. To follow this route is disaster. But we may also be tempted by the more subtle wile of the devil to stand pat, ignoring the workings of God's Holy Spirit which keeps bursting in upon our cozy world with new sounds and new inspirations. Unless we are willing to become professional (i.e., professing our faith with skill), knowledgeable of what is happening, critical in our evaluations, skillful in preparation and performance, and compassionate in leading the people into new paths, we may find that we have withered on the vine and will be cut down and cast aside.

For some people music is nothing more than an emotional experience, and there has been entirely too much emphasis on making every performance or worship service a happening. For others church music is mainly concerned with teaching, and words take precedence over music. In such cases poor music can undermine and undercut the text, and may even cancel out any learning by saying musically the exact opposite of what the words are attempting to say. For still others music is nothing more than a tool for evangelistic revivals, to be used in manipulating people into making responses on an emotional basis through the use of monotonous and repetitive tunes, chords, and rhythms. But worship is not limited to any one of these areas. Worship is not just experience, not merely instruction, not only an appeal to the will, but a drama which includes all these and fuses them into a living whole. Great church music always is great drama; it is concerned with experience, teaching, exhorting, prophesying, and with the totality of life. To be responsible for the choice of such music and its preparation calls for true ministry—service to God and man.

Finally, some practical advice. Use contemporary music in moderation. All-modern is just as bad as all-Bach. Keep a balanced diet. Use only that music you yourself are sold on. You cannot be convincing to choir or congregation if you are not convinced yourself. Inventory your resources before tackling a work that cannot succeed because of the size and ability of the choir, the instruments available, the acoustical situation, the cultural climate, or the ability of the congregation to understand. Be sure there is a right place and right time for the work. It must be valid liturgically. Learn the music thoroughly and do it well. Educate the congregation and prepare them in advance so they have at least a vague inkling of what it is all about and why you are presenting the music. Afterwards, evaluate. Was it worth the effort? If not, move on to something else. If the answer is yes, repeat the work enough times to allow ears to become attuned. Above all, work hand in hand with your minister and with the leadership of the church. You should pull together, not apart.

Carlton Young in an article in *Church Music* sums up the situation well:

The new direction for parish music is already set, and as Protestants we have three alternatives: (1) We can sit tight, close our eyes and ears, and cry in a loud voice "but we've been right all the time." (2) We can allow ourselves to be pushed into the new day with the false hope that yesterday's solutions will suffice for tomorrow's problems. (3) We can move together in faith and confidence into the unknown and untried in obedient response to the demands of Christ's Gospel.[5]

We are always tempted to follow the faddish route of shock for shock's sake, sensation for sensation's sake, beauty for beauty's sake, or relevance for relevance's sake. But the only route is to proceed with careful attention to the understanding and use of the new techniques, balanced by a sensitive pastoral concern for the people for whom music serves as a vehicle of prayer and praise.

[5] February 1967, p. 24.

XIV

In Spirit and in Truth

SOMEONE HAS SAID FACETIOUSLY THAT PLAYING A VIOLIN IS LIKE SCRAPING on the inside of a cat with the outside of a horse. This is hardly the whole truth, but the basic fact is that a violin would not make music unless there were an appropriate balance in tension between the catgut string and the horsehair bow.

In a thought-provoking article called "Pop Rock and Sacred," Herman Berlinski says,

Music is a kinetic art. It is and must be in a perpetual state of motion. The whole history of western music can be reduced to an analysis of the various agents of propulsion in music. The moving of the punctus contra punctum, the tension and motion generated within the melodic units created by contraction and expansion of its intervals, the establishment of tonal centers, the conscious alienation from and the eventual return to these centers, the interplay of consonance and dissonance, the multiple time division of the rhythmical elements, the accentuation and the suppression of the strong beat, the tempo changes, the variety of density in the choral fabric of music and eventually the never-ending succession of dynamic contrasts—these are the elements of propulsion which sustain music as a kinetic art.[1]

Then he relates this to the religious experience by saying that this principle of tension in music "corresponds well to the basic tenets of almost all religious thinkers, namely, that there is a relationship between resistance and value, or, to express it in religious terminology, between resistance and morals." [2]

The thrust of his article is that uncritical acceptance of rock music threatens the concept of holiness, and that ecstasy (which is rock's

[1] *Music/AGO*, January 1971, p. 47.
[2] *Ibid.*, p. 48.

most authentic claim) is not a suitable substitute for prophecy. He sees the movement as anti-intellectual, often succumbing to the temptation to substitute drug-induced ecstatic experiences for conscious thought process.

Yet it is doubtful that Dr. Berlinski was making an appeal against ecstasy in worship—certainly the Old Testament is full of examples. Rather, he is saying that when one side of the scales is tipped too far, when the tension slips badly, or when situations become either-or, music in worship falls upon evil times and true religion is poorly served.

The thrust of this final chapter is to suggest some of the basic balances and conflicts that form a framework within which we all must work.

The first is that of *Art—Science*. Music is both an art and a science, yet it cannot be truthfully said to be more one than the other. The artist usually is the aggressive or positive terminal. It is he who develops new sounds, new rhythms, new patterns. Then the theorist—sometimes the passive or negative terminal—tries to analyze, systematize, and concretize what the artist has done. For example, a theorist will earn a degree by analyzing all chordal progressions in every Bach chorale harmonization. But this does not exhaust the possibilities of harmony! *Musica ficta* was the way musicians handled scales; the theorists later figured out the laws. Theorists discover that composers avoid parallel fifths for quite good reasons, but when they create a rule outlawing all parallel fifths composers such as Ralph Vaughan Williams prove that they can be used very effectively and beautifully. When art and science are kept in tandem pulling together, great music can be developed.

Emotion—Reason. Here is an ancient battlefield. John Wesley was intrigued by the singing of the Moravians on shipboard, and as a result he studied their pietistic hymns carefully and even translated several. But when he came across Martin Luther's commentary on the book of Romans, he turned to the Lutheran appeal to reason rather than the pietistic appeal to emotions. This is not to say that religion or life should be devoid of emotions—far from it. But it is important that the mind be engaged before starting the emotional engine. "Place-kick me, Jesus, through the goalposts of life" may have a great emotional impact, but it would be hard to defend on any intellectual level. Charles

Wesley's hymns at their best are perfect balances of reason and emotion. They are filled with theology and scriptural references, but the language, rhyme, and meter combine to make them potent emotional experiences. For comparison, read twenty hymns by Charles Wesley, and twenty by Fanny Crosby. The need for a balance between emotion and reason will become crystal clear.

Form—Content. There are other companion words that are closely related, such as classic-romantic and objective-subjective. Organists can perhaps see the importance of this balance better than choral directors since they have been brought up on Baroque preludes and fugues where the form of the prelude or the fugue is heavily dependent upon the content of the subject matter. It is interesting to see what Bach did with the theme of the Passacaglia in C Minor for Organ. The melody is beautifully shaped and balanced, melodically and harmonically conceived to leave room for a rich rhythmic development in the eighteen contrapuntal variations. Bach was also the master of fugue writing, for he knew that the simpler the fugue subject harmonically (almost all are simply tonic-dominant) the easier the working out. He also knew that good counter-subjects were necessary to keep the interest to the end of the fugue. The whole subject of choral preludes is a study of the balance between the subject matter of the choral and the form chosen to develop the theological subject of the text. Jehan Alain's "Litanies" is a classic example of a modern treatment of the problem of crying out to the Lord. The famous Russian "Hospodi Pomilui," which used to be the touring *a cappella* choir *tour de force*, is in actuality a kind of tortured "Litanies" with the phrase, "Lord, have mercy on us," repeated twenty-seven times.

Classical music is often categorized as being primarily interested in form, while romantic music becomes amorphous as it tries to avoid too much control by form. Thus it has been said that Vivaldi did not write two thousand pieces, but wrote the same piece two thousand times. Much so-called classical music is more design than anything else— wallpaper music, as it were. But on the other extreme, one wearies of the yearnings, wanderings, emoting, and *sturm und drang* of the romantics. Franz Liszt attempts to hide his glaring paucity of ideas with a plethora of notes and keyboard pyrotechnics.

Music which is strong on form is usually called objective music, while

210

music which is long on content is often called subjective. Yet every great composer has struggled with this conflict, and the masterpieces are always those in which the listener is guided by a strong sense of form into which musical ideas are poured to become a powerful personal statement of faith and belief. Like the popular song "Love and Marriage" you can't have one without the other.

Music—Words. Which is more important in church music—words or music? In a hymn it can be said that the text and tune are equal, except that the text is more equal. This is to say that the words are the primary reason for the hymn's being written, but without the tune, the text could never have the impact that comes from being coupled with good music that adds a new dimension. He who sings prays twice—once with the words, and once with the music.

The history of church music is replete with examples of music and words fighting for pre-eminence. The *jubilus* was first of all an extension of the single syllable A at the end of an *Alleluia*, with pure vocalization and melody taking precedence. But because the singers could not always remember the melodic contour, words were added and the *trope* was born. The best of the tropes became the *sequences* of the Roman Church. It is a long journey from a simple plainsong setting of Kyrie Eleison with one note per syllable to the elaborate and overwhelming melismatic setting by Johann Sebastian Bach which opens the B Minor Mass. Which is better? Neither. For each attempts to do something different, but they do indicate the need for balance between words and music. Can one say that a simple homophonic setting of a text by Josquin des Prés is in any way inferior or superior to the incredible polyphonic settings by Palestrina? There is no answer to the problem of words versus music, but the church musician must be always on the alert to prevent the balance from swinging too violently in either direction.

Secular—Sacred. We have already said there is no real distinction between these two. Can anyone prove that a C major triad is either secular or sacred? Is the scale of E-flat major more sacred than that of E-major? (Some church organists who hate to play in four sharps might be tempted to say so!) Whenever the Church has tried to set rules for composers the "secular" has a way of sneaking in the back door. For example, look at masses such as "L'homme armé" that were actual-

211

ly built on secular popular songs. When composers were forbidden by the Church to write in thirds, they invented *faux bourdon* (false bass) in which the music was written as sixths but sung as thirds. The carols, with their dancing backgrounds, were brought into the Church for Christmas, and Martin Luther even said that he didn't think the devil should have all the good tunes. It is a bit amusing to find such a song as "Amazing Grace" hitting the top of the pop charts about the same time that most churches discontinued singing it because it was old-fashioned and out of date. There needs to be more conversation between the Church and the world in the area of sacred-secular music.

Instrumental—Vocal. The early Church, with perhaps good reason, did not trust instruments. After all, the flute had bad associations of illicit love, and the organ was played for bacchanals and other unholy revels. John Calvin banned the use of the organ and other instruments in the church in Geneva, even going so far as to melt down some of the metal pipes for other uses. He even distrusted singing in parts, lest the people have fun and take their minds off the serious business of "making a joyful noise to the Lord." Yet the Old Testament, and particularly the Psalms, urge the use of all musical instruments for the praise of God.

Today the Church of Christ still forbids organs, but there are few churches of other denominations where brass is not used along with guitars, drums, flutes, percussion, and other available instruments. The Moravians still support a church orchestra that accompanies anthems and oratorios, and their brass ensembles at the Easter sunrise service should be heard to be believed.

The Church has inherited great literature because certain composers were encouraged to write instrumental music for the liturgy. Mozart's sonatas for orchestra and organ, written for the Masses at Salzburg, are small masterpieces. Yet in all honesty it must be said that the Church has relied more heavily on vocal music than on instrumental. For one thing, it is easier to get together a successful group of singers than it is a group of good instrumentalists. Also the emphasis of the Church on words has made choral music and hymn singing primary activities in worship. Furthermore, the human voice is always handy and available, whereas one may not have a double bass available at all times. Since the primary musical impulse is vocal, the Church has encouraged its de-

212

velopment more than it has the instrumental. Perhaps the time has come for the greater use of instrumental music in worship to restore balance.

Choir—Congregation. Although the psalmist makes it plain that it is the duty of every person to praise God through singing, in most churches a highly successful choir program often sounds the death knell for hearty congregational participation. Subtly the idea takes hold that singing is only for those with good voices, the best singers, the professionals. Even the choir director can encourage this attitude by holding difficult auditions to keep out undesirable singers. The congregation is encouraged to sit passively and let the choir lead the music. Even a hearty Amen is squelched by the choir's Seven-fold Amen.

Yet the truth is that the congregation is always the first choir in every church, and all other choirs are subsidiary. Hymns are the true liturgy of the people; worship without hymn singing is almost inconceivable. While anthems *may* be sung, they do not necessarily have to be. The choir's first responsibility is to lead and encourage the congregation to sing hymns and other service music. It should sing hymns in unison so that everyone can hear the melody clearly, and hymns should be rehearsed so the choir is leading rather than sight-reading. The congregation is the whole choir for all worship; the choir is still part of that congregation when it moves to its priestly and prophetic functions of singing on behalf of the larger group or singing prophetic musical expositions of texts for the congregation. A sound music program will begin with the congregation, and then grow into the selected "Levitical" choirs.

New—Old. Just as the New Testament or the New Covenant does not supplant the Old Testament, there is no need to assume that only the new is good and the old passé. Yet the struggle between these two ideas is an ancient one. When the herald angels sang their new song, "Glory to God in the highest," they announced something new coming into the world, but the theme of peace to men of good will is a theme which is found in the prophets. Always the old is the basis for the new, even though the new often seems startling and strange to those who have been too blind to read the signs of the times. The "spirit bloweth where it listeth," and the Holy Spirit's work in the world is certainly related to the new.

213

Music history is filled with examples of the new bursting out of the old. The term "ars nova" means the new art, and composers have always experimented with new forms after they have assimilated the old. The true innovators attract the eager students, who then move on in their own directions. When Isaac Watts wrote his hymns of human composure, he was moving in a new field even though his psalm paraphrases started him in the search for the new song which came with faith in Christ. Those who would cling to the old songs must face the fact that if the early Christians had done this there would have been no Christian hymns—just the Psalms of David. Clinging to the old hymns would have precluded "A Mighty Fortress," "Dear Lord and Father of mankind," "God of grace and God of glory," and every other favorite hymn now sung. As the song says, "Make new friends, but keep the old; one is silver, and the other is gold."

Sir Walford Davies and Harvey Grace in their book *Music and Worship* make the telling point that great church music always has the qualities of newness and oldness in balance. The newest piece has the quality of stating a truth which is eternal, no matter how recently it has been stated. Likewise, the great old works are always new, sparkling with fresh insights, no matter how many times they are sung.

Music—People. At first glance this may seem to be a strange tension, and yet it may be one of the most critical of all. What is a director's first concern? Do you teach music, or do you teach people? Unfortunately, there are too many choir directors in the Church who hate people, and there is no way these people can be ministers. Obviously, a director is concerned that a choir sing the right notes, have a pleasing tone, keep together rhythmically, and interpret the music with proper concern for style. But if this is the only concern, many people will soon depart from the choir because they do not find the pastoral concern that is necessary to develop a group of individuals into a body of singing believers. The sound of a great choir is love—the ability to work together as a team to make sounds that say the music has been mastered and the message is true and beautiful. A director can browbeat a choir for a while, but eventually the fact that he really doesn't like people will take its toll.

An organist can easily choose music for his own gratification and glory, without the slightest concern for whether it means anything to

214

the people. Hymns can be chosen which have no meaning to the singer although the tune is "good music." Hymns can be played too fast (or too slow) without concern for people. Music is merely the medium and material with which a director works. He must be concerned primarily with people, yet equally with music.

Professional—Amateur. The first word too often has the connotation of snobishness—a high-brow musician who cannot be bothered with just plain folks. Another definition of a professional musician is a person who can perform well even when he doesn't feel like it! Still another definition is: "one belonging to a skilled profession, one who makes a business of an occupation, as in the arts, where amateurs engage for amusement or recreation." A better definition might be a person who professes what he believes, and declares openly before others that his belief is strong enough to lead him to take whatever steps are necessary to make his artistry a matter of skill and stewardship.

An amateur on the other hand is often thought of as a pleasant but bumbling person who plays at music but really does not want to take the necessary steps to achieve perfection. The dictionary defines the amateur as "one who cultivates an art or activity for personal pleasure instead of for gain." Synonyms are "dilettante," "tyro," and "novice"—all with a negative connotation. But the word *amateur* comes from the Latin for "love"—one who loves what he does!"

The Church needs both professionals and amateurs—the professional to lead, to guide, to encourage, to train, to cajole, to excite, until the amateurs, through hard work done because they love it, actually go beyond their capacities to make great music for the glory of God. A dedicated group of skilled amateurs often will be much more moving and exciting in a performance than a group of ultra-skilled professional singers who do not love what they are doing. Together a professional director and an amateur choir often find that they are "going on to perfection" together, and the harder the climb the greater the joy at the end of the road.

Freedom—Discipline. The word *discipline* usually has a negative meaning—"punishment," "correction," "subjection," and "chastisement." But the original meaning of the word is "instruction." Train up a child in the way he should go and when he is older he will not depart from it. A pianist disciplines his fingers to play scales, arpeggios, octaves,

215

and difficult patterns to the end that these patterns will become so easy, so much a second nature, that the pianist may then be free to play music. A choir which learns to sing vowels correctly finds that its tone and blend has improved; it is then free to sing beautifully. An organist practices pedal passages so that the feet may be free to play melodies in a fugue with the same ease as the hands. Often a person with a physical handicap disciplines himself so that he not only overcomes the difficulty but excels others with no similar handicap.

Music history is full of illustrations of limitations that have disciplined music making, thus creating new forms of great effectiveness. Chant, with its limitation of pitches and range, was found to be the most effective way to keep tuned speech comprehensible in long cathedrals with several seconds of reverberation. The half close and full close were clues to the listener to the developing thought. Palestrina's counterpoint with interweaving sections was a perfect answer for the acoustics in which he worked. Giovanni Gabrieli's great experiments with multi-choral and multi-brass media grew out of rather unusual architectural arrangements in St. Mark's in Venice. The French organ music of César Franck reflects his concern for the reverberation factors and the type of organ on which he played. When Heinrich Schuetz found his choirs decimated by wars, he wrote music for one or two voices. Russian composers, having no pipe organs, wrote music for basso profundos who sound like great organ pipes. If we can recognize the limitations and disciplines under which we must work and can put them to use as advantages, we become free to scale the mountains rather than be blocked by them.

Crucifixion—Resurrection. While many people claim to love the "old rugged cross," they really prefer to have it on a hill and very far away. Crucifixion is not a pleasant word, for it means the ultimate sacrifice. Christians do not pretend that they can be crucified and take away the sins of mankind, but Christians must accept the idea of sacrifice. In the hymn, "For the beauty of the earth," the correct form of the refrain is "Lord of all, to Thee we raise This our *sacrifice* of praise." Too many people like to celebrate the joy of victory and resurrection, but prefer to bypass the cross. When a composer goes the low road, writing what everyone is buying and what is popular for the moment, he is bypassing the cross. When a choir is unwilling to make the effort to be present regularly and to work diligently under the leadership of the director,

216

they are expressing their unwillingness to lose their lives so that they may find them. Discipline is the requisite for freedom; taking up the cross daily is the way to eternal life.

Daniel Moe in a small pamphlet, *Responsibilities of the Choir Member* states, "Technique, accuracy and precision, acquired through the *discipline* of rehearsal, provide the ensemble with the necessary freedom to re-create music authentically. Without this freedom—without re-creative spontaneity—Revelation is impossible. Artistic singing is a *synthesis* of *all* the elements of technical proficiency and stylistic awareness. These elements are the *Servants* of *Revelation* and must not be mistaken for Revelation itself. When a synthesis of necessary elements has been achieved—both *individually* and *corporately*—Music can become a Meaningful Sonorous Symbol. We have then earned the right to become the instruments of Disclosure and Revelation." [3]

Law—Grace. In his book *Church Music and Theology* Erik Routley states as one of his interim conclusions "that the criticism of church music in practice should proceed from the ground of doctrine, should avoid facile legalism, and should be constructive enough to encourage the good, before being repressive enough to ensure the avoidance of error." [4] In his second and third chapters he compares and contrasts the different emphases of Law in the Old Testament, and the principle of Grace in the New. The mere avoidance of error is an inadequate basis for Christian living or for music-making. When Christ says that we must go the second mile, he is stating a principle that involves the whole dimension of living—the law of the first mile still stands, but if we are gracious we go beyond what is required.

Perhaps another illustration is that of the conductor as an enabler rather than a controller. No doubt you have seen directors who insist on controlling everything a choir does—all dynamics must be scaled by the director, each section must use a specific tone color regardless of voice differences, each consonant is carefully delineated, and the choir is expected to respond to every tiny flick of the finger or eyebrow. The choir may sing with absolute perfection of detail; but there is no life, no graciousness, no excitement, no spirit. Another director will work just as carefully on tone, dynamics, phrasing, diction, and all the rest; but

---

[3] Minneapolis: Augsburg Publishing House, 1965.
[4] (London: SCM Press, 1959), p. 108.

when the time comes for performance he encourages the choir to move beyond the law to the realm of grace, and the result is a glowing, spirit-filled revelation of the intent of the composer. The first director is a controller; he follows the law to the letter and kills the spirit. The second director is an enabler; he also observes the law, but he permits and enables the choir to move beyond legalism to the realm of grace. They go beyond the first mile because they want and are able to do so; the law has made them free. Because what they desire is the same as what God wills they are blessed, and their singing reveals a joy and spirit that can never be found in merely following the rules.

Spirit—Truth. When Jesus spoke to the woman at the well in Samaria he said, "The hour is coming, and now is, when the true worshipers will worship the Father in spirit and truth, for such the Father seeks to worship him. God is spirit, and those who worship him must worship in spirit and truth" (John 4:23, 24).

These two words sum up the principles that are the basis for every pair of words in this chapter. It is not a case of either-or, but of both being two sides of one coin. It is human nature to try to avoid facing the greater realities of life. Religiosity easily becomes a mechanism to avoid being truly religious. Arthur John Gossip says that people can be busy, diligent in organization matters, interested in the program, well versed in doctrines and theology, and still have no vital relationship to God. It is "possible to haunt the holy place, and bustle about its precincts, yet catch no vision of the Holy One." [5]

The central fact of worship is that while we think we are seeking God and his truth, he is seeking us first. Our highest and best is our obedient and joyful response to God's reaching out to us. If we interpret the word "spirit" as the highest part of man's nature, then God wants worshipers who worship in spirit the realities of God. In *The Word of God and of Man* Karl Barth says, "The Bible is expectant of people who have eyes to see what eye hath not seen, and ears to hear what ear hath not heard, and hearts to understand what hath not entered into the heart of man." [6] Such mysteries are too much for us, and yet it is given to those who are open to God's guidance to share in things eternal in this mortal life.

[5] *The Interpreter's Bible* (Nashville: Abingdon, 1952), vol. 8, p. 527.
[6] Tr. Douglas Horton (Boston: Pilgrim Press, 1928), p. 121.

Theologian—Artist. Theologians (ministers) are often suspicious of artists, yet in their own way they are artists also. A good sermon is a matter of consummate artistry, and the art of counseling and ministering takes a finesse and artistry which defies analysis. But artists (musicians) are also often suspicious of the clergy. Yet a church musician cannot serve as a minister through the medium of music unless he understands the theological implications of his work. The music chosen and performed will state a theological position whether the artist realizes it or not. If he is not careful, he may be promoting in his choice of music an opposite viewpoint from that of everything else that is said and done.

The musician may be highly trained and a paid staff member; or he may be a fill-in organist or director because no one else is available. In either case the musician in the church is a minister, or a servant, with a higher loyalty than mere music-making. The cause of more effective church music is waiting for a deeper communication between theologian and artist. "As long as the theologian regards the artist as fundamentally a temperamental trifler, and the artist the theologian as an obstinate and ignorant theorist, the best we shall get is patronage from church to music, together with tentative moralisms from musicians to musicians. . . . Men, as men, are bound together in the body of humanity, and in the body of Christ. Where they accept with penitent gratitude their common humanity and rejoice together in their common Christhood, the work of the Lord will be done." [7]

---

[7] Routley, *Church Music*, p. 110.

Glossary

Much of the following material was taken from *Dictionary of Worship*, prepared by Frank M. McKibben, instructor, for the class "Worship in the Church and the Church School" at Northwestern University in 1934-35. This was revised by Bob Wigington and Fred Wilken for "Worship in the Church" at Garrett Theological Seminary in December, 1951. G. W. Stubbings' *A Dictionary of Church Music* (New York: Philosophical Library, 1950) served as an added source of information. Items marked (S) are quoted from Stubbings. The third principal source was Willi Apel's *Harvard Dictionary of Music and Musicians* (Cambridge, Mass.: Harvard University Press, 1944). Items marked (H) are taken from the *Harvard Dictionary*.

A Cappella—Vocal music sung unaccompanied.

Acoustics—the sound producing qualities of a given room. Also the science of sound.

Agnus Dei—A hymn beginning "O Lamb of God"; an image or representation of a lamb as an emblem of Christ, especially one bearing a cross or banner; the final movement in Mass composition.

Agogic Accent—Accent by longer duration rather than by emphasis.

Aisle—the side passage or part of the church which connects the vestibule with the apse.

Aleatoric—Unplanned; music produced spontaneously, sometimes by chance.

Alleluia (S)—"Praise ye the Lord." An ejaculation used frequently in religious worship in festival seasons, particularly Eastertide. Many well-known Easter hymns have "Alleluia" either as a refrain or following each line of the hymn.

Altar—The whole combination of the reredos with its dossal curtain. The retable and the communion table may be properly referred to as the altar,

220

which is the center of worship in many evangelical churches. In a high liturgical church, the altar cannot be moved, whereas, the communion table, as employed in many churches, will be movable. It is the raised structure on which the elements of the Eucharist are consecrated; a place of prayer; a symbol of artistic and religious unification.

ALTO (S)—The next higher vocal part to the tenor, which was originally the principal melody. In modern vocal four-part choir music the principal part is in the treble or the third above the tenor, and the alto part is that immediately below the melody. In a mixed choir of men and women the alto part is sung by women's voices, usually called contralto. The musical effect of an alto part sung by men is strikingly different from the same part sung by women; the male alto voice sounds higher than the tenor, the women's contralto voice sounds lower than the treble.

AMEN—A hymn of peculiar structure, which owes its name to its position in the Mass. It appears there as the continuation of the Gradual or Alleluia. It was originally a long melody without words attached to the Alleluia. Dresden Amen—a twofold amen beginning very softly and increasing in volume of tone. Sequence Amen—a fivefold amen for women's voices. Fourfold and sevenfold contain four and seven amens respectively; the term means "so be it."

ANGLICAN CHANT (S)—In its simplest form, the single chant, a short musical formula, consisting of two sections, one of three and the other of four bars, which is used for the musical recitation of the psalms and other prose passages of scripture.

ANTIPHON—A versicle or sentence sung by one choir in response to another; an anthem; a short piece of plainsong introduced before a psalm, the meaning of which it illustrates and enforces.

ANTIPHONAL—Responses made by one part of the choir to another or by the congregation to the minister, in the church. Also alternate singing.

APSE—The eastern or altar end of a church, semicircular and covered with a semidome; in ancient churches, the bishop's seat.

ARIA—A solo song, usually accompanied. The operatic or oratorio aria is often florid and embellished.

ATONAL—Having no recognizable key center.

BENEDICITE—The canticle beginning, "O all ye works of the Lord, bless ye the Lord." It is called the "Song of the Three Children" taken from the book of Daniel.

BENEDICTUS—The fifth movement in the service of the Mass, beginning with

221

the words "Benedictus qui venit"; the song of Zacharias (Luke 1:68), used as a canticle in the Book of Common Prayer, 1552. This Benedictus is to follow the lessons in the morning service of the Anglican Church. Used also by the Roman Church.

BENEDICTUS ES—"Blessed Art Thou, O Lord God of Our Fathers." Not to be confused with the two preceding terms.

CALL TO WORSHIP—In formal worship, usually a scriptural admonition spoken by the leader when oral, or by the choir when choral, in order to call attention to the purpose of the gathering and focus attention upon the corporate nature of worship. The call to worship is distinguished from the introit, in that usually it is distinctly an exhortation to worship and seek God, whereas the latter is a proclamation or declaration of God's presence and his quest of the worshiper.

CANON (S)—A musical composition so contrived that one part is repeated later in time by another part, either at the same pitch or at a constant interval therewith. There may be further repetitions by third and fourth parts, and each repetition is called a canonic imitation. Otherwise two separate and distinct melodies by two parts may each be imitated canonically by two other parts.

CANTATA—Formerly a narrative poem set to recitative, or alternate recitative and melody, for a single voice accompanied by one or more instruments; now, a choral composition comprising choruses, solos, recitatives, interludes, arranged in a somewhat dramatic manner. It may be either sacred, resembling a short oratorio, or secular, as a lyric drama or story set to music, but not intended to be acted.

CANTICLE—A little song or hymn; especially a hymn or chant consisting of a psalm occurring in the Scriptures, appointed to be used in public church services. In the Book of Common Prayer, the term is applied only to the Benedicite, but it is also used with reference to the Magnificat, Nunc Dimittis, and others.

CANTOR—A leader of church choir; a precentor. Musician of the temple; soloist in the synagogue.

CANTORIS (S)—The section or side of a cathedral choir which is placed on that side of the structural choir containing the precentor's stall. The other section or side, corresponding to that containing the dean's stall, is known as the decani. As the precentor's stall is on the north side of the choir, the half of an Anglican church choir on the ritual north side of the chancel, or that to the left facing the altar, is called the cantoris, the other half of the choir on the south side being called the decani.

CANTUS FIRMUS (H)—Literally, a fixed melody. A pre-existent melody which

222

is made the basis of a polyphonic composition by the addition of contrapuntal voices.

CASSOCK—A tailored black robe worn by the clergyman, chorister, or acolyte under other vestments.

CHANCEL—The portion of a church immediately in front of the congregation containing an elevated altar, pulpit, lectern, and the choir stalls.

CHANCEL SCREEN—A screen separating the chancel at the floor level from the remainder of the church.

CHANT—To utter, repeat a statement monotonously; a short or simple melody or phrase characterized by the reciting of an indefinite number of syllables to one tone. Used in public worship in singing unmetrical psalms, canticles, et cetera; most ancient form of choral music.

CHOIR—The part of the chancel reserved for singers; also the singers.

CHOIR STALLS—The seats provided for the singers in cruciform churches, usually arranged in two groups, one to each side of the approach to the altar, an arrangement adapted to antiphonal singing.

CHORAL—Pertains to choir, full, or many voices; also the name given to the hymn tunes of the early German Protestant Church.

CHORAL SPEECH—The choir speaking the words instead of singing them; e.g., the scripture.

CHORALE OR CHORAL—A hymn tune; a simple sacred tune sung in unison as by the congregation in Lutheran service, where the choral is characterized by a plain vigorous harmony, and stateliness. E.g., "A mighty fortress is our God."

CHURCH YEAR—A twelve-month recapitulation of the significant events in the life of Christ and the Christian Church. As generally accepted, its seasons include Advent, Christmastide, Epiphany, Lent, Eastertide, Whitsuntide, and Kingdomtide.

COLORS—Used to emphasize various parts of the church year. White speaks to us of the complete revelation of God's love in Christ Jesus since it is not really a color at all but it is the sum of all the colors and hues of the spectrum. Because of its purity and completeness it is natural to associate it with the high feasts of the Lord.

Black—stands for the symbol of sin and has been associated with death, especially the death of our Lord.

Red—symbolizes the sacrificial life of God's children and especially the original sacrifice of the Lord Jesus Christ. It typifies the shed blood of the church's martyrs. It is the color of the Holy Spirit.

Violet—properly reminds men that sin results in death and has come to be associated with times of repentance. It is nearest black in the spectrum.

Green—speaks of eternity and permanence of our Christian faith and the freshness of our religious hope.

COMMUNION—One of the names given the ordinance or sacrament observed in different forms by nearly all Christian sects in remembrance of the Saviorhood of Christ. It is also called the Lord's Supper, because instituted by him, and Eucharist, or giving thanks, because the breaking of bread and passing of the cup is always accompanied by a prayer of thanksgiving. The term Eucharist is derived from the Lord's giving thanks at the Last Supper. The ordinance is also called "breaking of bread," "cup of blessing," "communion of the body of Christ," and "the Lord's table"; it is a term used to denote religious fellowship among Christians or with God; an act of individual participation in worship. "Closed Communion" is a term employed by religious bodies to describe the practice of admitting to their Holy Communion only those who are regular members in good standing of the group. (See also Mass.)

COMMUNION TABLE—A raised structure of stone or wood, within the chancel, on which are usually placed the vessels and elements used during administration of the Lord's Supper or Holy Communion.

CONFESSION OF FAITH (Declaration of Faith)—A form in public worship to be used in general acknowledgment of sin; in liturgical bodies it has special reference to the confession as an act of preparation for the receiving of the Holy Communion; a declaration in worship of belief, i.e., a creed. When so used in Protestant groups, the term Declaration of Faith, or Affirmation of Faith, is more appropriate although Confession of Faith occurs in a non-sacramental connection.

CONGREGATION—An organized local group meeting regularly for worship and other religious purposes.

CONSONANCE—An interval that is satisfying and pleasing to the ear.

CORPORATE WORSHIP—An expression of worship in which the church collectively considered as the body of Christ, or the family of God, offers up its devotion to that power which gives it significance as a group.

COTTA—A short, white, choir surplice.

COUNTERPOINT (S)—A melody which added to and sung or played with a principal melody makes satisfactory harmony with it. The counterpoint must essentially have melodic interest, either of an independent character or by imitation of the principal melody.

CREED (Credo)—A confession of faith. A form or summary of the fundamental points of religious belief; an authoritative statement of doctrine on points held to be vital, usually representing the views of a religious body.

DECANI—See Cantoris.

DESCANT—A varied melody or song; an ornamental melody written above the soprano part giving brilliance to hymns.

DIAPASON—A type of organ tone, produced by so-called flue pipes, without a vibrating metal reed, which is intermediate between the duller flute tone of some registers and the keen pungent string tone of others supposed to be imitative of the orchestral strings. Diapason tone is the foundation of the organ; its characteristics are weight and dignity with due brilliancy, and it is best produced from pipes made of an alloy of tin and lead.

DISSONANCE—An interval that causes unrest to the ear.

DOXOLOGY—A short formula of praise to God. E.g., the "Gloria in Excelsis" or "Praise God from Whom all blessings flow." Some nonliturgical churches use the term to mean a congregational response often sung at the time of the offering.

EPISTLE—One of the apostolic letters in the New Testament; a selection, usually from one of the Epistles in the New Testament, appointed to be read between the collect and the Gospel in various liturgies.

EPISTLE SIDE—The side of the chancel to the right of the altar when one is facing the altar.

FAUX BOURDON (S)—A harmonized arrangement of a psalm tune or a Gregorian chant, with the principal melody in the tenor part. The Genevan and the early English tunes for the metrical psalms were harmonized in this way, as were the Gregorian chants by some Tudor composers.

FERIAL (S)—A term applicable to the service of a day which is not a festival. The term is often also applied to simple harmonized settings of the responses at the Anglican services of Morning and Evening Prayer, to distinguish them from the more elaborate setting by Tallis which is often designated festal. The only essential difference between such settings of the responses is their elaboration.

FUGUE (H)—The latest and most mature form of imitative counterpoint, developed during the seventeenth century and brought to its highest perfection by J. S. Bach. A fugue is always written in contrapuntal style. A certain number of voices (usually three or four) take up a short melody called the "subject" or "theme," at first singing in imitation and later in various combinations as the "subject" is developed.

FONT—The container for the water of baptism.

GLORIA IN EXCELSIS (S)—"Glory be to God on high." An ancient hymn sung after the Kyrie Eleison in the opening part of the Mass. The English form of this hymn occupied this position in the Communion Service of the first vernacular prayer book of 1549, but it was transferred to the end of the service in the next (1552) book, which position it has occupied in subsequent Anglican liturgies.

GLORIA PATRI—The doxology beginning "Glory be to the Father."

GLORIA TIBI—The doxology "Glory be to Thee, O Lord" which is sung in response to the announcement of the Gospel.

GOSPEL—The good news; in the New Testament it means the message of salvation through Jesus Christ, preached by the apostles and evangelists of the early Church; part of the scripture lesson which usually follows the reading of the Epistle.

GOSPEL SIDE—The side of the chancel to the left of the altar when one is facing the altar.

GOTHIC ARCHITECTURE—One of the leading types of church architecture, characterized by the pointed arch, clustered columns, traceried windows, stained glass, vaulted roof, flying buttresses, spires, and pinnacles. One of the best examples of this is the Cathedral of Cologne, Germany.

GRADUAL (S)—A liturgical anthem, the words of which are appointed for the day in the Roman ritual, sung antiphonally by cantors (q.v.) and choir to a plainsong melody immediately after the Epistle at Mass. During festival seasons Alleluia is interpolated in the Gradual. The plainsong music of the Gradual is of great complexity.

GREGORIAN MUSIC—A type of unison or plainsong chant developed under the auspices of Gregory the Great.

HARMONY (H)—In general, any simultaneous combination of sounds. Specifically, a succession of chords, and the relationships between them. Harmony denotes vertical (chordal) structure, whereas counterpoint refers to horizontal (melodic) structure.

HOMILY—Pastoral preaching; the address given by the minister which is intended to give instruction in the things of the spiritual life.

HOMOPHONY—Literally, voices in unison. Often used to describe music written in harmony rather than polyphony.

HYMN—An ode or song of praise or adoration; praise or thanksgiving intended to be used in a religious service, sung by the congregation.

IMPROVISATION—The art of singing or playing music extemporaneously. The organist often does this between parts of the service of worship to help make it one continuous whole.

INTERLUDE—A short musical passage played between the verses of a hymn, a song, or between parts of the service, as when late arrivals are being seated.

INTROIT—In liturgical churches, one or more verses, mostly from the psalms, sung at the entrance of the clergy into the sanctuary, for the celebration of the Mass, or Holy Communion. It is sung as an act of preparation for the service which follows. An introit consists of two parts, the antiphon or anthem and the psalm; in nonliturgical churches, a choral annunciation of the presence of God in the sanctuary designed to call attention of the worshiper to his helpful and solicitous spirit. (See Call to Worship.)

INVITATION—The general invitation is a liturgic form employed by the leaders of worship to emphasize the requirements of repentance, obedience, charity, and faith for all who would receive the Holy Communion. It usually concludes with an exhortation to make "humble confession and absolution." In liturgic communions it is followed by the General Confession and Absolution; when employed informally, as in Protestant bodies in connection other than with the sacrament, the term may be used in the sense of an invitation to participate with the worshiping group in various ways, such as uniting in membership, participation in prayer, and similar appeals to individual and corporate participation.

JUBILATE DEO (S)—"O be joyful in the Lord, all ye lands." Ps. 100, which is set as an alternative to the Gospel canticle Benedictus, in the Anglican service of Morning Prayer.

KYRIE ELEISON—The words of a short petition used in Eastern and Roman Churches especially at the beginning of the Mass; represented in the Anglican service by the words, "Lord, have mercy upon us." Also the musical setting of the words, "Lord, have mercy upon us."

LAITY—The people as distinguished from the clergy.

LECTERN—The reading desk from which the scripture lessons are read at services of worship.

LECTIONARY—A book containing a list of lessons or portions of scripture appointed to be read at divine worship.

LECTIONS—A passage from Scripture, the writings of the fathers or the lives of the saints, read in the service of the church, particularly in the Eucharist and in Matins.

LITANY—A form of prayer or supplication in which fixed and frequent responses are made by the people to short biddings or petitions said or sung by the minister, priest, deacon, or cantor.

LITURGICAL COLORS—(See Colors.)

LITURGY—The service of the Holy Eucharist in the Eastern Church; a collection of the formularies for the conduct of public worship.

MACARONIC—The use of alternating phrases of Latin and the people's language, especially in carols.

MAGNIFICAT (S)—The Gospel canticle, "My soul doth magnify the Lord," which occurs in the Office of Vespers, and in the Anglican service of Evening Prayer.

MAJOR MODE (S)—A mode or tonality of modern music corresponding to the white-note scale starting with C of a keyed instrument. The characteristics of the major mode are the wide or major third on the tonic, and the major common chord on the fifth note or dominant of the scale, due to the leading note, a semitone below the tonic. The old name for this mode is the Ionian mode.

MATINS (also Mattings)—In the Anglican Church the service of Morning Prayer as distinguished from Evensong; in the Roman Church one of the daily offices properly recited at midnight; the order for public morning prayer in the Episcopal Church in America; the musical arrangement of a matin service; the first of the canonical hours used in the Roman Catholic and Anglican services.

MAUNDY THURSDAY—(Latin, *mandatum*, command; the new command, "Love one another.") Holy Thursday, the Thursday preceding Good Friday. It commemorates Christ's washing the feet of the disciples and his instituting the Holy Supper. The color is violet or red. (See Colors.)

METER or METRE—The arrangement of poetical feet, or of long and short syllables in verse. The succession of accents in music. Meter is the rhythm of the phrases and not of the measure. Meters most frequently used are common, short, and long. *Common meter*, a stanza of four lines in iambic measure, the syllables of each being in order as follows: 8. 6. 8. 6. *Long meter*, four lines in iambic measure each containing eight syllables. *Short meter*, four lines in iambic measure, 6. 6. 8. 6.

MINISTER OF MUSIC—A title of recent origin which applies to that person responsible for the music program in a local, nonliturgical church. Usually a full-time employee; may be a layman or an ordained minister.

MINOR MODE (S)—The mode represented by a scale having the characteristic interval of a minor third, or three semitones, between the tonic and the mediant or third note. The diatonic minor scale, identical with that of the Aeolian mode, is given by the white notes between two A's on a pianoforte. The modern melodic minor scale has the sixth and seventh notes sharpened in the ascending form, but is diatonic descending. In the modern harmonic form of the minor scale, the seventh note only is sharpened, and the ascending and descending forms of the scale are the same. The harmonic minor scale gives the notes of the diminished seventh chord, which was so much used in Victorian harmony.

MODULATION—A transition from one key to another by a certain succession of related chords in a natural flowing manner. It makes for smoother transition from one number to another. A skilled organist frequently modulates from the offertory number to the doxology, between the prelude and the first hymn if there is no break, or between the anthem and the Gloria.

MOMENT MUSIC—Music designed to fill an immediate need and not intended to last.

MOOG SYNTHESIZER—An electronic device made up of sound sources and modifiers, usually combined with a piano-type keyboard. It is capable of reproducing an unlimited variety of sounds in various combinations, colors, and sequences.

MULTI-MEDIA—The use of two or more performance media that stimulate hearing, seeing, feeling—even smelling.

NARTHEX—A vestibule or portico stretching across the western (back) end of the church, divided from the nave by wall, screen, or railing.

NAVE—The central division or body of the church extending from the inner door to the choir or chancel, usually separated from the aisles by pillars. The part of the church in which most of the congregation is seated.

NUNC DIMITTIS—The canticle using the words of the song of Simeon found in Luke 2:29. One of the evening canticles.

OBLIGATO—An ornamental instrumental or vocal part that appears to be added to a selection.

OFFERTORY—A hymn, prayer, anthem, or instrumental piece sung or played during the gathering of the offering; a term applied generally to that stage in worship in which an offering is made by the people as an act of homage; specifically used in reference to particular parts of this stage of the service including the *offertorium*, or offertory chant of sentences of scripture, or non-biblical materials, while people offer, or offertory sentences usually of scripture spoken by the minister to emphasize the duty of almsgiving, maintenance of clergy, or relief of poor; the offertory prayer or prayers said before receiving the offering; and choral responses by the choir or people, usually standing.

OFFICE (S)—A term generally meaning the order of a liturgical service, but more particularly indicative of those services called choir offices, which normally are said or sung in the choir of a cathedral or the chancel of a parish church. The Anglican choir offices are the services of Morning and Evening Prayer.

ORATORIO—A more or less dramatic text or poem usually based on some scriptural theme set to music in recitative, aria, choruses, et cetera, with an orchestral accompaniment but without action or scenery. Oratorio includes the developed form of Passion music as in that of Bach, and sometimes has secular subjects.

ORATORY—A small chapel for prayer connected often with churches and used many times for presentation of oratorios.

ORDER OF SERVICE—The order of service as contained in the bulletin which the people are given as they enter for worship.

ORGAN—A wind instrument, the most powerful and most varied in resources of musical instruments consisting of from one to many hundred sets of pipes, and played by means of one or more keyboards from the organ console. The pipe organ is distinguished from a reed or electronic organ.

ORGAN POINT—A single tone, either high or low in pitch, sustained at length against moving parts.

ORGANUM—Earliest polyphonic music, usually in parallel fourths and fifths. Originated in the ninth century.

PEDAL POINT—A single bass tone sustained at length against moving parts.

PLAINSONG (S)—Non-mensural or unbarred melody in one or other of the ecclesiastical modes traditionally used for the singing of the liturgical services of the Church. Plainsong varies greatly in complexity, the simplest being the inflected monotone for versicles and responses, collect and Scripture lections, and for the chanting of the psalms to the Gregorian tones; the most complex are the melodies for the graduals and the responds or anthems of the choir offices, while the antiphons and the hymn melodies are intermediate in character. Plainsong flourished in the Middle Ages, and in the more complex varieties it was generally melismatic in structure, groups of three or more notes being often assigned to a single syllable of the words. Toward the end of this period the structure of new plainsong melodies became simpler and tended to be syllabic in character—that is, to have one note only to a syllable. Plainsong is essentially melodic, and it does not depend for its effectiveness on any instrumental accompaniment.

POLYTONAL—Having two or more recognizable key centers.

POSTLUDE—The after piece or concluding number of a service of worship usually played on the organ. In a well-planned service, this number will be in harmony with the thought which has gone before. It may be a hymn, the melody and thought of which will go with the people as they leave the church.

PRAYER MEETING—Group worship with no regular procedure wherein all are free to take part as they are moved. Freshness, spontaneity, novelty, enthusiasm, holy eagerness, intimacy, informality, and brotherhood are some ideal characteristics of the service.

PRECENTOR—The leader of a choir in a cathedral. Also a leader of congregational singing in churches which have no choir and especially in those which have no instrumental accompaniment to the singing.

PRELUDE—The introductory musical composition to prepare for the succeeding movements or elements in a service. Its purpose is to create an atmosphere of worship and bring unity to the group.

PROCESSIONAL—A hymn or other selection sung at the opening of a worship service during the orderly and ceremonial process of the choir and clergy to their places; organ or piano music played at the beginning of a worship service during the movement down the aisle by the choir or other participants; a book containing hymns to be sung in processionals.

PSALTER—A translation or particular version of the book of Psalms. A copy of the Psalms as arranged especially for liturgical or devotional use.

PULPIT—A raised structure or enclosed platform in a church or chapel from which the preacher delivers the sermon, usually supplied with a desk and seat.

RECESSIONAL—A hymn sung as the clergy and choir retire formally from the church at the close of a church service; organ or piano music played during the withdrawal or a processional at the close of a church service, as at a wedding. At a funeral the designation is usually "a march."

RECITATIVE—A solo that depends primarily upon the inflections and rhythms of the spoken word.

REREDOS—The term for the wall or screen back of the altar, whether of carved stone, metal, woodwork, or drapery. The wall or screen is sometimes painted, sometimes enriched with a profusion of statues, pinnacles, and other ornaments. The reredos differs from a dossal in that a dossal is a piece of embroidered cloth, used as a screen when there is no reredos.

RESPONSE—Part of the liturgy said or sung by the congregation in reply to the minister; as a part of an order of worship, a choir office in which choral response is made to versicles of scripture, to prayers, or to the utterances by the leader of worship, such as to the call to worship, at the close of prayers. Responses and versicles are largely employed in Protestant usage as transitional devices in the service.

RESPONSIVE READING—An alternate or antiphonal reading between the leader of worship and the congregation in unison, usually a biblical passage.

RESPONSIVE PRAYER—Prayer in which the leader of worship and the congregation engage alternately.

RHYTHMIC CHOIR—A choir which uses symbolic bodily movement as a medium for religious interpretations.

RITE—A religious ceremony; a ceremonious act or observance.

RITUAL—A prescribed method for the performance of religious ceremony; also a book setting forth such a system of rites.

ROBE—Covering worn by ministers and members of the choir.

ROCK MUSIC—A type of popular music that is almost entirely dependent upon the beat. It grew out of a combination of blues and country music and was recognized as a separate art-form in the mid-50s. Rock originally used a 4/4 meter with the beats (accents) falling on 2 and 4. Pure rock depended strongly upon amplified guitars—amplified to a body-shattering level. Rock has had many forms:

Psychedelia—A drug-oriented catalyst for the flower-power movement in San Francisco. It began its short life about 1967. Distortion, feedback, and special audio and visual effects were used by such groups as "The Jefferson Airplane," "Moby Grape," "Vanilla Fudge," and others.

Acid Rock—Another short-lived style that grew out of the psychedelic era. It glorified the use of drugs with texts that were often quite explicit. Sometimes innocent sounding phrases were used to imply acceptance of drug usage.

Soul Rock—A combination of "soul music," which had grown out of the blues, with pure rock. Soul bands were originally rather large, depending mainly upon saxophones, trumpets, and rhythm for their kind of sound. The music was played and sung for Blacks by Blacks. The addition of electronic devices produced a distinctive sound now identified as soul rock, with a strong flavor of Black gospel music.

Folk Rock—Music that combines the effects of folk music and rock to produce a distinctive effect. Bob Dylan is a good example of a folk musician whose success came when he was backed by a rock band.

232

Jazz Rock—The addition of trumpets, trombones, and saxophones to rock guitar bands brought jazz back in a new form. Jazz rock groups emphasize improvisation and overall good musicianship.

Electronic Rock—The Moog synthesizer and other electronic devices have made possible the production of an incredible variety of sounds and rhythms in rock style.

ROSTRUM—A platform; stage; a stand adapted for public speaking; a pulpit.

SACRAMENT—(1) A solemn religious ceremony enjoined by the church, for the spiritual benefit of the church or of the individual Christian by which special relation to Christ is created or freshly recognized and obligations to him are renewed and ratified. (2) A means of grace acting directly upon the heart and life, irrespective of the faith of the one who receives it. This allows the impenitent to receive the sacraments as a means of converting him. (3) The sacrament, though not in itself a means of grace, is nevertheless a solemn ratification of a covenant between God and the individual soul and is in itself efficacious and significant. (4) The sacrament is simply a visible representation of something spiritual and invisible, and is significant only when the spiritual and invisible reality is present. It is in the nature of a solemn oath in confirmation of an agreement.

SACRISTY—A room in a religious house or church where the sacred vessels and vestments are kept.

SANCTUARY—The correct ecclesiastical name for that portion of a church which is reserved for the altar or communion table and in which the clergy minister. This does not include the choir. Popular use permits the use of this term for the entire place of assemblage for worship. An appropriate place of worship as contrasted with a mere auditorium; an environment suggestive of the beauty of holiness.

SANCTUS—The "angelic" hymn from Isa. 6:3 beginning with the words, "Holy, Holy, Holy." It forms the conclusion of the Eucharist preface.

SERMON—The discourse delivered by the minister or leader of worship for the purpose of instruction and illumination, dealing with some phase of religious truth.

STOLE—A long strip of cloth in various colors worn around the neck. Many churches change the stole of the minister with the change of the seasons, corresponding to the church year. It symbolizes the cross of Christ resting and carried on his shoulders.

SURPLICE—A long flowing robe worn by clergy of the Roman Church, for use in the choir and in the administration of the sacraments; a robe also worn by Anglican clergymen in various offices.

SURSUM CORDA—"Lift up your hearts," the first words of a versicle beginning the preface of the Mass.

SYMBOLISM—The use of conventional or traditional signs to direct attention, awaken responses, and guide behavior in dealing with realities too complex, intimate, or otherwise inaccessible to precise designation.

TABERNACLE—A temporary place of worship as distinguished from a church. Formerly a meetinghouse or place of worship of Protestant nonconformists which was not of ecclesiastical architecture; a canopied niche or recess in a wall to contain an image; a part of the altar on which a cross is mounted and in which the sacrament is kept.

TE DEUM LAUDAMUS—"We praise Thee, O God," an ancient Latin hymn of praise in the form of a psalm sung or chanted as thanksgiving on special occasions, as after victory.

TESSITURA—The average pitch level of a vocal part.

TONALITY—A feeling for a particular key.

TRANSEPT—The lateral projections between the nave and the choir of the church; that section of a cruciform church building forming the arms of the cross.

USHER—One who escorts worshipers to seats in the church.

UNISON READING—The people and the minister read in unison the scripture, prayers, et cetera.

VENITE—The Ninety-fifth Psalm, beginning "O come let us sing unto the Lord." It is an invitatory psalm; also a musical setting of this phrase.

VERSICLE—One of a series of short sentences, said or sung antiphonally in religious services, especially one said by the officiant and followed by the response of the congregation. The versicles, in most instances, are passages from the Psalms and are thus distinguished from other suffrages which are neither verses from the Psalms, nor form in each petition and response a continuous sentence.

VESPER—An evening service; a twilight service; the next to the last of the canonical hours in the Roman and Anglican Churches.

VESTMENT—A term applied to any of the garments worn in addition to the regular dress by the clergy and their assistants when performing religious services.

VESTRY—A room or part of the church in which the vestments, vessels, and records are kept and in which the clergy and choir go before the service of worship. (See Sacristy.) Also the governing body of certain churches.

VOLUNTARY—A musical selection usually played on the organ, often extemporaneously, and so called because the choice of the music is left to the will of the organist; an organ solo played before, during, or after divine worship.

(See also *Music Educators Journal*, November 1968, p. 169 ff. for a glossary of electronic terms.)

Bibliography

I. Church Music—History and General

Apel, Willi. *Harvard Dictionary of Music*. Cambridge: Harvard University Press, 1944.

Ashton, J. N. *Music in Worship*. Boston: Pilgrim Press, 1943.

Bacon, A. *The True Function of Church Music*. Stockton: Printwell Press, 1953.

BMI. *The Many Worlds of Music; Electronic Music Special*. New York: BMI Public Relations Department, 589 Fifth Avenue, 10017, Summer 1970.

Caravan, Guy, and Caravan, Canelie. *We Shall Overcome!* New York: Oak Publications, 1963.

Clokey, J. W. *In Every Corner Sing*. New York: Morehouse-Barlow Company, 1948.

Cope, David. *New Directions in Music*. Dubuque, Iowa: William C. Brown Co. 1971.

Cross, Lowell M. *A Bibliography of Electronic Music*. University of Toronto Press, 1967.

Curry, L. H., and Wetzel, C. M. *Worship Services Using the Arts*. Philadelphia: The Westminster Press, 1961.

Davies, W., and Grace, H. *Music and Worship*. New York: H. W. Gray Company, 1925.

Davison, A. T. *Church Music: Illusion and Reality*. Cambridge, Mass.: Harvard University Press, 1952.

————. *Protestant Church Music in America*. Boston: E. C. Schirmer, 1933.

Dickinson, H. A., Dickinson, C., and Wolfe, P. A. *The Choir Loft and the Pulpit*. New York: H. W. Gray Company, 1943.

Douglas, W. *Church Music in History and Practice*. New York: Charles Scribner's Sons, 1937.

Ellinwood, L. *The History of American Church Music*. New York: Morehouse-Barlow Company, 1953.

Eschman, Karl. *Changing Forms in Modern Music*, 2nd ed. Boston: E. C. Schirmer, 1967.

Etherington, C. L. *Protestant Worship Music*. New York: Holt, Rinehart, & Winston, 1962.

Halter, Carl. *God and Man in Music*. St. Louis: Concordia Publishing House, 1963.

————. *The Practice of Sacred Music*. St. Louis: Concordia Publishing House, 1955.

Hartley, Kenneth R. *Bibliography of Theses and Dissertations in Sacred Music*. Detroit: Information Coordinators, 1966.

Hooper, William L. *Church Music in Transition*. Nashville: Broadman Press, 1963.

Hutchings, Arthur. *Church Music in the Nineteenth Century*. New York: Oxford University Press, 1967.

Irwin, K., and Ortmayer, R. *Worship and the Arts*. Nashville: Board of Education of The Methodist Church, 1953.

Josephs, Jess J. *The Physics of Musical Sound*, No. 13. Princeton: Van Nostrand Momentum Books, 1967.

Kettring, D. D. *Steps Toward a Singing Church*. Philadelphia: The Westminster Press, 1948.

Liemohn, E. *The Chorale*. Philadelphia: Muhlenburg Press, 1953.

Long, Kenneth R. *The Music of the English Church*. New York: St. Martins, 1972.

Lovell, John, Jr. *Black Song: The Forge and the Flame*. New York: The Macmillan Company, 1972.

Lydon, Michael. *Rock Folk*. New York: Dial Press, 1971.

McAll, May deForest. *Melodic Index to the Works of Johann Sebastian Bach*. New York: C. F. Peters, 1962.

Manual of Church Praise. Edinburgh, Scotland: The Church of Scotland Committee on Publications, 1932.

Maus, C. P. *The Church and the Fine Arts*. New York: Harper & Row, 1960.

Mendl, R. W. S. *The Divine Quest in Music*. New York: Philosophical Library, 1957.

Miller, William R. *The World of Pop Music and Jazz*. St. Louis: Concordia Publishing House, 1965.

Music Educators Journal, November 1968. Washington, D.C.: Music Educators National Conference (1201 16th Street, 20036. Issue devoted to Electronic Music, including extensive listing of books, records and materials.)

Nininger, R. *Church Music Comes of Age.* New York: Carl Fischer, 1957.

Ode, James A. *Brass Instruments in Church Services.* Minneapolis: Augsburg Publishing House, 1970.

Peyser, John. *The New Music; The Sense Behind the Sound.* New York: Dell Books, 1971.

Phillips, C. H. *The Singing Church.* London: Faber & Faber, 1945.

Pratt, W. S. *Musical Ministries in the Church.* New York: G. Schirmer, 1923.

Routley, Erik. *Church Music and Theology.* London: SCM Press, 1959.

_____. *Music Leadership in the Church.* Nashville: Abingdon Press, 1967.

_____. *Music, Sacred and Profane.* London: Independent Press, 1960.

_____. *The Church and Music.* London: Duckworth and Co., 1950.

_____. *Twentieth-Century Church Music.* New York: Oxford University Press, 1964.

_____. *Words, Music, and the Church.* Nashville: Abingdon Press, 1968.

Sessions, Roger. *The Musical Experience of Composer, Performer, Listener.* New York: Atheneum, 1962.

Smith, H. A. *Lyric Religion.* Westwood, N.J.: Fleming H. Revell, 1931.

Squire, R. N. *Church Music.* St. Louis: Bethany Press, 1962.

Steere, D. *Music in Protestant Worship.* Richmond: John Knox Press, 1960.

Stevenson, R. M. *Patterns of Protestant Church Music.* Durham, N.C.: Duke University Press, 1953.

_____. *Protestant Church Music in America.* New York: W. W. Norton & Co., 1966.

Stubbings, G. W. *A Dictionary of Church Music.* New York: Philosophical Library, 1950.

Swisher, W. S. *Music in Worship.* Bryn Mawr, Pa.: Oliver Ditson Company, 1929.

Taylor, H. V., and Kelly, J. M. *Our Singing Church.* Philadelphia: Board of Christian Education, Presbyterian Church in the U.S.A., 1951.

Trobian, Helen. *The Instrumental Ensemble in the Church.* Nashville: Abingdon Press, 1963.

Werner, Eric. *The Sacred Bridge.* New York: Schocken Books, 1970.

Whittlesey, F. L. *A Comprehensive Program of Church Music.* Philadelphia: The Westminster Press, 1957.

_____. *Music and Worship.* Philadelphia: Board of Christian Education, Presbyterian Church in the U.S.A., 1951.

_____. *The Ministry of Music.* Philadelphia: Board of Christian Education, Presbyterian Church in the U.S.A.

II. Music in Christian Education

Humphreys, Louise, and Ross, Jerold. *Interpreting Music Through Movement.* Englewood Cliffs, N.J.: Prentice-Hall, 1964.

Ingram, Madeline. *Organizing and Directing Children's Choirs.* Nashville: Abingdon Press, 1959.

Ingram, Madeline, and Rice, W. C. *Vocal Technique for Children and Youth.* Nashville: Abingdon Press, 1962.

Marvel, L. M. *Music Resources Guide.* Minneapolis: Schmitt, Hall, and McCreary, 1961.

Morsch, V. *The Use of Music in Christian Education.* Philadelphia: The Westminster Press, 1956.

Moyer, J. Edward. *The Voice of His Praise.* Nashville: Graded Press, 1965.

Shields, E. McE. *Music in the Religious Growth of Children.* Nashville: Abingdon Press, 1943.

Terry, R. Harold, ed. *Children Sing.* Philadelphia: Fortress Press, 1972.

Thomas, E. L. *Music in Christian Education.* Nashville: Abingdon Press, 1953.

For Beginners:
A First Book in Hymns and Worship. E. L. Thomas. Abingdon Press.
Another Singing Time. Satis Coleman. Reynal and Hitchcock.
Child's First Songs in Religious Education. Oglevee. Vaile Company.
Fun For Every Day. Wrenn and Wrenn. Willis Music Co.
Martin and Judy Songs. E. L. Thomas. Beacon Press.
Mother Goose. Elliott. McLaughlin Brothers.
140 Folksongs for Children. Concord Series No. 7. E. C. Schirmer.
Singing Time. Satis Coleman. Reynal and Hitchcock.
Singing Time. Dearmer and Shaw. Oxford University Press.
Songs for Little People. Danielson and Conant. Pilgrim Press.
Walk the World Together. Crowninshield. Boston Music Company.
When the Little Child Wants to Sing. Laufer. The Westminster Press.

For Primaries:
As Children Worship. Perkins. Pilgrim Press.
Children's Worship in the Church School. Perkins. Harper & Brothers.
Folksongs of All Nations. Marzo. G. Schirmer.
Hymns for Primary Worship. Laufer. The Westminster Press.
Music for Young Children. Alice G. Thorn. Charles Scribner's Sons.
Sing, Children, Sing. E. L. Thomas. Abingdon Press.
Songs and Hymns for Children's Voices. D. and G. Malmin. Augsburg Publishing House.

Songs of Praise for Children. Dearmer, Williams, and Shaw. Oxford University Press.

The Canyon Hymnal for Boys and Girls, Primary Ed. Demarest. Canyon Press.

The Hymnal for Boys and Girls. Parker and Richards. Appleton-Century-Crofts.

The Primary Worship Guide. Perkins. Pilgrim Press.

For Juniors:
Hymns for Children and Grownups. Bristol and Friedell. Farrar, Straus and Young.

Hymns for Junior Worship. Curry. The Westminster Press.

Singing Worship. E. L. Thomas. Abingdon Press.

The Canyon Hymnal for Boys and Girls, Junior Ed. Demarest. Canyon Press.

For Youth:
Beacon Hymnal. Beacon Press.

Hymnal for American Youth. H. A. Smith. Century House.

Hymnal for Young People. Abingdon Press.

Hymnal for Youth. The Westminster Press.

III. Organist and Pianist

Aldrich, Putnam. *Ornamentation in J. S. Bach's Organ Works.* New York: Coleman-Ross Company, 1950.

Arnold, Corliss. *Organ Literature: A Comprehensive Survey.* Metuchen, N.J.: Scarecrow Press, 1973.

Barnes, W. H. *The Contemporary American Organ,* 7th ed. Glen Rock, N.J.: J. Fischer and Brother, 1959.

Bender, Jan. *Organ Improvisation for Beginners.* St. Louis: Concordia Publishing House, 1975.

Biddle, Perry. *Abingdon Marriage Manual.* Nashville: Abingdon, 1974.

————. *Abingdon Funeral Manual.* Nashville: Abingdon, 1976.

Blanton, Joseph. *The Organ in Church Design.* Albany, Texas: Venture Press, 1957.

Boyd, C. *The Organist and the Choirmaster.* Nashville: Abingdon Press, 1936.

Clutton, C., and Dixon, G. *The Organ.* London: Grenville Publishing Company, 1950.

Conely, James. *A Guide to Improvisation.* Nashville: Abingdon Press, 1975.

Conway, M. P. *Church Organ Accompaniment.* London: Canterbury Press, 1952.

Dannreuther, Edward. *Musical Ornamentation* (reprint). New York: Edwin F. Kalmus, n.d.

Donington, Robert. *The Interpretation of Early Music.* London: Faber & Faber, 1963.

———. *Tempo and Rhythm in Bach's Organ Music.* London: Hinrichsen Edition, 1960.

Edson, Jean Slater. *Organ—Preludes.* Vol. I. Metuchen, N.J.: Scarecrow Press, 1970.

———. *Organ—Tune Names Index.* Vol. II. Metuchen, N.J.: Scarecrow Press, 1970.

Emery, W. *Bach's Ornaments.* London: Novello, 1953.

Geer, E. H. *Organ Registration.* Glen Rock, N.J.: Fischer and Brothers, 1957.

Goode, Jack C. *Pipe Organ Registration.* Nashville: Abingdon Press, 1964.

Grace, H. *The Complete Organist.* London: Richards Press Ltd., 1947, 3rd ed.

———. *The Organ Works of Bach.* London: Novello 1922.

Hymnal 1940, The Companion. New York: Church Pension Fund, 1949.

Irwin, Stevens. *Dictionary of Electronic Organ Stops.* New York: G. Schirmer, 1968.

Johnson, David N. *Organ Teachers Guide.* Minneapolis: Augsburg Publishing House, 1971.

Keller, Hermann. *The Organ Works of Bach.* New York: C. F. Peters, 1967.

Koch, C. *The Organ Student's Gradus Ad Parnassum.* Glen Rock, N.J.: J. Fischer and Brother, 1945.

Krapf, Gerhard. *Liturgical Organ Playing.* Minneapolis: Augsburg Publishing House, 1964.

———. *Organ Improvisation: A Practical Approach to Chorale Elaboration for the Service.* Minneapolis: Augsburg Publishing House, 1967.

Lovelace, A. C. *The Organist and Hymn Playing.* Nashville: Abingdon Press, 1962.

Lutkin, P. C. *Hymn Singing and Hymn Playing.* Bulletin 3. Evanston: Northwestern University, Department of Church Music, 1930.

Mathis, W. S. *The Pianist and Church Music.* Nashville: Abingdon Press, 1962.

Music for Church Funerals. Greenwich: The Seabury Press, 1952.

Nicholson, S. H. *Quires and Places Where They Sing.* London: S.P.C.K., 1950.

241

Ode, James. *Brass Instruments in Church Services*. Minneapolis: Augsburg Publishing House, 1970.

Rowley, A. *Extemporisation*. London: Joseph Williams, 1955.

Schouten, H. *Improvisation on the Organ*. London: W. Paxton and Company, n.d.

Snell, Frederick A. *Music for Church Funerals and Memorial Services*. Philadelphia: Fortress Press, 1966.

Stellhorn, M. H., comp. *Index to Hymn Preludes*. St. Louis: Concordia Publishing House, 1948.

Sumner, W. L. *Bach's Organ Registration*. London: Hinrichsen Edition, 1961.

————. *The Organ*. London: Macdonald and Company, 1952.

Taylor, S. D. B. *The Chorale Preludes of J. S. Bach*. London: Oxford University Press, 1942.

Thiman, E. H. *The Beginning Organist*. London: Ascherberg, Hopwood, and Crew, 1954.

Trobian, Helen R. *The Instrumental Ensemble in the Church*. Nashville: Abingdon Press, 1963.

Walter, Samuel. *Basic Principles of Service Playing*. Nashville: Abingdon Press, 1963.

IV. Choir Director and Choir Training

Ades, Hawley. *Choral Arranging*. Delaware Water Gap, Pa.: Shawnee Press, 1966.

Andrews, Frances M., and Leeder, Joseph A. *Guiding Junior High School Pupils in Music Experiences*. Englewood Cliffs, N.J.: Prentice-Hall, Inc., 1953.

Christiansen, O. C. *Voice Builder* (pamphlet). Park Ridge, Illinois: Neil A. Kjos Music Company.

Christensen, Helga. *Better Choir Singing*. Dallas: Choristers Guild, 1973.

Cleall, C. *The Training of Mixed Choirs*. London: Independent Press, 1960.

Coleman, H. *The Church Choir Trainer*. London: Oxford University Press, 1964.

Coward, H. *Choral Techniques and Interpretation*. London: Novello, 1914.

————. *"C.T.I." The Secret*. London: Novello, 1938.

DeVinney, Richard. *There's More to Church Music Than Meets the Ear*. Philadelphia: Fortress Press, 1972.

Ehmann, Wilhelm. *Choral Conducting*. Minneapolis: Augsburg Publishing House, 1968.

Eisenberg, H., and Eisenberg, L. *How to Lead Group Singing*. New York: Association Press, 1965.

242

Field-Hyde, F. C. *The Art and Science of Voice Training*. London: Oxford University Press, 1950.

Finn, W. J. *The Art of the Choral Conductor*. Boston: C. C. Birchard and Company, 1939.

Garrettson, R. L. *Conducting Choral Music*. Boston: Allyn and Bacon, 1961.

Halter, C. *The Christian Choir Member*. St. Louis: Concordia Publishing House, 1959.

Hardy, T. M. *How to Train Children's Voices* (19th ed.). London: J. Curwen and Sons, n.d.

Harper, E. E. *Church Music and Worship*. New York: Abingdon Press, 1924.

Heaton, C. H. *How to Build a Church Choir*. St. Louis: Bethany Press, 1959.

Herz, Gerhard, ed. *Bach: Cantata No. 4*. New York: W. W. Norton & Co., 1967.

Hjortsvang, C. *The Amateur Choir Director*. Nashville: Abingdon Press, 1941.

Hoffelt, Robert O. *How to Lead Informal Singing*. Nashville: Abingdon Press, 1961.

Hoffland, R. D. *The Ministry to Youth Through Music*. Minneapolis: Augsburg Publishing House, 1956.

Ingram, Madeline D. *A Guide for Youth Choirs*. Nashville: Abingdon Press, 1967.

————. *Organizing and Directing Children's Choirs*. Nashville: Abingdon Press, 1959.

————, and Rice. W. C. *Vocal Technique for Children and Youth*. Nashville: Abingdon Press, 1962.

Jacobs, Arthur, ed. *Choral Music, A Symposium*. Baltimore: Penguin Books, 1963.

Jacobs, R. K., comp. *The Children's Choir*. Rock Island, Ill.: Augustana Book Concern, 1958.

————. *The Successful Children's Choir*. Chicago: H. T. FitzSimons, 1948.

Kortkamp, I. *One Hundred Things a Choir Member Should Know*. Decorah, Iowa: Published by the author, 1954.

Lorenz, Ellen Jane. *The Learning Choir*. Nashville: Abingdon Press, 1968.

Lovelace, A. C. *The Youth Choir*. Nashville: Abingdon Press, 1964.

Lundstrom, Linden J. *The Choir School*. Minneapolis: Augsburg Publishing House, 1957, 1963.

McElheran, Brock. *Conducting Technique for Beginners and Professionals.* New York: Oxford University Press, 1966.

McKenzie, Duncan. *Training the Boy's Changing Voice.* New Brunswick, N.J.: Rutgers University Press, 1956.

Marshall, M. *The Singer's Manual of English Diction.* New York: G. Schirmer, 1946.

Miller, P. J. *Youth Choirs.* New York: Harold Flammer, 1953.

Moe, Daniel. *Basic Choral Concepts.* Minneapolis: Augsburg Publishing House, 1972.

_____. *Problems in Conducting.* Minneapolis: Augsburg Publishing House, 1968.

_____. *Responsibilities of the Choir Member:* Augsburg Publishing House, 1965.

Nicholson, S. H. *Boys Choirs.* London: Paterson Publication, n.d.

_____. *Quires and Places Where They Sing.* London: S.P.C.K., 1950.

Noble, T. T. *Training the Boy Chorister.* New York: G. Schirmer, 1943.

Nordin, D. W. *The Choirmaster's Workbook.* Rock Island, Ill.: Augustana Book Concern.

_____. *How to Organize and Direct the Church Choir.* West Nyack, N.Y.: Parker Publishing Co., 1973.

Pfautsch, Lloyd. *Mental Warmups for the Choral Director.* New York: Lawson-Gould, 1969.

Pooler, Frank, and Pierce, Brent. *New Choral Notation.* New York: Walton Music Corp., 1971.

Rice, W. C. *Basic Principles of Singing.* Nashville: Abingdon Press, 1961.

Riedel, Johannes, ed. *Cantors at the Crossroads.* St. Louis: Concordia Publishing House, 1967.

Salzer, Felix. *Structural Hearing: Tonal Coherence in Music.* New York: Dover Publications, 1961.

Sateren, Leland B. *The New Song: A Guide to Modern Music for Use in the Church Choir.* Minneapolis: Augsburg Publishing House, 1958.

Scherchen, H. *Handbook of Conducting* (8th ed.). London: Oxford University Press, 1956.

Shanet, Howard. *Learn to Read Music.* New York: Simon & Schuster, 1956.

Sims, M. A. *Sight Reading for Choir-boys.* London: Novello, n.d.

Sunderman, L. F. *Organization of the Church Choir.* Rockville Center, N.Y.: Belwin, Inc., 1957.

Sydnor, James R. *The Training of Church Choirs.* Nashville: Abingdon Press, 1963.

Thomas, Kurt. *The Choral Conductor*. New York: Associated Music Publishers, 1971.

Vosseller, E. V. J. *Junior Choirs—More Helps and Suggestions*. Flemington: Democrat Printing Office, 1939.

Walter, Samuel. *Music Composition and Arranging*. Nashville: Abingdon Press, 1965.

Wienandt, Elwyn A. *Choral Music of the Church*. New York: Free Press, 1965.

Wilson, H. R., and Lyall, J. L. *Building a Church Choir*. Minneapolis: Hall & McCreary Company, 1957.

Witherspoon, H. *Singing*. New York: G. Schirmer, 1925.

Wright, E. *Basic Choirtraining*. Croydon, England: Royal School of Church Music, 1955.

V. Ministers

Abba, R. *Principles of Christian Worship*. New York: Oxford University Press, 1957.

Abbott, Walter M., S. J., ed. *The Documents of Vatican II*. New York: Guild Press, America Press, and Association Press, 1966.

Bailey, A. E., ed. *The Arts and Religion*. New York: The Macmillan Company, 1944.

Bailey, Wilfred M. *Awakened Worship*. Nashville: Abingdon Press, 1972.

Benson, Dennis C. *Electric Liturgy*. Richmond: John Knox Press, 1972.

Blackwood, A. W. *The Fine Art of Public Worship*. Nashville: Abingdon Press, 1934.

Bloy, Myron, ed. *Multi-Media Worship*. Greenwich: The Seabury Press, 1969.

Coffin, H. S. *The Public Worship of God*. Philadelphia: The Westminster Press, 1946.

Davies, J. G. *A Select Liturgical Lexicon*. (Ecumenical Studies in Worship, No. 14) Richmond: John Knox Press, 1965.

Devan, S. A. *Ascent to Zion*. New York: The Macmillan Company, 1942.

Dunkle, William F., Jr., Quillian, Joseph D., Jr., eds. *Companion to the Book of Worship*. Nashville: Abingdon Press, 1970.

Gealy, Fred D. *Celebration*. Nashville: Graded Press, 1969.

Goldsworthy, E. A. *Plain Thoughts on Worship*. Chicago and New York: Willett, Clark, and Company, 1936.

Hedley G. *Christian Worship*. New York: The Macmillan Company, 1953.

Hislop, D. H. *Our Heritage in Public Worship*. Edinburgh, Scotland: T. and T. Clark, 1935.

Horn, Henry E. *Worship in Crisis*. Philadelphia: Fortress Press, 1972.

Hughes, Anselm. *Liturgical Terms for Music Students*. Boston: McLaughlin & Reilly Co., 1940.

I.C.E.T. *Prayers We Have in Common*. Philadelphia: Fortress Press, 1972.

Irwin, K., and Ortmayer, R. *Worship and the Arts*. Nashville: Board of Education of The Methodist Church, 1953.

Jowett, J. H. *The Preacher: His Life and Work*. New York: Harper & Brothers, 1912.

Kleinhans, Theodore J. *The Year of the Lord*. St. Louis: Concordia Publishing House, 1967.

Lomas, Bernard T., and Parsons, George A. *Worship Aids for a Space Age*. Lima, Ohio: C. S. S. Publishing Co. n.d.

Marxhausen, Reinhold. *Please Dispose After Use: Disposable Forms for Worship*. St. Louis: Youth Ministry Materials, P.O. Box 14325.

Maxwell, W. D. *An Outline of Christian Worship*. New York: Oxford University Press, 1936.

―――. *Concerning Worship*. New York: Oxford University Press, 1948.

Micklem, N., ed. *Christian Worship: Studies in Its History and Meaning*. Oxford: Clarendon Press, 1936.

Nicholls, W. *Jacob's Ladder: The Meaning of Worship*. Richmond: John Knox Press, 1958.

Palmer, A. *O Come Let Us Worship*. New York: The Macmillan Company, 1941.

―――. *The Art of Conducting Public Worship*. New York: The Macmillan Company, 1939.

Randolph, David J., ed. *Ventures in Worship (Vols. 1, 2, and 3)*. Nashville: Abingdon Press, 1969, 1970, 1973.

Routley, Erik. *Church Music and Theology*. London: SCM Press, 1959.

Seidenspinner, C. *Form and Freedom in Worship*. Chicago and New York: Willett, Clark, and Company, 1941.

Shepherd, Massey H., Jr. *The Worship of the Church*. Greenwich: The Seabury Press, 1952.

Snyder, Ross. *Contemporary Celebration*. Nashville: Abingdon Press, 1971.

Sperry, W. L. *Reality in Worship*. New York: The Macmillan Company, 1926.

Thompson, Bard, ed. *Liturgies of the Western Church*. New York: World Publishing Co., 1961.

Underhill, E. *Worship*. New York: Harper & Brothers, 1937.

Vogt, V. O. *Modern Worship*. New Haven, Conn.: Yale University Press, 1927.

White, James F. *New Forms of Worship.* Nashville: Abingdon Press, 1971.
Wilkinson, R. S., ed. *Worship in a Changing Church.* New York: Morehouse-Barlow Company, 1965.
Zdenek, Marilee, and Champion, Marge. *Catch the New Wind.* Waco, Texas: Word Books, 1972.
Ziegler, E. K. *A Book of Worship for Village Churches.* New York: Agricultural Mission Foundation, 1939.

VI. Music Committee

Anderson, R. W., and Caemmerer, R. R., Jr. *Banners, Banners, Banners, Etc.* Chicago: Christian Art Associates, 1967.
Ashton, J. N. *Music in Worship.* Boston: Pilgrim Press, 1943.
Bacon, A. *The True Function of Church Music.* Stockton: Printwell Press, 1953.
Bartholomew, W. T. *Acoustics of Music.* Englewood Cliffs, N.J.: Prentice-Hall, 1942.
Biddle, Perry. *Abingdon Marriage Manual.* Nashville: Abingdon, 1974.
———. *Abingdon Funeral Manual.* Nashville: Abingdon, 1976.
Blanton, J. *The Organ in Church Design.* Albany, Tex.: Venture Press, 1957.
Clokey, J. W. *In Every Corner Sing.* New York: Morehouse-Barlow Company, 1948.
Davies, W., and Grace, H. *Music and Worship.* New York: H. W. Gray Company, 1925.
Davison, A. T. *Church Music: Illusion and Reality.* Cambridge, Mass.: Harvard University Press, 1952.
———. *Protestant Church Music in America.* Boston: E. C. Schirmer, 1933.
DeVinney, Richard. *Bridging the Gap Between Choir Loft and Pew.* Nashville: Board of Education, The United Methodist Church, 1970.
Fryxell, R. *Wedding Music.* Rock Island, Ill.: Augustana Book Concern, 1956.
Halter, C. *The Practice of Sacred Music.* St. Louis: Concordia Publishing House, 1956.
Ireland, Marion P. *Textile Art in the Church.* Nashville: Abingdon Press, 1971.
Jensen, Donald F. *Raise a Jubilee—Music in Youth Ministry.* Nashville: Graded Press, 1970.
Kettring, D. D. *Steps Toward a Singing Church.* Philadelphia: The Westminster Press, 1948.

Laliberté, Norman, and McIlhaney, Sterling. *Banners and Hangings.* New York: Reinhold Publishing Co., 1966.

Morsch, V. *The Use of Music in Christian Education.* Philadelphia: The Westminster Press, 1956.

Music for Church Weddings. Greenwich, Conn.: The Seabury Press, 1952.

Music for Funerals. Greenwich, Conn.: The Seabury Press, 1952.

A Prelude to the Purchase of a Church Organ. Philadelphia: Fortress Press, 1964.

Routley, Erik. *Music Leadership in the Church.* Nashville: Abingdon Press, 1967.

Snell, Frederick A. *Funeral Music.* Philadelphia: Fortress Press, 1966.

Sydnor, J. R. *Planning for Church Music.* Nashville: Abingdon Press, 1961.

Whittlesey, F. L. *A Comprehensive Program of Church Music.* Philadelphia: The Westminster Press, 1957.

VII. Choir's Music

Carols for Today. London: Oxford University Press, 1965.

Halsey, Lewis, and Ramsey, Basil, eds. *Sing Nowell: 51 Carols New and Arranged.* London: Novello, 1963.

Nardone, Thomas R., Nye, James H., Resnick, Mark. *Choral Music in Print. Vol. I. Sacred Choral Music.* Philadelphia: Musicdata, 1974.

Palmer, Larry. *Hugo Distler and His Church Music.* St. Louis: Concordia Publishing House, 1967.

Poston, Elizabeth, ed. *The Second Penguin Book of Christmas Carols.* Baltimore: Penguin Books, 1970.

Routley, Erik, ed. *University Carol Book.* Brighton: H. Freeman & Co., 1961.

Sacred Choral Music. Vol. I. Philadelphia: Musicdata, 1974.

Sateren, L. B. *The New Song.* Minneapolis: Augsburg Publishing House, 1958.

Steere, D. *Music for the Protestant Church Choir.* Richmond: John Knox Press, 1955.

Ulrich, Homer. *A Survey of Choral Music.* New York: Harcourt Brace Jovanovich, 1973.

Wienandt, Elwyn A., and Young, Robert H. *The Anthem in England and America.* New York: Free Press, 1970.

VIII. Soloist

Christiansen, O. C. *Voice Builder* (pamphlet). Park Ridge, Illinois: Neil A. Kjos Music Company.

Christy, Van A. *Expressive Singing* (Vol. I, *Basic Textbook*; Vol. II, *Advanced Textbook*). Dubuque, Ia.: William C. Brown Co., 1961.

Coffin, B. "The Sacred Solo, Its Significant Composers and Trends," *The Bulletin* (March, April, 1952). (NATS)

Espina, Noni. *Vocal Solos for Protestant Services*, 2nd ed. revised and enlarged. Bronx, New York: Published privately, 1974.

Garcia, Manuel. *Hints on Singing*. Tr. from the French by Beata Garcia. London: Ascherberg, Hopwood, and Crew, New York: E. Schuberth and Company, 1894.

Gerts, A. "The Sacred Solo," *The Bulletin* (October, 1956). (NATS)

Henderson, William J. *The Art of the Singer*. New York: Charles Scribner's Sons, 1906.

Huls, H. S. "Song List: For Adolescent Voices; Beginning Students." St. Cloud, Minn.: Mimeographed by author, 1961.

Koopman, John. *Selected Sacred Solos in Modern Idiom*. Minneapolis: Augsburg Publishing House, 1965.

Lamperti, G. B. *Vocal Wisdom*. Ed. William Earl Brown. New York: Hudson Offset Company, 1953 (1931).

Marshall, M. *The Singer's Manual of English Diction*. New York: G. Schirmer, 1953.

Newton, G. "Qualifications and Shortcomings of Church Soloists," *The Bulletin* (March, April, 1952). (NATS)

Nicholas, L. "Choosing Solos for the Worship Service," *The Bulletin* (March, April, 1953). (NATS)

Peterson, Paul W., rev. Blair, John F. *Natural Singing and Expressive Conducting*: Winston-Salem: John F. Blair, 1955.

Pfautsch, Lloyd. *English Diction for the Singer*. New York: Lawson-Gould, 1971.

Rice, W. C. *Basic Principles of Singing*. Nashville: Abingdon Press, 1961.

Schiotz, Aksel. *The Singer and His Art*. New York: Harper & Row, 1970.

Shakespeare, William. *The Art of Singing*. Byrn Mawr, Pa.: Oliver Ditson Company, 1898, rev. 1921.

Siebel, Katherine. *Sacred Songs—A Guide to Repertory*. New York: H. W. Gray, 1966.

Uris, Dorothy. *To Sing in English: A Guide to Improved Diction*. Oceanside, N.Y.: Boosey & Hawkes, 1971.

Vennard, William. *Singing, The Mechanism and the Technique* (revised). New York: Carl Fischer, 1967.

Witherspoon, Herbert. *Thirty-six Lessons in Singing*. Chicago: Miessner Institute, 1930.

IX. Hymnody

Allen, Cecil J. *Hymns and the Christian Faith.* London: Pickering and Inglis, 1966.

Bailey, A. E. *The Gospel in Hymns.* New York: Charles Scribner's Sons, 1950.

Benson, L. F. *The English Hymn.* Richmond: John Knox Press, 1962.

————. *The Hymnody of the Christian Church* (reprint). Richmond: John Knox Press, 1956.

Bodley, D. E. *The Index.* Detroit: Religious Publications, 1958.

Daries, F. R., comp. *Book of Chorales and Supplementary Hymns.* St. Louis: Eden Publishing House, 1957.

Davis, A. P. *Isaac Watts, His Life and Works.* New York: Dryden Press, 1943.

Dearmer, P., comp. *Songs of Praise Discussed.* London: Oxford University Press, 1933.

Demarest, A., ed. *The Canyon Hymnal for Boys and Girls.* East Orange: Canyon Press, 1958.

Diehl, Katharine Smith. *Hymns and Tunes—An Index.* Metuchen, N.J.: Scarecrow Press, 1966.

Ellinwood, L., ed. *The Hymnal Companion.* New York: Episcopal Church, 1949.

Farlander, A. W. *The Hymnal: How It Grew* (pamphlet). New York: Episcopal Church, 1951.

————. *The Hymnal: How to Use It* (pamphlet). New York: Episcopal Church, 1951.

————. *The Hymnal Outsings the Ages* (pamphlet). New York: Episcopal Church, 1951.

————. *The Hymnal: What It Is* (pamphlet). New York: Episcopal Church, 1951.

Flew, R. N. *The Hymns of Charles Wesley.* London: Epworth Press, 1953.

Foote, H. W. *Three Centuries of American Hymnody.* Hamden, Conn.: Shoe String Press, 1961.

Frost, M. *English and Scottish Psalm and Hymn Tunes.* London: Oxford University Press, 1953.

Gealy, Fred; Lovelace, A. C.; Young, Carlton R. *Companion to the Hymnal.* Nashville: Abingdon Press, 1970.

Haeussler, A. *The Story of Our Hymns.* St. Louis: Eden Publishing House, 1952.

Horn, Dorothy D. *Sing to Me of Heaven.* Gainesville, Fla.: University of Florida Press, 1970.

Hostetler, L., ed. *Handbook to the Mennonite Hymnary*. Newton, Kan.: 1949.

Hymns Ancient and Modern, Historical Edition. Clowes, 1909.

Julian, J., ed. A *Dictionary of Hymnology* (revised ed.). London: Murray, 1908.

Leupold, Ulrich S., ed. *Laudamus, Hymnal for the Lutheran World Federation*. Geneva: Lutheran World Federation, 1970.

Liemohn, E. *The Singing Church*. Columbus, Ohio: Wartburg Press, 1959.

Lovelace, A. C. *The Anatomy of Hymnody*. Nashville: Abingdon Press, 1965.

McCutchan, R. G. *Hymn Tune Names*. Nashville: Abingdon Press, 1957.

———. *Hymns in the Lives of Men*. Nashville: Abingdon Press, 1945.

———. *Our Hymnody: A Manual of the Methodist Hymnal*. Nashville: Abingdon Press, 1937.

Macmillan, Alexander. *Hymns of the Church*. Toronto: United Church Publishing House, 1935.

Manning, B. L. *The Hymns of Wesley and Watts*. London: Epworth Press, 1942.

Messenger, R. E. *The Medieval Latin Hymn*. Washington: Capital Press, 1953.

Moffatt, J., and Patrick, M., eds. *Handbook of the Church Hymnary*. London: Oxford University Press, 1933.

Moyer, J. Edward. *The Voice of His Praise*. Nashville: Graded Press, 1965.

Ninde, E. S. *Nineteen Centuries of Christian Song*. Westwood, N.J.: Fleming H. Revell, 1938.

Northcott, Cecil. *Hymns in Christian Worship* (Ecumenical Studies in Worship). Richmond: John Knox Press, 1962.

Parks, Edna D. *Early English Hymns: An Index*. Metuchen, N.J.: Scarecrow Press, 1972.

Parry, K. L., and Routley, E. *Companion to Congregational Praise*. London: Independent Press, 1953.

———. *Christian Hymns*. London: SCM Press, 1956.

Patrick, M. *Four Centuries of Scottish Psalmody*. London: Oxford University Press, 1949.

———. *The Story of the Church's Song*. J. R. Sydnor. Richmond: John Knox Press, 1962.

Phillips, C. S. *Hymnody Past and Present*. London: SPCK, 1937.

Polack, W. G., ed. *Handbook to the Lutheran Hymnal*. St. Louis: Concordia Publishing House, 1942.

Reynolds, William J. *A Survey of Christian Hymnody.* New York: Holt, Rinehart & Winston, 1963.

Riedel, Johannes. *The Lutheran Chorale, Its Basic Traditions.* Minneapolis: Augsburg Publishing House, 1967.

Routley, E. *The English Carol.* London: Jenkins, 1958.

_____. *Hymns and Human Life.* New York: The Philosophical Library, 1952.

_____. *Hymns and the Faith.* London: Murray, 1955.

_____. *I'll Praise My Maker.* London: Independent Press, 1951.

_____. *The Music of Christian Hymnody.* London: Independent Press, 1957.

_____. *The Musical Wesleys.* New York: Oxford University Press, 1968.

Ryden, E. E. *The Story of Christian Hymnody.* Rock Island, Ill.: Augustana Book Concern, 1959.

Smith, F. A. *Lyric Religion.* New York: Appleton-Century-Crofts, 1931.

Songs for Liturgy and More Hymns and Spiritual Songs. New York: Walton Music, 1971.

Sydnor, James R. *The Hymn and Congregational Singing.* Richmond: John Knox Press, 1960.

Thomson, Ronald William. *Who's Who of Hymn Writers.* London: Epworth Press, 1967.

Whitley, W. T. *Congregational Hymn Singing.* London: J. M. Dent & Sons, 1933.

Worship Supplement. St. Louis: Concordia Publishing House, 1969.

Publications

American Choral Review. (Journal of the American Choral Foundation, 130 West 56th Street., New York, New York 10019.)

American Music Teacher. Music Teachers National Association. Frank S. Stillings, ed., School of Fine and Applied Arts, Central Michigan University, Mt. Pleasant, Michigan 48858.

Bulletin, The. National Association of Teachers of Singing, Harvey Ringel, ed., 430 South Michigan Avenue, Chicago, Illinois. 60605.

Church Music. 3558 South Jefferson Ave., St. Louis, Missouri 63118.

Clavier. 1418 Lake Street, Evanston, Illinois. 60204.

The Diapason. 434 South Wabash Avenue, Chicago, Illinois 60605.

The Hymn. Hymn Society of America. William Watkins Reid, ed., 475 Riverside Drive, New York, New York 10027.

The Hymn Society Bulletin. 30 East Meads, Guildford, Surrey GU2 5SP, England.

Journal of Church Music. Fortress Press, 2900 Queen Lane, Philadelphia, Pennsylvania 19129.

Musart. (National Catholic Music Educators Association), 4637 Eastern Avenue, NE, Washington, D.C. 20018.

Music Educators Journal. Music Educators National Conference. 1201 16th Street, NW, Washington, D.C. 20036.

The Musical Heritage of the Church, Vols. 5-7, Concordia Publishing House, St. Louis, Missouri 63118.

The Musical Quarterly. G. Schirmer, New York, New York.

Music: AGO and R.C.C.O. Magazine, 630 Fifth Avenue, New York, New York 10020.

Music Ministry. 201 Eighth Avenue, South, Nashville, Tennessee 37202.

Notes. (Quarterly Journal of the Music Library Association), W. F. Humphrey Press, Geneva, New York.

Response. (Journal of the Lutheran Society for Worship, Music, and the Arts), Valparaiso University, Valparaiso, Indiana.

Worship and Arts. P.O. Box 1026, Huntington Park, California 90255.

Index